WITNESS IDENTIFICATI
IN CRIMINAL CASES

WITNESS IDENTIFICATION IN CRIMINAL CASES

PSYCHOLOGY AND PRACTICE

RACHEL WILCOCK
RAY BULL
REBECCA MILNE

OXFORD
UNIVERSITY PRESS

OXFORD
UNIVERSITY PRESS

Great Clarendon Street, Oxford OX2 6DP

Oxford University Press is a department of the University of Oxford.
It furthers the University's objective of excellence in research, scholarship,
and education by publishing worldwide in

Oxford New York

Auckland Cape Town Dar es Salaam Hong Kong Karachi
Kuala Lumpur Madrid Melbourne Mexico City Nairobi
New Delhi Shanghai Taipei Toronto

With offices in

Argentina Austria Brazil Chile Czech Republic France Greece
Guatemala Hungary Italy Japan Poland Portugal Singapore
South Korea Switzerland Thailand Turkey Ukraine Vietnam

Oxford is a registered trade mark of Oxford University Press
in the UK and in certain other countries

Published in the United States
by Oxford University Press Inc., New York

British Library Cataloging in Publication Data

Data available

Library of Congress Cataloging-in-Publication Data

Wilcock, Rachel.
   Witness identification in criminal cases : psychology and practice / Rachel Wilcock,
Ray Bull, Rebecca Milne.
      p. cm.
   Includes bibliographical references and index.
   ISBN 978–0–19–921693–2 (pbk. : alk. paper) 1. Eyewitness identification. 2.
Witnesses. 3. Criminals—Identification. 4. Recognition (Psychology) I. Bull, Ray.
II. Milne, Rebecca. III. Title.
   HV8073.W5253 2008
   363.25'8—dc22

2008027096

Typeset by Laserwords Private Ltd, Chennai, India
Printed in Great Britain
on acid-free paper by
Biddles Ltd., King's Lynn

ISBN 978–0–19–921693–2

1 3 5 7 9 10 8 6 4 2

FOREWORD

It is exactly 100 years since Hugo Munsterberg's highly aspirational *On the Witness Stand*[1] was published in which the possible contributions of psychology to law were laid out. The current book presents an up-to-date account of one aspect of that aspiration—how psychology can aid the criminal justice system overcome the myriad problems associated with person identification in criminal cases.

Within this particular area of research the relation between law and psychology can be seen to have passed through a number of positive and negative phases. The initial phase was essentially negative: law relied heavily on eyewitness testimony; psychology tended to indicate such evidence was fragile and fallible. The second phase can be seen as less fraught: psychology began broadening its methodology to include case and field studies where testimony and identification were seen to be less fallible than laboratory-based studies would suggest; for their part, law was beginning to accept that such evidence could be problematical and should be the subject of judicial guidance. The third phase can be seen to be a natural outcome of this mutual accommodation to the facts of identification evidence: law now talks to psychology, and psychology increasingly tries to improve the relevance and ecological validity of its experimentation. This welcomed third-phase reciprocity has been hastened by the increasing presence of children as valued, valuable but vulnerable witnesses and victims in the courts.

The current book focuses on the interaction of laws, legal practices, and current psychological knowledge. It shows how procedures based on psychological theory can be put in place which attempt to maximize the opportunity for accurate identification. The book makes the point that information is the critical currency of the criminal justice system and process. Specifically, information about a criminal incident and the person or persons involved is crucial. However, such evidence has to endure an obstacle course that involves many hurdles and pitfalls. The authors argue that it thus behoves everyone in the criminal justice system—from the initial call handler, through police and social work interviewers, to eventually judges and juries—to learn and appreciate how easily the various personnel can influence what interviewees/witnesses report. Every information- and evidence-gathering process has a different impact on human memory and in turn on the resultant quantity and quality of information gained.

In the light of this insight the book makes the perspicacious point that memory needs to be treated in the same way as physical trace evidence as it also is a crime scene needing to be protected. To date, unlike physical trace evidence, eyewitness evidence does not have the same rigorous procedures in place to provide the most optimal ways of collecting, recording, preserving, and interpreting such evidence.

There is a need for robust scientific models to prevent such miscarriages of justice as are known to have occurred, predicated as they were predominantly upon faulty

---

[1] Munsterberg, H. (1908). *On the Witness Stand: Essays on Psychology and Crime.* New York: Clark Boardman.

eyewitness testimony and identification. However, researchers must always take great care not to draw premature conclusions and to make recommendations to the criminal justice system before developing adequate theoretical understandings and empirical underpinnings. It has often been said that the most practical aid to any applied endeavour is a valid general theory. If such a general theory were to exist, then much experimentation could be dispersed with, because the general covering laws of the theory could predict a priori what the outcome of such experimentation would be.

It is one of the many strengths of this book that the authors demonstrate clearly that no such general theory of eyewitness identification yet exists. They go further and lay bare the current status, nature, and quality of the empirical database to which a legal practitioner or an expert witness on identification could make recourse. That database is shown to be somewhat uncertain in terms of its reliability and validity. As a case in point the authors document the valiant attempts made to improve vulnerable witnesses' performance, but are forced to conclude that most such attempts have, to date, been unsuccessful.

This candid appraisal of what is sound and what is not in the various facets of current identification research and practice is a leitmotif that sets this book apart as an informative and valuable primer for both psychologists and legal personnel who have a genuine desire to improve justice for all. It is, in short, a book which Munsterberg would recognize as beginning to truly realize his aspirations for the applied discipline of forensic psychology.

Brian R. Clifford

Emeritus Professor, University of East London

Honorary Professor, University of Aberdeen

May 2008

ACKNOWLEDGEMENTS

We would like to thank our families for their continual support and understanding. Rachel and Becky would also like to say a special thank you to Ray for being an inspirational mentor over the years. It is our hope that this book will be of benefit to those directly or indirectly involved in Criminal Justice.

Rachel Wilcock
Ray Bull
Rebecca Milne

CONTENTS

TABLE OF CASES

TABLE OF STATUTES AND CODES OF PRACTICE

ABOUT THE AUTHORS

Rachel Wilcock Senior lecturer in Psychology at London South Bank University. Eyewitness identification is her major research interest and in particular, investigating methods to improve the performance of older adult witnesses. She has worked with a number of police forces across England and Wales, collecting research data on the identification decisions made by elderly witnesses, and examining the experiences and beliefs of witnesses and victims prior to them viewing identification procedures. She has just finished developing, in collaboration with Surrey Police, a multi-media presentation to show to witnesses prior to them viewing an identification parade to help inform them about police procedures and allay any fears they have about viewing an identification parade. She has published widely in international peer-reviewed journals and presented at a number of national and international conferences on the subject of identification procedures.

Ray Bull Professor of Forensic Psychology at the University of Leicester. His major research topic is police investigative procedures and he was part of the team commissioned by the Home Office to write 'Achieving Best Evidence in Criminal Proceedings: Guidance for Vulnerable or Intimidated Witnesses, Including Children (ABE)'. Professor Bull has advised a number of police forces on investigative procedures, and he has testified as an Expert Witness in a number of trials, several of which involved witness identification. In 2005 he received a Commendation from the London Metropolitan Police for his assistance in a complex rape investigation. He has authored and co-authored a large number of papers in research journals and has co-authored and co-edited many books, including *Investigative Interviewing: Psychology and Practice*.

Rebecca Milne Principal Lecturer at the Institute of Criminal Justice Studies, University of Portsmouth. She has trained a wide range of professions, including police officers, in witness interviewing issues, and has performed consultancy work in the UK and abroad. Dr Milne is the Academic Lead of the ACPO Investigative Interviewing Strategic Steering Group and is chair of the associated research sub-committee. She was part of the team that wrote a national training package to support 'Achieving Best Evidence' and is currently part of the team writing the 'Achieving Best Evidence: Part 2' document. She is a chartered Forensic Psychologist, an Associate Fellow of the British Psychological Society, and an Associate Editor of the *International Journal of Police Science and Management*.

1

INTRODUCTION

THE IMPORTANCE OF EYEWITNESS IDENTIFICATION EVIDENCE

When an eyewitness points a finger at a defendant and says, 'he did it! I saw him. I was so shocked I'll never forget that face!' the case is as good as over.

(Loftus, 1996, v.)

When a crime is committed and the identity of the crime perpetrator is unknown, the victim(s) or witness(es) to the crime may be asked to attend an identification parade (referred to in the United States as a line-up) to see if they can identify the police suspect as the perpetrator of the crime. As illustrated in the above quotation, eyewitness identification evidence when presented in court can have a significant impact on the outcome of a case. Indeed, research demonstrates that mock juries strongly believe in identification evidence given by confident witnesses, and in turn are likely to convict the defendants in such cases (Cutler, Penrod and Stuve, 1988). Additional research suggests that identification evidence is the second most incriminating type of evidence after confession evidence (Kassin and Neuman, 1997). Part of the reason for this is that for some people (ie jurors), eyewitness identification evidence has a common-sense appeal about it. Recognizing faces is an everyday task. Thus, if a juror observes a witness stating that they identified the perpetrator from an identification parade, they can understand and relate to that evidence. However, as will be described below, and discussed in the following chapters, eyewitness identification evidence is not always accurate.

PROBLEMATIC IDENTIFICATION EVIDENCE

Brandon and Davies (1973) claimed that the identification of innocent people from identification parades is the main cause of wrongful convictions in the United States and in England. Evidence that mistaken identification could contribute to miscarriages of justice comes from Huff, Rattner and Sagarin (1986) who reviewed 500 cases of wrongful convictions in the United States (US) and found that almost 60% of the cases involved faulty identification evidence given by primarily confident witnesses. Further evidence that misidentifications play a role in wrongful convictions comes from cases of DNA exoneration. This occurs when a biological specimen from a crime such as blood, semen, or hair is compared with the DNA of the person previously convicted of the crime (when DNA matching was not available) and the DNA from the crime is found not to match the convicted person's DNA. Since 1989, when the first person was exonerated on the basis of DNA evidence, there have so far been 208 DNA exonerations in the US. Mistaken eyewitness identification was a factor in 77% of these post-conviction DNA exoneration cases in the US, making it the leading cause of wrongful convictions (see <http://www.innocenceproject.org>). Misidentifications have also guided the legislation which has evolved through the history of identification evidence.

HISTORY OF IDENTIFICATION EVIDENCE

Wills (1912; cited by Shepherd, Ellis and Davies, 1982, 9) discusses a number of cases dating back to 1735 where witnesses have mistakenly identified innocent people as the crime perpetrator. Possibly due to these cases of misidentification, formal identity parades were introduced by the Metropolitan Police in London in about 1860 (Shepherd et al, 1982). Since this time, the notion of placing a suspect among a group of his or her peers and asking the witness to see if they can identify the perpetrator has remained the same. However, the exact procedures for constructing and delivering such identification parades have evolved over the years largely as a result of a number of miscarriages of justice. For example, in England in 1895 Adolf Beck was found guilty of a series of thefts from women. He was falsely identified by 10 out of the 15 victims and imprisoned. However, after the true perpetrator had been found, a Court of Enquiry in 1904 noted that the identity parade was composed of eight or nine men but only two had grey hair similar to Beck and neither of them bore any physical resemblance to him. In light of Beck's case the Home Office revised the Metropolitan Police Codes of Practice for identification parades and recommended that they be used by all Chief Constables. However, the rules were only advisory and were not publicly available.

In 1925 a Court of Enquiry was conducted (in England) in the case of Major Shepherd, a senior Officer in the Army who had been falsely identified from an unfair identification parade. As a result of the enquiry, the 1925 Circular on Parades was revised to emphasize: (i) the importance of foils (ie known to be innocent members of the parade) bearing a good resemblance to the suspect; and (ii) that the suspect should be advised that they could have a legal representative present during a parade. Between 1925 and 1969, although there were cases involving misidentification, there were no changes in the guidelines, which still remained advisory. In March 1968, 15 cases, most involving people convicted on the basis of mistaken identification, were sent to the Home Secretary by the National Council of Civil Liberties. As a result the Home Office (the relevant part of the government) in 1969 issued new advisory guidelines for the conduct of identification parades. These included much of what had gone before, but also that: (i) the police officer conducting the parade should be of Inspector rank and not have knowledge of the case, and (ii) that witnesses should be explicitly told that they should say if they cannot make a positive identification.

Despite the 1969 guidelines, a series of high profile cases involving misidentifications (for example, George Davis and Peter Hain, see Shepherd et al 1982 for details) led to the setting up by the Home Office of the 'Devlin Committee' to conduct an in-depth review of the law and procedures related to identification parades. The Devlin

Report (1976) was the first thorough report on issues related to eyewitness identification and contained statistics showing the prevalence of cases which had involved eyewitness identification evidence and also the number of cases where convictions have been overturned on the basis of faulty identification evidence. Since the Second World War this figure was believed to be 38, although some believe this figure to be an underestimate (Shepherd et al, 1982). There were two main recommendations contained in the Devlin Report. First, that cases based only on identification evidence should not proceed to Court unless there were very exceptional circumstances. Second, should such a case proceed, the judge should point out to the jury the problems with relying on identification evidence alone. Additionally, if identification evidence did play a prominent role in a case, the judge should point out to the jury any problems with the identification evidence specific to that particular case, such as, if the perpetrator had been viewed by the witness only briefly and in poor light.

Following the Devlin Report judicial guidance was given in a review by the Court of Appeal of a number of cases concerning identification evidence. The judgment, known as the Turnbull Judgment (*R v Turnbull* (1977) QB 224) after a defendant in one of the cases, provided specific guidelines for judges to give to juries in cases that involved disputed identification evidence. (Note that the Turnbull Judgment did not follow the Devlin Report suggestion that cases involving identification evidence alone should not continue unless the identification evidence was exceptional.) An example of exceptional identification could be if the witness was in the presence of the perpetrator for a long period of time. Conversely, an example of poor-quality identification evidence could be if the witness only glimpsed the perpetrator for a few seconds. To help juries assess whether an identification is likely to be of good or poor quality the Turnbull Judgment requires that judges direct the jury to relevant circumstances in which the crime initially occurred and the later identification took place. These circumstances can be remembered by the acronym ADVOKATE and police officers in England and Wales were required (and still are) to cover the following areas when eliciting eyewitness accounts (Kebbell and Wagstaff, 1999):

- Amount of time the perpetrator was observed for.
- Distance from where the crime was witnessed to the perpetrator.
- Visibility at the time of the crime, for example, did it occur in broad daylight or darkness.
- Obstructions, for example, did the witness have a clear view of the perpetrator or was it obstructed by something such as passing traffic.
- Known perpetrator, for example, did the witness either know the perpetrator or had they seen them before.
- Any reason to remember, for example, was the perpetrator in any way distinctive looking.
- Time lapse between witnessing the crime and viewing the identification parade.
- Errors in the identification as proven by other independent evidence.

Although the Turnbull guidelines given to juries in court commenced in 1977, legislation for constructing and delivering identification parades did not come into force until 1985 with Code D of the Police and Criminal Evidence Act 1984 (known as PACE) which governs police conduct in all police forces in England, Wales, Northern Ireland, the Channel Islands, and the Isle of Man. (Scotland has slightly different legislation for the conduct of identification parades.) Since 1984 there have been various revisions to Code D. Currently the 2005 edition is in use, although a new edition is about to be published and will come into force late in 2008. Code D stipulates various methods of identifying people (in connection with the investigation of crimes) such as by finger-prints, footwear impressions, bodily samples, taking photographs of arrested people to check their identity, examining detained suspects to find distinctive features such as scars or tattoos to help establish identity, and visual identification from parades. (Whilst the code does not give specific guidance for voice identification parades it does not preclude their use where appropriate (see Chapter 5). Code D contains a number of annexes which give guidance for conducting identification parades. Annex A pro-vides guidance for video identification parades and will be referred to in greater detail in Chapter 7.

In the US, the Department of Justice document *Eyewitness Evidence: A Guide for Law Enforcement* (Technical Working Group, 1999) gives guidance on eliciting evi-dence from witnesses. The guide includes recommendations for conducting identi-fication parades. Again, parts of this document will be referred to in greater detail in Chapter 7.

Some of the documents that have evolved to deal with eliciting identification evidence and reviewing identification evidence in court have referred to the contri-bution that behavioural scientists including psychologists can make to aid under-standing the complexities relating to identification evidence. For example, contained in the Devlin Report was a request for psychological research that could inform the conduct of identification parades and how identification evidence may be used in court. Furthermore, *Eyewitness Evidence: A Guide for Law Enforcement* was produced by a group of experienced professionals which included psychologists. However, the relationship between psychological research and identification practices and pro-cedures has not always been easy, and in some countries there still seems to be an ignorance of relevant psychological research.

APPLICATION OF PSYCHOLOGICAL RESEARCH
TO IDENTIFICATION

Psychologists demonstrated an interest in legal issues at the beginning of the 20th cen-tury. This began with Freud who made a speech to Austrian judges in 1906 suggesting that psychologists could help in establishing the likely truthfulness of witness testi-mony (Clifford and Bull, 1978). Following on from this, Hugo Von Munsterberg (an experimental psychologist at Harvard University in the US) made the first substantial attempt to bridge the gap between psychology and law. In 1908 he published a book entitled *On the Witness Stand*. In this he reviewed a number of topics relating to psy-chology and law, raising important issues about witness testimony and accuracy. He called for scientific research to guide legal reform. Psychologists then began to conduct research using methods which are the basis for much of the research still conducted today. For example, Stern (1939) investigated people's memory for simulated crime events and this methodology was developed in the 1970s by leading researchers on the accuracy of eyewitness testimony including, amongst others, Professor Elizabeth Loftus in the US, and members of the Psychology Department at North East London Polytechnic (now the University of East London). In 1978, Brian Clifford and Ray Bull (the second author of the present book), whilst at North East London Polytechnic, published their book entitled *The Psychology of Person Identification*. This was the first 'modern' comprehensive overview of the contribution that psychology could make to understanding witnesses identification performance.

When a witness is asked to view an identification parade to see if they can recognize the crime perpetrator they have to rely on their perception and memory of that crime. Perception, memory, and recognition are significant areas encompassed within the wider area of 'cognitive psychology' which can be defined as 'internal processes involved in making sense of the environment, and deciding what action might be appropriate. These processes include attention, perception, learning, memory, language, problem solving, reasoning, and thinking'. (Eysenck and Keane, 2005, 1). Another area of psychology relevant to eyewitness identification is 'social psychology' which can be defined as 'trying to understand the social behaviour of individuals in terms of both internal characteristics of the person (eg personality, mental processes) and external influences (the effect of the social environment)' (Crisp and Turner, 2007, xv). Thus, although perception, memory, and recognition are key processes for witnesses, it is important to remember that we are social beings and therefore cognitive processes are coloured by social factors such as attitudes, stereotypes and expectations, and conformity to other people.

Research in both cognitive and social psychology can be carried out in a laboratory setting. For example, research investigating face recognition ability could involve participants going to a quiet room without any distractions and viewing a large set of unknown faces. After a delay the participants are asked to respond to a test set of faces containing some of the faces they saw earlier along with some new faces not seen before. Using this method researchers are able to manipulate various factors that they believe may affect face recognition performance. For example, age or the interaction between ethnicity of participant and ethnicity of the 'to be recognized' faces. The results of this type of highly controlled experiment are informative but we need to remember that face recognition ability is also affected by additional factors that may not be present in a laboratory situation.

Another way in which we can look at face recognition ability in the more applied real world situation of eyewitness identification is to use a mock witness identification paradigm where participants (ie mock witnesses) view a simulated crime event. This crime event can be a staged event shown live or on videotape, or it can be a reconstruction of a real crime (similar to those shown on television such as the BBC's *Crimewatch* that tries to solve certain crimes by showing high quality reconstructions of the particular crime in question). After a delay, 'mock witnesses' view an identification parade/line-up which can either be live, shown on videotape or photographically. The parade can be either be target present (TP) which simulates a real life situation in which the police suspect is the perpetrator, or the line-up can be target absent (TA) which simulates a real life situation in which the police suspect is innocent. This mock witness identification paradigm is closer to real world conditions and therefore has more ecological validity (more closely replicates real world conditions) but generally researchers only use one parade and therefore it may be difficult to generalize findings from one target face to other faces (Wells and Windschitl, 1999).

Another way in which we can conduct research to investigate eyewitness identification is via field studies. Here, for example, researchers examine police records of witness performance on identification parades and can investigate whether certain factors lead to greater or fewer suspect identifications. Whilst this method has the greatest ecological validity, researchers do not have the control they have in mock witness and face recognition studies. For example, they may not be able to isolate all the factors that could be affecting the identifications. They also may not know for sure whether the suspect is in fact the perpetrator of the crime or innocent.

Whilst one method's advantage is another method's weakness, there is a demand for research which employs all three. Only by examining results (i) from cognitive psychology laboratory studies and (ii) from more applied research are we are able to build up a reliable picture of the psychological factors affecting witness identification performance. Thus, this book will especially discuss research which encompasses these three different methods.

AIMS OF THIS BOOK

The main aim of this book is to provide a practical guide to identifying crime perpetrators based on psychological theory and research. Based on current knowledge at the time, Clifford and Bull did this very effectively in their 1978 book *The Psychology of Person Identification*. However, a great deal of very relevant research has been conducted since the 1970s, and we felt that an up-to-date review was sorely needed. This book discusses research and theories that are relevant to current legislation and guidelines concerned with person identification and outlines what psychologists currently know about constructing and delivering identification parades from the point of view of the suspect and the witness/victim.

Chapter 2 outlines important theories derived from cognitive psychology which are important for helping us understand both how witnesses remember crime and recognize crime perpetrators. With regard to eyewitness memory we examine how memory can be thought of as including three key stages: perception and encoding of a crime, storage of information about the crime in memory, and retrieval, including verbal recall of the crime and visual person recognition. We consider the constructive nature of eyewitness memory and how learning incorrect information related to the crime and poor questioning can affect the quality of our memory for the crime event. We also briefly discuss ways in which we can aid witness memory. The remainder of the chapter is focused on psychological theory and research relating to face recognition. Various models of face recognition are outlined and we discuss how these are helpful in considering factors likely to affect witness performance on identification parades. Having outlined models of face recognition, discussion moves to problems that can occur in face recognition. Finally, we consider the role of decision-making processes and judgements involved when people recognize faces.

Chapter 3 focuses on giving person descriptions which play a vital role in many criminal investigations and witnesses typically volunteer such information spontaneously. Thus, it is important to consider the factors likely to affect the accuracy of person descriptions. Identification parades generally occur after verbal descriptions have been given, and so how person descriptions relate to witnesses' subsequent identification performance is also examined. The chapter begins by discussing how to elicit person descriptions at each phase of the investigative process, from an initial description ascertained during the first call made to the police to report a crime, through to the stage when a witness is formally interviewed by the police, and if a witness is asked to help construct a facial composite of the perpetrator. When considering the quality of person descriptions, we discuss factors likely to affect them, such as age of the witness and the conditions under which the crime was viewed. The remainder of the chapter is devoted to discussion of the relationship between person descriptions and person identification. This is of interest because processes underlying verbal recall and visual recognition differ. Indeed, some research that is discussed demonstrates that describing a face can negatively impact on the ability subsequently to correctly recognize that face.

Chapter 4 goes on to discuss further factors that may affect our ability to correctly identify perpetrators of crime. These factors include variables relating to the witness, such as how confident they are that they have made a correct decision on the identification parade, variables relating to the perpetrator, such as whether they were wearing some form of disguise, and variables relating to the situation in which the crime was committed, such as whether the crime was committed during daylight or darkness. These factors are referred to as estimator variables because their effect on identification performance can only be estimated after the crime has been witnessed. Recent research investigating the effect of such estimator variables on identification performance is considered in this chapter.

In Chapters 1 to 4 we have largely focused on the performance of eyewitnesses. However, in Chapter 5 we turn to other methods of identification, apart from face identification. These other methods include voice identification and gait identification. For example, an ear witness (the witness has only heard the perpetrator's voice but not seen them) would only be able to take part in a voice identification parade. We consider the effect of factors relating to the voice that was heard, such as regional accent, and factors relating to the ear witness, for example whether the witness was blind. Finally, with respect to voice identification parades we discuss how best to conduct them and some current guidelines. The next part of the chapter is devoted to another method of identification, identification via walk/gait. Whilst relatively little research has considered identification of a perpetrator by their gait, there is some which suggests we are able to some extent to discriminate between individuals' gait. This research is evaluated before finally considering research examining witness performance on multiple identification line-ups for different aspects of the perpetrator including both voice and face.

Chapter 6 examines the effects of expectancies and stereotypes on identification performance. It begins by examining research concerned with professionals who examine fingerprints to determine whether the sample from the 'crime scene' and that from the 'suspect' are similar enough to arrive at the decision that they are from the same person. Pioneering recent research is discussed which demonstrates that even professionals' decisions as to the identity of fingerprints can be subject to expectations they hold on the basis of psychological and cognitive factors. The chapter proceeds to discuss research which examines the effect of expectations and stereotypes on identification performance. Psychological research has demonstrated that people believe that nasty things are done by ugly people. Therefore, when trying to identify or describe crime perpetrators witnesses may let their expectations of what criminals look like (and their stereotypes about what certain types of criminals look like) influence their descriptions and identifications.

Chapter 7 gives an overview of current legislation and guidelines related to the conduct of identification procedures. In England and Wales, PACE Code D provides stipulations as to how identification procedures should be conducted and in the US, as mentioned above, there is the US Department of Justice's *Eyewitness Evidence: A Guide for Law Enforcement*. The content of these documents is discussed in terms of the empirical research which has guided some of the recommendations. Key areas include construction, presentation, and administering identification parades/lineups, as well as the instructions given to witnesses. Finally, in this chapter we consider alternative identification procedures.

In Chapter 8 the identification performance of witnesses who are deemed vulnerable, including children, the elderly, and people with learning disabilities, is discussed. This area of research is particularly important due to the Youth Justice and Criminal Evidence Act 1999 (in England and Wales) and the Vulnerable Witnesses (Scotland) Act 2004. These Acts stress that methods urgently need to be developed to assist vulnerable witnesses/victims to play a fuller role in the criminal justice system, especially to assist them to provide evidence against crime perpetrators. We, therefore, also consider in this chapter the limited amount of research that has investigated possible methods to aid child and elderly witnesses.

In Chapter 9 we outline new technologies involved in identification procedures. A historical overview is given examining the technological advancements of the tools used to provide facial composites. An evaluation is also made of the efficacy of such tools for an investigation. The merits of video identification parades using both VIPER and PROMAT (the two systems currently used by police in the UK) are discussed over the more traditional methods of live identification parades. The discussion then ends with an examination of how CCTV images help or hinder recognition performance.

Finally, in Chapter 10, we draw upon the previous chapters to make some final conclusions regarding the contribution of psychology to identification, theory, and practice. We comment on the issue of applying findings from psychological research to police practice. Recommendations are made regarding the future of identification procedures and also future directions in identification research. Finally, we end with a discussion of the importance of police professionals and academics working more closely together to ensure that accurate identification evidence is elicited. This is especially important in the many counties where such 'working together' rarely or never occurs at present.

It is our hope that this book will be a useful guide for professionals whose work involves identification procedures (such as police officers, judges, and lawyers) or those who have an interest in the area. Although the PACE Code D and the Department of Justice *Eyewitness Evidence: A Guide for Law Enforcement* are significant steps in the right direction, currently there is no comprehensive document for professionals regarding psychology behind the various recommendations, the psychological factors affecting identification, and psychology underpinning recent innovations in the area. We hope that the overviews in the following chapters will go a considerable way in helping to address this gap. We also hope that this book will be a very useful learning resource for psychology students, law students, and policing studies students who should have an interest in the crucially important topic of identification.

REFERENCES

BRANDON, R. and DAVIES, C. (1973). *Wrongful Imprisonment: Mistaken Convictions and Their Consequences.* London: Allen and Unwin.

CLIFFORD, B.R. and BULL, R. (1978). *The Psychology of Person Identification.* London: Routledge and Kegan Paul.

CRISP, R.J. and TURNER, R.N. (2007). *Essential Social Psychology.* London: Sage Publications.

CUTLER, B.L., PENROD, S.D. and STUVE, T.E. (1988). Juror decision making in eyewitness identification cases. *Law and Human Behavior, 12,* 41–55.

DEVLIN, LORD P. (1976). *Report to the Secretary of State for the Home Department of the Departmental Committee on Evidence on Identification in Criminal Cases.* London: HMSO.

EYSENCK, M.W. and KEANE, M.T. (2005). *Cognitive Psychology: A Student's Handbook* (5th edn). Hove: Lawrence Earlbaum Association.

HUFF, C.R., RATTNER, A. and SAGARIN, E. (1986). Guilty until proven innocent: Wrongful conviction and public policy. *Crime and Deliquency, 32,* 518–544.

Innocence Project available at <http://www.innocenceproject.org> (accessed 26 November 2007).

KASSIN, S.M. and NEUMAN, K. (1988). On the power of confession evidence: An experimental test of the fundamental difference hypothesis. *Law and Human Behavior, 21,* 469–484.

KEBBELL, M.R. and WAGSTAFF, G.F. (1999). *Face Value? Evaluating the Accuracy of Eyewitness Information.* Police Research Series, Paper 102. Research Development and Statistics Directorate, Home Office.

LOFTUS, E. (1996). *Eyewitness Testimony.* Cambridge, Massachusetts: Harvard University Press.

MUNSTERBERG, H. (1908). *On the Witness Stand: Essays on Psychology and Crime.* New York: Clark Boardman.

Police and Criminal Evidence Act 1984. Codes of practice, edition of 2005, available at <http://police.homeoffice.gov.uk/operational-policing/powers-pace-codes/pace-code-intro> (accessed 1 September 2006).

SHEPHERD, J.W., ELLIS, H.D. and DAVIES, G.M. (1982). *Identification Evidence: A Psychological Evaluation.* Aberdeen: Aberdeen University Press.

STERN, W. (1939). The psychology of testimony. *Journal of Abnormal and Social Psychology, 34,* 3–20.

TECHNICAL WORKING GROUP FOR EYEWITNESS EVIDENCE (1999). *Eyewitness Evidence: A Guide For Law Enforcement.* Washington, DC: Office of Justice Programs, National Institute of Justice.

WELLS, G.L. and WINDSCHITL, P.D. (1999). Stimulus sampling and social psychological experimentation. *Personality and Social Psychology Bulletin, 25,* 1115–1125.

2

PERCEPTION, MEMORY, AND RECOGNITION INVOLVED IN WITNESS IDENTIFICATION

INTRODUCTION

Remembering and recognizing faces is something we do on a day-to-day basis, usually without giving it much thought. It therefore may come as a surprise when people who have witnessed a crime are not always able to give accurate accounts of what happened during the crime or to correctly identify the crime perpetrator. Psychologists have conducted research on memory and recognition which gives possible explanations as to why witnesses may not always be accurate and why it is such a difficult task. This chapter will outline key theories on eyewitness memory and recognition which are important for understanding the performance of eyewitnesses.

WHAT IS MEMORY?

Memory contains a vast amount of vital information which allows us to make sense of the world around us and of new information that we come across on a daily basis. Memory contains a wealth of information such as language, who we are, where we have come from, and events in our lives. Psychologists have termed our memory for specific events 'episodic' memory (Tulving, 1972). Hence a memory for a crime (episode) would usually be referred to as an episodic memory. However, episodic memory is not like a video camera that records an event onto a videotape which can then simply be rewound to the appropriate point and played back, rather memory for a specific event is reconstructed using stored information about the particular event in time, in conjunction with the more general knowledge we have about the world. The *processes* underlying memory can be thought of as comprising three different components. Initially there is *encoding* where the perceived information first enters memory. In the context of a crime, this is when a witness views a crime (for example, the face of the perpetrator) and that information is put into or represented in memory. The second phase occurs between encoding and remembering the information and it is referred to as *storage*, where the encoded face of the perpetrator is stored in memory. The final phase occurs when the witness tries to *retrieve* information about the face of the perpetrator (for example, when giving a description of him/her and what happened during the crime to the police (a recall task) or when viewing an identification parade (a recognition task)). Although recall and recognition both rely on a witness' ability to retrieve information, slightly different processes are involved (as will be discussed later on in this chapter).

Problems can occur at any or all of these three stages. For example, witnesses may not have perceived all the crime information or they were not able to adequately encode it. There may be problems that occur during the storage of information, and/or witnesses may have difficulty retrieving information. Each stage will now be discussed.

ENCODING

In order for a witness to perceive and encode a crime they must be in a position where they are able to view and experience the crime adequately. If a witness is too far away from the crime scene to be able to accurately perceive all that occurred, then while their subsequent report may well contain details that they were able to perceive (such as a car driving off at high speed and a lady lying in the middle of the road), it may also contain details that they presume must have happened but which they did not directly perceive (such as the car hitting the lady).

Assuming that the witness is in a position where they are able to perceive the crime (in order for it to be encoded into memory) they must attend to it (ie focus on it and pay attention to it). There are vast amounts of both external and internal information that are picked up by our senses at any given time. For example, as I'm writing this paragraph I can hear birds singing, I'm a little bit cold, I'm aware that the chair I'm sitting on is hard, I have a little scratch on my finger that is sore, I can taste the remains in my mouth of the coffee I have just finished. All of this sensory information that we receive every minute has the potential to be encoded into memory. However, because there is so much of it, our brain cannot encode all of it. Therefore, attention is selective and we encode only that information which we attend to. For example, when I am working on my laptop computer I don't generally attend to the humming noise it routinely makes. Thus a vast amount of information in our environment is not encoded in the first place and therefore is not available for retrieval at a later time.

We have the ability to rapidly change the focus of our attention and encode new things in our environment that suddenly occur. For example, when we are driving a car we are paying attention to the road ahead of us and we may be talking to a passenger. However, if there is suddenly a new piece of important sensory information in our environment, such as a loud police siren, we automatically attend to it, possibly at the expense of not being able to remember what our passenger had just been talking about (because we switched attention from passenger to siren). In addition to our attention being automatically focused (as described above with the effect of the police siren) we have the ability to be able to focus our attention on particular things in our environment. This is known as 'Selective Attention' and in the context of witnessing a crime, a witness must 'selectively attend' to the crime in order to encode it successfully so that a memory of it can be retrieved at a later time. If a mugging took place on a busy high street, in order for a witness to successfully recall important aspects of the mugging they would need to selectively attend to the mugger and victim and ignore other information such as other shoppers, shop deliveries, people busking etc. Assuming that we are able to selectively attend to a crime, we may also find that some specific aspect of the crime particularly grabs our attention and this may be at the cost of us not being able to encode other crime-relevant information. For example, if a weapon is present during a crime, research has shown that our attention can be focused largely on the gun and because of that we are less likely to be able to correctly identify the perpetrator (Steblay, 1992). (For an in-depth discussion on the weapon focus effect see Chapter 4.)

In addition to where our attention is focused, there are other factors that affect the quantity and quality of encoding. For example, we are more likely to encode information that is meaningful to us. Imagine that a witness to a crime was a hairdresser by profession, it may be likely they would have encoded the perpetrator's hair because, due to their job experience, hair is salient to them and they know a lot about it. If they were to be later asked for a description of the perpetrator, it may also be likely that they would be able to give a very detailed account of the colour and texture of hair as well as the hair style. Conversely, if another witness were asked for a description of the perpetrator, they may only be able to give a limited description of the perpetrator's hair because hair is not something that is meaningful to them.

We know that knowledge affects encoding, and related to this is research that has found that life experience also affects encoding. Christianson, Karlsson and Persson (1998) examined the effect of experience on memory by studying experienced police officers', recruit police officers', teachers', and university students' memories of a violent crime. Experienced police officers were significantly better at remembering information about the crime compared to the other three groups, probably because they had more experience of viewing crime scenes and were thus better able to process the information.

If a crime is witnessed by several people it is likely there will be several different accounts of that crime due to the different things witnesses were able to perceive, attend to, their experience, and knowledge. Additionally there are factors (not already mentioned) which occur at the time of encoding that also determine whether a crime is remembered and what aspects of it are remembered. These factors include, the amount of time a witness viewed the perpetrator, how salient the perpetrator was, how far away from the perpetrator the witness was standing, how violent the crime was, and the levels of stress the witness experienced. (For an in-depth discussion of the effect of these factors on person descriptions see Chapter 3 and on identification see Chapter 4.)

STORAGE

Once a memory has been encoded it is available for storage. The length of time the memory is stored for can have an effect on how much of it can subsequently be remembered. Ebbinghaus was the first person to study the effect of delay on memory (back in 1879). Using himself as a subject, he found that his memory for nonsense syllables dropped quickly soon after learning the syllables and then decreased more gradually as time went on. Other research using larger numbers of participants has also found that memory appears to decline over time. For example, Bahrick (1984) tested teachers' memory of names and faces of their pupils from eight years ago, four years ago, one year ago, and two weeks ago. Performance declined over time. In the context of a crime there are cases where witnesses are not identified by the police until many months or even years after the crime has occurred. In these sorts of situations it is likely that the witness will have more problems remembering what happened the longer time goes on compared to a witness who is asked to recall the crime soon after it occurred.

Such problems could be due to issues that occur during storage such as learning new information about a crime. For example, a witness may read an account of the crime in a newspaper which could contain correct information but could also contain some incorrect information (known as misinformation, see below for a discussion of this). Another process that could occur during storage is self-rehearsal where we go through what happened in our mind to try to make sense of and remember the crime. During self-rehearsal our own knowledge and expectations of the world will affect how and what we think about the crime (known as scripts or schema; see below for a discussion of this). These issues that occur during storage are likely to influence retrieval.

RETRIEVAL OF VERBAL INFORMATION

When we are asked to remember something we are not able to simply press rewind and play the original memory. In actual fact memory, as already noted, is constructive. That is, it is composed of stored information about the particular event, but it also contains more general knowledge we have about the world. We tend to have expectations in our mind as to what happens in a certain situation, whether or not we have actually experienced such a situation, and these are known within psychology as scripts or schema. For example, recent research shows that 82% of people believe that during a mugging a robber approaches a victim by running up from behind and 51% believe that a robber is always with a gang of other people (Dando, Wilcock and Milne, in preparation, 2008). In light of this, a victim who is mugged will remember what they actually saw and experienced (eg the robber snatching their mobile phone or bag) but may also 'recall' other actions such as the perpetrator having run up behind them (although they did not actually see the perpetrator do that and the perpetrator may not have done that). The scripts/schema help them to make sense of what happened in terms of their knowledge and understanding of what occurs during a mugging and allows them to fill in gaps in their memory of the crime.

In addition to memory being constructed from our encoding of the event and our own schema for that type of event, it may also contain new information that we have since learnt which relates to the event. Indeed, established research literature suggests that without realizing we can incorporate related *external* information (which may be correct or incorrect) when we reconstruct our memory of an event. Professor Elizabeth Loftus has been instrumental in raising our awareness of the existence of the 'misinformation effect'. This effect has been tested using a research paradigm in which participants initially view an event. Subsequently, half the participants are deliberately given some incorrect information (misinformation) for example, in a question about the event or in a report of the event. Later on all participants are asked to recall what happened in the event either by giving an account of it or by answering questions about it. For example, Loftus (1975) showed participants a videotape of a road traffic accident and then half the participants received a question containing misleading information asking participants how fast the car was travelling along the country road when it passed the barn (when in fact no barn existed). The other half of the participants were simply asked how fast the car was travelling along the country road. A week later participants were asked whether they had seen a barn and 17.3% of participants who had received the question which mentioned the barn reported seeing one compared to just 2.7% of participants who had received the question which did not mention the barn.

Even something more subtle such as the precise wording of a question can lead people to give different accounts of an event. Loftus and Palmer (1974) showed participants slides depicting a road traffic accident. Participants were then asked a number of questions about the event including a question asking participants about the speed the cars were travelling when the accident happened. Specifically, some were asked how fast the cars were going when they hit each other. For other participants 'hit' was replaced with either 'smashed', 'collided', 'bumped', or 'contacted'. Participants' estimates of speed altered depending upon which verb was used in the question. Participants who heard 'smashed' gave the highest estimate of speed compared to participants who heard 'contacted' who gave the lowest estimate of speed. Additionally, a week later participants who heard 'smashed' were significantly more likely to report seeing glass in the slide sequence (when there was none) compared to those participants who heard the other verbs used to describe the moment of impact when the cars came together.

Research has also investigated the circumstances under which people are particularly likely to be susceptible to misinformation. For example, when the memory for the event is weaker (ie the witness viewed the crime under poor conditions such as darkness and they were standing a long way from the crime scene) misinformation effects are more likely to occur (Reyna and Titcomb, 1997). Once misinformation is taken into the memory, the more occasions on which a witness is asked to give the account containing the misinformation, the more likely it is to remain in the account of the actual event (Haber and Haber, 2000) and be repeated as part of the original memory, and maybe even confidently!

Thus our memory for an event is likely to contain originally encoded information, information that we hold in our own schema which relates to the event, and new information (correct or incorrect) that we have learnt since the event. We should now also consider what happens after witnesses have given their initial account of what happened. Later they may be asked to go through their account again, possibly by people who do not know how to interview properly (Milne and Bull, 1999). In fact, during the course of an investigation a witness may be repeatedly asked to report what happened, so by the time a case gets to court the witness will have been through their account on numerous occasions, including with family and friends. Each time the memory for the crime is reported it is not simply recounted in an identical fashion each time of telling (Haber and Haber, 2000). Instead, the account of the crime will change slightly. It will contain many aspects of the original encoding but also new pieces of information based on other people's reactions to what the witness has said. If there is some element of the crime that does not really make sense, the witness may add some explanation or inference to make the account seem more coherent (even though, for example, the actions of the perpetrator may well have not made sense). The witness may under or over emphasize certain parts of the account according to whom their audience is. Thus, each time the witness relays the crime, different pieces of information may be added and other bits of information forgotten and, the resulting memory will be rather different from the original memory for the crime. However, the witness will have little insight into how their memory has changed over the repeated retrieval attempts (Haber and Haber, 2000).

Improving Retrieval

One of the best ways in which we can help to obtain as accurate an account of what happened as possible is to use appropriate questioning. For example, by the use of open-ended questions such as: 'Tell me everything that happened.' Related to this principle, psychologists have developed the 'Cognitive Interview' (Fisher and Geiselman, 1992), which is a memory-enhancing interview technique that aims to improve both the quality and quantity of information recalled by witnesses. The 'Cognitive Interview' has proven to be very successful and is now used by police forces in several countries around the world (see Milne and Bull, 1999).

Recall can also be aided by giving appropriate retrieval cues. These are relevant pieces of information that are linked with the to-be-remembered event and which aid the process of remembering the particular event. For example, if a relative asks whether you remember a particular holiday cottage from your childhood you may struggle until they give you another piece of information (ie a retrieval cue) such as: 'Remember it was the cottage where your father put his slipper on and there was a mouse in it which bit his toe.' The effectiveness of retrieval cues in aiding recall for an event depends on how appropriate they are. The more overlap there is between encoding and information provided by retrieval cues, the more likely a person will be able to remember other relevant aspects of the event (Thomson and Tulving, 1970). Research has found that at the time of retrieval, if aspects of the encoding context can be reinstated (for example, by taking someone back to the physical location where the information was learnt) this can aid recall. Godden and Baddeley (1975) demonstrated this by asking divers to learn a list of words either under water or on land. After a delay the divers were either asked to recall the words on land or under water. Those divers who were in the same context at recall as at encoding (eg on land at both encoding and recall) remembered significantly more words than those who were in a different context (eg on land at encoding but under water at recall). Mental context reinstatement has also been found to be successful at enhancing recall whereby a person is instructed to mentally recreate in their mind the original context, both physical (what the environment looked like), and personal (how they were feeling) in which they encoded the information (Dando, Wilcock and Milne, in press, 2008). Furthermore, mental reinstatement of context helps to overcome the practical problem of taking someone back to a crime scene which may, for example be too traumatizing or have changed. Mental context reinstatement is a very important component of the Cognitive Interview.

RETRIEVAL OF VERBAL INFORMATION VERSUS RECOGNITION

Thus far we have discussed retrieval only in terms of remembering verbal information. However, when someone is asked to view a line-up to see if they can recognize the crime perpetrator they rely on somewhat different processes to recognize a face compared to if they are asked to verbally recall what happened during the crime. Asking a witness to recall what happened is a very demanding task because they are being asked to actively retrieve information from memory to tell the police officer. Conversely when a witness is asked 'Do you recognize this face?' the face stimulus is directly in front of them and they are simply trying to determine whether the face matches their memory. Thus, asking a witness to describe the perpetrator's face is likely to be a more difficult task than recognizing the perpetrator's face from a line-up (see Chapter 3 for a discussion on the relationship between descriptions of faces and identification). From this it sounds like recognition is a simple task, however, as we will see in the next section, recognizing faces creates its own problems.

FACE RECOGNITION

Before we consider how we recognize faces, there is an important distinction that must be made between recognizing known faces and unknown faces (referred to in research, respectively, as familiar and unfamiliar faces). Generally people are able to successfully recognize the faces of people they know well such as friends and family very easily (Bruce, Burton and Hancock, 2007). Less familiar faces are more problematic for people to recognize and this poses a problem for witnesses. Most crimes for which a line-up would be required, are committed by people that witnesses have not seen before and therefore at a line-up they will be searching for an unfamiliar face seen only once before. During the process of face recognition the recognizer initially considers: Is this face known to me? If the answer is yes, the next crucial question in terms of eyewitness identification is: From where or how do I know this person? Even if a face seems somewhat familiar to a witness, in terms of identification that is not sufficient because they need to go beyond that feeling of knowing, and say not only 'Yes this person is known to me', but also 'Yes this is the perpetrator of the crime whom I saw break into a car last Saturday night'. It is precisely this latter part of the process that many people have difficulty with. For example, I was travelling to work on the train and by chance sat down opposite a lady whose face was known to me but I was unable to determine where or when I had seen her before. A day later when I was walking my dog it came to me that I had met her before (and her two dogs) out dog walking on a few occasions. When we see a known face that is out of context (as the above example illustrates) we are less likely to be able to determine where or when we know the face from.

In order to understand how we recognize faces psychologists have put forward a number of theories/models. These models have been developed using empirical research findings gained through studying the performance of participants on face recognition tasks in laboratory situations, problems of face recognition in everyday life, and people with brain damage which has resulted in deficits in face recognition (such as prosopagnosia whereby people are unable to recognize faces that are known to them). The first very influential model of face recognition was put forward by Bruce and Young in 1986. They suggested that there are seven different types of information or *codes* which can be sought from faces. These are pictorial codes, structural codes, visually derived semantic codes, identity specific codes, name code, expression code, and facial speech code (see Table 2.1). If many of the codes are present it is more likely that a face will be recognized.

Table 2.1 Bruce and Young's Facial Codes

Facial Codes	Definition
Pictorial	A record of any particular static visual pattern, picture, or event. For example, a pictorial code of a mug shot will include details of the face, pose, and expression, as well as any information about lighting, graininess of image, or flaw in the mug shot.
Structural	A representation of areas of the face and features of the face and how they relate to one another. When we look at faces we process the face as a whole in a 'configural or holistic' manner rather than focusing on individual features of the face such as the nose, eyes etc.
Visually derived semantic	Visually derived semantic information refers to things such as gender and age, which can be derived simply by looking at a face. We can also look at a face and consider whether it reminds us of a person that we know.
Identity specific semantic	Identity specific semantic refers to information that is known about a familiar person such as their occupation, whom they socialize with, where they live etc.
Name	The name code provides information that tells us what a person's name is.
Expression	The expression code refers to information that we can glean from a face by looking at the arrangement of features, whether a person is happy, sad, angry etc.
Facial speech	Observation of a person's lip movements when they are speaking helps us to correctly perceive what they are saying.

The Bruce and Young (1986) model also offers an explanation of how the facial codes are generated and accessed (see Figure 2.1). *Facial Recognition Units* contain structural codes for a known face. If there is a high degree of resemblance between the stored description and the encoded input a signal to the *Cognitive System* will be activated. Facial recognition units can access *Person Identity Nodes* which contain identity specific semantic information about a known person which allows us to identify who

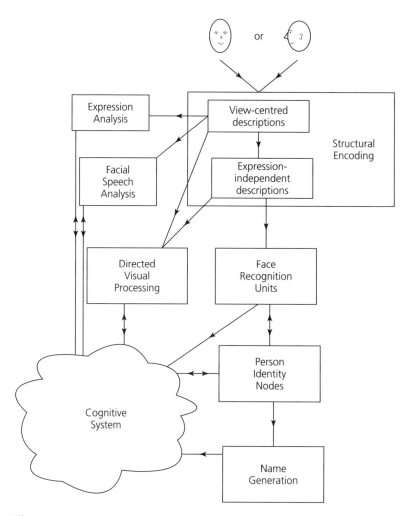

Fig 2.1

the person is. Through the person identity nodes *Name Generation* can be reached.
The *Cognitive System* has several purposes: it contains additional associated general
information that is beyond the scope of the person identity nodes (eg associated person information that is not essential for identifying a person); it is responsible for
different decision processes (eg using information from different facial codes); and
it receives information from different components of the system such as *Face Recognition Units* (and equally it can influence those same components). One such component is *Directed Visual Processing* which occurs when we selectively encode visual
information. For example, if a person witnesses a crime they may actively concentrate
on what the perpetrator's face looks like so that they will (hopefully) later be able to
give a good description to police.

One key aspect of Bruce and Young's model which is important when thinking about witnesses identifying perpetrators of crime is that it assumes that familiar and unfamiliar faces are processed differently. (Bear in mind that for most witnesses who are asked to view a line-up, the face of the perpetrator is likely not to be of a very familiar person.) With unfamiliar faces only certain codes are likely to be involved (pictorial, structural, visually derived semantic, expression, and facial speech). Conversely, with familiar faces additional identity specific and name codes could be involved. With unfamiliar faces recognition may only get as far as a face recognition unit being activated and the person simply knowing that the face is familiar but not being able to say why or how. However, with familiar faces it is more likely that if a face recognition unit is activated it will go on and access a person identity node and possibly the name of the person.

Bruce et al (1999) examined performance on a face matching task in which participants were asked to view high quality video frames of unfamiliar male faces and state whether the same stimulus face was present in an array of similar looking photographs of faces shown alongside the stimulus face to allow for comparisons to be made. When view point (full face or 30 degrees) and expression (smiling or neutral expression) matched, rather surprisingly accuracy was only 70%. The researchers suggested that the low accuracy rates may be due to differences in pictorial quality and detail. Of more interest is the finding that, if view point or expression changed accuracy dropped further. This research suggests that even if the initial image of an unfamiliar face is very clear, even subtle changes regarding the face at test will affect recognition accuracy. Bruce et al (2007) suggest that familiarity with a face is a result of viewing many different images of the same face which contribute to an average for that face represented in memory. Thus, when we view a face that is familiar to us the fact that the expression is slightly different is unlikely to affect our ability to recognize the face.

Since Bruce and Young's model of face recognition, there have been other models of face recognition put forward, for example by Valentine, Bredart, Lawson and Ward (1991), Burton and Bruce (1993), and Burton, Bruce and Hancock (1999). These models of face recognition are also really concerned with how we recognize familiar faces and the role that semantic information and name identification play in this process. Generally, when witnesses attempt to identify a perpetrator of a crime they are not privy to this sort of knowledge about a perpetrator and hence these models go beyond (and may not directly apply to) what we need to know for understanding how a witness is able to identify a perpetrator of crime who is unfamiliar to them.

A model of face recognition has also been developed to deal with factors that affect people's ability to accurately recognize familiar and unfamiliar faces. For example, we know from research looking at the performance of mock witnesses in laboratory tasks investigating eyewitness identification performance that their performance is likely to be affected by (i) race of face (own race faces may be more likely to be correctly identified than other race faces—Meissner and Brigham, 2001) and (ii) distinctiveness of face (a face rated as distinctive is more likely to be correctly identified compared to a face rated as typical—Going and Read, 1974). (See Chapter 4 for a fuller discussion of such effects.) Additionally, we know that the orientation in which a face is seen has an effect on the accuracy of a subsequent recognition (people are usually less accurate at recognizing a face if the face was initially presented upside down (Valentine, 1988). As a result, to account for all this Valentine (1991) put forward a *Multidimensional Space Framework* which offers explanations of how faces are encoded and of the effects of distinctiveness, race, and inversion. He suggested that we encode faces within a *Multi-dimensional Space* where faces are defined by a number of dimensions which serve to distinguish between different faces. Examples of dimensions could be hair length, eye colour, face shape etc. 'The origin of the multidimensional space is defined as the central tendency of the dimensions' (1991, 166). Thus, typical looking faces (that we are more likely to see) will generally cluster around the central tendency where there will be lots of other typical looking faces. Conversely, more distinctive faces will be more distant from the central tendency where there will be far fewer faces. The multidimensional space includes both familiar and unfamiliar faces. Within the framework two models are identified, a *Norm-based Model* and an *Exemplar-based Model*. The *Norm-based Model* assumes that when a face is viewed it is encoded on the basis of how far it deviates from a single general norm face which is at the origin/central tendency of the multidimensional space. The *Exemplar-based Model* assumes there is no single general norm face and each face is encoded as a point in the multidimensional space and the origin of the multidimensional space merely represents where the maximum number of points/faces exist.

Valentine (1991) used the framework to make predictions as to why there are effects of distinctiveness, inversion, and race on face recognition performance. Distinctive faces will be contained in regions of the multidimensional space where there are fewer points, so if an unfamiliar but distinctive face is seen it is unlikely to be confused with a previously seen face and it should therefore be easier to accurately and more quickly reject the face as not seen before. Conversely, a typical looking unfamiliar face is more likely to be confused with the many other typical looking faces encoded in a region of high density in the multidimensional space and should therefore (i) take a longer time to reject or (ii) incorrectly be classified as familiar. Valentine also made predictions as to the effect of showing a face upside down on the recognition of distinctive versus typical faces. He suggested that inverting a face is likely to be equivalent to poor encoding conditions, thus the effect of viewing a perpetrator under poor viewing conditions (such as among a crowd of other people) could possibly lead to similar effects as inversion. Valentine suggested that inverted faces may be more likely to be incorrectly located in the multidimensional space compared with upright faces. Thus, when an unfamiliar but typical face is inverted, it is likely to be mistakenly judged as familiar because (i) there is a region of high density points/faces and (ii) the inverted face may be incorrectly located in the multidimensional space. With an inverted unfamiliar but distinctive face the same applies, but because distinctive faces are in a region of low density it is less likely that errors will be made. Evidence was found to support these predictions for the effects of inversion on typical/distinctive faces (Valentine, 1991).

The multidimensional space framework also provides us with a way to understand how other race faces may be encoded (assuming that the multidimensional space is based largely on experience of faces from one race). Valentine suggests that the dimensions (such as hair and face shape) used to encode own race faces may not be appropriate dimensions for other race faces and that we have no or limited dimensions relevant to other race faces. This may result in other race faces being less likely to be accurately recognized because they are densely clustered (using inappropriate dimensions for other race faces) within the existing multidimensional space, meaning it is more difficult to distinguish among other race faces than among own race faces. The norm-based model suggests that the cluster of other race faces will be distant from the centre of the multidimensional space (central tendency) where typical (own race) faces are located, thus, recognizing other race faces will be more difficult. The exemplar-based model suggests that because there are more exemplars of own race faces than other race faces, own race faces will be better recognized than other race faces. Valentine also predicted that inversion would be more disruptive for other race faces than own race faces and this was supported by research by Valentine and Bruce (1986).

The Multidimensional Space Framework offers an explanation as to how faces are encoded and how both familiar and unfamiliar faces are recognized. More importantly, this model of face recognition can cater for the effects of race and distinctiveness of face that we know can occur in eyewitness identification situations.

MISTAKES IN FACE RECOGNITION

Although such models of face recognition give us some idea as to how we can recognize faces, we know that mistakes nevertheless sometimes occur when we are asked to recognize unfamiliar faces. Many factors affect identification accuracy especially those relating to the witness, the perpetrator, the situation, and the procedures involved in identification line-ups. These will be discussed in detail in the following chapters. However, there are two factors that are relevant to eyewitness identification situations that are directly the result of problems with our memory.

The effect of misleading information on verbal recall of an event was discussed above. Loftus and Greene (1980) extended this research to look at the effect of misinformation contained in a description of a perpetrator on subsequent identification performance. In an initial study participants viewed a short film and after a delay read a one page narrative of the film. There were four different versions of the narrative. One was accurate, and the other three narratives each contained one inaccurate detail relating to the description of the perpetrator: (i) the perpetrator had wavy hair when in fact it was straight, or (ii) the perpetrator had a thin moustache when in fact he had no moustache, or (iii) the perpetrator had crooked teeth when they were straight. After a further delay participants were instructed to write their own narrative of the event including a description of the perpetrator. Additionally they were instructed that their accounts should be their own, as accurate as possible, and if the narrative they had already read contained something they did not see themselves in the event they should not include it in their account. The result was that 34% of participants who had read narratives containing an inaccurate detail reported it using the exact wording from the inaccurate narrative (compared to just 5% of participants who read the accurate narrative). This demonstrates that it would be possible for a witness to hear from another witness or read in the newspaper an inaccurate description of a perpetrator and adopt that incorrect information and give it as part of their own description of the suspect. (Also see Chapter 3 for the effect of inappropriate questioning on eliciting descriptions of the perpetrator.)

In a follow-up study, Loftus and Greene (1980) asked participants to look at a photograph of a group of people at a party. After a delay half of the participants read a narrative about the photograph that included a description of one particular person which was entirely accurate. The other half of the participants read the same narrative save that the description of the particular person incorrectly stated that he had a moustache. After a further delay participants were shown 12 mug shots and were asked to pick out the person. Half the men in the photographs had moustaches and half did not and the particular person was not present. Despite participants explicitly being given the option not to choose, 69% of participants who had read the description containing the inaccurate detail that the culprit had a moustache identified an individual with a moustache. Furthermore, when these participants viewed the same line-up a few days later (which also contained six new photos including the actual person), 89% nevertheless chose the same (wrong) mug shot they had before. These findings suggest not only that we can adopt misinformation about a description of a perpetrator but also that such misinformation may affect the accuracy of a subsequent identification.

Another problem that can occur in identification which directly relates to problems with our memory is when a witness later identifies an innocent bystander to a crime as the perpetrator of the crime (referred to as the 'Bystander Effect'). For example, Read, Tollestrup, Hammersley, McFadzen and Christensen (1990) cite a famous UK case where a robbery occurred at the ticket office of a railway station. The ticket seller viewed a line-up and identified a sailor (who had an alibi for the time of the incident). When the ticket seller was asked why he had identified the sailor he responded that the face looked familiar. It transpired that the sailor had bought tickets from the ticket seller prior to the robbery. Previously researchers have used the term 'Unconscious Transference' to explain the 'bystander effect'. 'Unconscious Transference' is defined as 'the transfer of one person's identity to that of another person from a different setting, time or context' (Read et al, 1990, 3). It is 'unconscious' because the person has not purposely confused/transferred the innocent bystander for the robber. Ross, Ceci, Dunning and Toglia (1994) subsequently reviewed the evidence for and against 'unconscious transference'. They noted that Read et al (1990) found the effect in only one out of five studies. A possible reason for the mixed findings could be that unconscious transference only occurs in quite specific circumstances. Ross et al (1994) suggest that when the memory trace for the bystander and perpetrator are equal (and they are neither very strong nor very weak) witnesses may be more likely to misidentify an innocent bystander. Conversely, if both memory traces are very strong (for example, the bystander and perpetrator were seen in daylight, close up, for a long period of time) then the witness will accurately remember both individuals. If both memory traces are very weak (for example, the bystander and perpetrator were seen for just a few seconds) then the witness may not judge the bystander (in the line-up) as looking familiar.

Ross et al (1994) also put forward an alternative explanation to unconscious transference to aid our understanding of the bystander effect. They called this 'Memory

Blending' where the witness 'remembers' having seen the two people involved but incorrectly infers they are the same person. The authors use the ticket seller case (described above) to illustrate that the ticket seller may have viewed the robber and thought he looked very familiar because he was so similar to the sailor he had previously sold tickets to. The ticket seller being fully aware that he had sold tickets to the sailor may incorrectly infer that the sailor and robber were in fact the same person. They conducted a series of five experiments and found evidence for the 'memory blending' notion. For example, when participants were told that the perpetrator and bystander were two separate people the bystander effect disappeared. (See the related discussion on viewing mug shots prior to a line-up in Chapter 4.)

In summary, recognition of unfamiliar faces is a very difficult task. Additionally, we know that our memory can be distorted by post-event misinformation that relates to the perpetrator. Furthermore, we can mistakenly transfer an unfamiliar face from one set of circumstances to a crime situation. In all the research discussed above participants have been asked to make decisions as to whether they recognize or can identify a face. It is to these decisions that we now turn.

JUDGEMENT STRATEGIES

Thus far in this chapter we have been largely concerned with how we perceive, encode, and retrieve information about an event and recognize a person. However, there is an additional stage that we should consider when thinking about identification performance. When we view a line-up we have to come to a decision as to whether the perpetrator is present (for example, number six) or whether the perpetrator is not present. Researchers have looked at how we come to make such decisions and have examined the different judgement strategies that we may use.

Nisbett and Wilson (1977) reviewed evidence of people's abilities to report upon their own cognitive processes. They contended that sometimes people are able to accurately report about these cognitive processes. For example, if we are asked why we chose person number six in the line-up, most people will be able to say something about their decision processes that they believe led them to choose that particular person. However, sometimes, although people can report their decision processes which they believe led them to choose a particular person they have not been able to accurately report their actual cognitive processes (Nisbett and Wilson, 1977).

On the basis of research which has examined peoples' reports of cognitive processes when completing a recognition task there is some evidence to suggest that recognition involves two different processes. One that is based on recollection of the exact details of an item and another that is based on an assessment of familiarity of the item (see Yonelinas 2002 for a review). In the context of person recognition these two different processes (usually referred to as 'Remember versus Know') can be illustrated by examples of occasions where a person immediately recognizes a face and knows that they know the person but is unable to remember where they have seen the face before and thus who the person is (Know). Conversely, a person may look at a face and actively retrieve specific information from memory about a person which leads them to recognize the person (Remember).

In terms of a line-up situation (where all the faces are viewed simultaneously) sometimes a witnesses will make a very rapid identification and when asked about why they identified the person they will respond along the lines of 'The face just popped out at me'. However, sometimes a witness will look at a line-up for a considerable length of time before making an identification, and when asked about why they identified the person they may be likely to report that they looked at all the line-up members together, compared them, and then eliminated faces until they were left with the face they identified. The automatic 'pop out' and the more deliberative elimination decision processes are clearly different from one another, and pop out could be seen as akin to 'Know' and elimination similar to 'Remember'. (See Chapter 4 for a discussion of decision strategies on accuracy.)

Research has looked at the differences in decision-making processes when line-ups are presented either simultaneously or sequentially. Lindsay and Wells (1985) suggested that such different line-up presentations may be likely to lead to people using different decision strategies. As stated above, when witnesses can look at all the faces together in a simultaneous presentation it is more likely that they will examine each member of the line-up but then compare them with one another. This may result in them identifying the member of the line-up who looks most similar to their memory of the perpetrator relative to the other line-up members (Lindsay and Wells, 1985). This sort of decision strategy is known as a 'Relative Decision Strategy'. Conversely, when witnesses view each line-up member one at a time in a sequential fashion they are less likely to be able to adopt a relative decision strategy. Instead they may be more likely to compare each line-up member directly with their own memory of the perpetrator. Lindsay and Wells (1985) termed this an 'Absolute Decision Strategy'. (See Chapter 7 for a discussion of the effect of decision strategies in sequential versus simultaneous line-ups on identification accuracy.)

People are likely to use different judgement strategies according to different situations and they will also differ according to their own cognitive processes involved on each specific occasion. Decision strategies may be able to give investigators additional information about the nature of an identification. However, we should bear in mind that such strategies may be unlikely to reflect the true cognitive processes involved in making a decision on a line-up because we are not always able to accurately report our own cognitive processes (Nisbett and Wilson, 1977).

CONCLUSION

In this chapter we have examined some psychological theories and models which may help us to understand how we recognize perpetrators of crime. This research serves as a good basis from which to try to understand and offer solutions to complex issues that arise from the applied problem of recognizing perpetrators of crime. For example, we have seen how fragile memory is and how this can also apply to recognizing faces. However, as will be seen throughout this book, procedures based on psychological theory can be put in place which attempt to maximize the opportunities for accurate identifications.

FURTHER READING

BRUCE, V. and YOUNG, A. (1986). Understanding face recognition. *British Journal of Psychology, 77*, 305–327.

EYSENCK, M.W. and KEANE, M.T. (2005). *Cognitive Psychology: A Student's Handbook* (5th edn). Hove: Lawrence Earlbaum Association.

ROSS, D.F., CECI, S.J., DUNNING, D. and TOGLIA, M.P. (1994). Unconscious Transference and Lineup Identification: Toward a Memory Blending Approach. In J.D. Read, D.F. Ross and M.P. Toglia (eds) *Adult Eyewitness Testimony: Current Trends and Developments*. New York: Cambridge University Press, 80–100.

VALENTINE, T. (1991). A unified account of the effects of distinctiveness, inversion, and race in face recognition. *The Quarterly Journal of Experimental Psychology, 43A*, 161–204.

REFERENCES

BAHRICK, H.P. (1984). Memory for people. In J.E. Harris and P.E. Morris (eds) *Everyday Memory, Actions and Absent-Mindedness*. London: Academic Press, 19–34.

BRUCE, V., BURTON, M. and HANCOCK, P. (2007). Remembering faces. In R. Lindsay, R. Ross, D. Read, and M. Toglia (eds) *Handbook of Eyewitness Psychology: Memory for People*. Mahwah, NJ: Lawrence Erlbuam Associates, 87–100.

——, HENDERSON, Z., GREENWOOD, K., HANCOCK, P.J.B., BURTON, A.M. and MILLER, P. (1999). Verification of face identities from images captured on video. *Journal of Experimental Psychology: Applied, 5*, 339–360.

—— and YOUNG, A. (1986). Understanding face recognition. *British Journal of Psychology, 77*, 305–327.

BURTON, A.M. and BRUCE, V. (1993). Naming faces and naming names: exploring an interactive activation model of person recognition. *Memory, 1*, 457–480.

——, BRUCE, V. and HANCOCK, P.J.B. (1999). From Pixels to People: A Model of Familiar Face Recognition. *Cognitive Science, 23*, 1–31.

CHRISTIANSON, S-A, KARLSSON, I. and PERSSON, L.G.W. (1998). Police Personnel as Eyewitnesses to a Violent Crime. *Legal and Criminological Psychology, 3*, 59–72.

DANDO, C.J., WILCOCK, R. and MILNE, R. (in press, 2008). The cognitive interview: The efficacy of a modified mental reinstatement of context procedure for frontline police investigators. *Applied Cognitive Psychology, 13*, 59–70.

——, —— and —— (2008). *Eyewitness recall of a script based crime event using the change temporal order technique*. Manuscript in preparation.

FISHER, R.P. and GEISELMAN, R.E. (1992). *Memory-enhancing Techniques for Investigative Interviewing: The Cognitive Interview*. Springfield, IL: Charles Thomas.

GODDEN, D.R. and BADDELEY, A. (1975). Context dependent memory in two natural environments: On land and underwater. *British Journal of Psychology, 66*, 325–331.

GOING, M. and READ, J.D. (1974). Effects of uniqueness, sex of subject, and sex of photograph on facial recognition. *Perceptual and Motor Skills, 39*, 109–110.

HABER, R.N. and HABER, L. (2000). Experiencing, remembering and reporting events. *Psychology, Public Policy and Law, 6*, 1057–1097.

LOFTUS, E.F. (1975). Leading questions and the eyewitness report. *Cognitive Psychology, 7*, 560–572.

—— and GREENE, E. (1980). Warning: Even memory for faces may be contagious. *Law and Human Behavior, 4*, 323–334.

—— and PALMER, J.C. (1974). Reconstruction of Automobile Destruction: An example of the interaction between language and memory. *Journal of Verbal Learning and Verbal Behaviour, 13*, 585–589.

LINDSAY, R.C.L and WELLS, G.L. (1985). Improving eyewitness identifications from lineups: Simultaneous versus sequential lineup presentation. *Journal of Applied Psychology, 70*, 556–564.

MEISSNER, C.A. and BRIGHAM, J.C. (2001). Thirty years of investigating the own race bias in memory for faces. *Psychology, Public Policy and Law, 7*, 3–35.

MILNE, R. and BULL, R. (1999). *Investigative Interviewing: Psychology and Practice.* Chichester: John Wiley.

NISBETT, R.E. and WILSON, T.D. (1977). Telling more than we can know: Verbal reports on mental processes. *Psychological Review, 84*, 231–259.

READ, J.D., TOLLESTRUP, P., HAMMERSLEY, R., MCFADZEN, E. and CHRISTENSEN, A. (1990). The unconscious transference effect: Are innocent bystanders ever misidentified? *Applied Cognitive Psychology, 4*, 3–31.

REYNA, V.F. and TITCOMB, A.L. (1997). Constraints on the Suggestibility of Eyewitness Testimony: A Fuzzy-Trace Theory Analysis. In D.G. Payne and F.G. Conrad (eds) *A Synthesis of Basic and Applied Approaches to Human Memory.* Hillsdale, NJ: Earlbaum, 157–174.

ROSS, D.F., CECI, S.J., DUNNING, D. and TOGLIA, M.P. (1994). Unconscious Transference and Lineup Identification: Toward a Memory Blending Approach. In J.D. Read, D.F. Ross and M.P. Toglia (eds) *Adult Eyewitness Testimony: Current Trends and Developments.* New York: Cambridge University Press, 80–100.

STEBLAY, N.M. (1992). A meta-analytic review of the weapon focus effect. *Law and Human Behavior, 16*, 413–424.

THOMSON, D.M. and TULVING, E. (1970). Associative encoding and retrieval: Weak and strong cues. *Journal of Experimental Psychology, 86*, 255–262.

TULVING, E. (1972). Episodic and Semantic Memory. In E. Tulving and W. Donaldson. *Organization and Memory.* New York: Academic Press, 381–403.

VALENTINE, T. (1988). Upside-down faces: A review of the effect of inversion upon face recognition. *British Journal of Psychology, 79*, 471–491.

—— (1991). A unified account of the effects of distinctiveness, inversion, and race in face recognition. *The Quarterly Journal of Experimental Psychology, 43A*, 161–204.

——, BREDART, S., LAWSON, R. and WARD, G. (1991). What's in a name? Access to information from people's names. *European Journal of Cognitive Psychology, 3*, 147–176.

—— and BRUCE, V. (1986). The effect of race, inversion and encoding activity upon face recognition. *Acta Psychologica, 61*, 259–273.

YONELINAS, A.P. (2002). The nature of recollection and familiarity: A review of 30 years of research. *Journal of Memory and Language, 46*, 444–517.

3

GIVING PERSON DESCRIPTIONS AND THE EFFECT OF THIS ON THE IDENTIFICATION PROCESS

INTRODUCTION

This chapter will outline the importance of witnesses and victims to the investigative process. It will go on to examine the *way* in which information about persons within the to-be-remembered incident is gathered from witnesses and victims, with regard the interviewing procedures in the first instance and the identification process in the second. The chapter will then examine how the nature of these two distinct investigative processes can affect both the quantity and quality of information gained. The discussion will conclude with recommendations for best practice.

IMPORTANCE OF WITNESSES AND VICTIMS: THE INVESTIGATION PROCESS

It is upheld by academics and practitioners alike that the main goal of an investigation is to answer two primary investigative questions: (i) what happened (if anything did indeed occur); and (ii) who committed the offence (Milne and Bull, 2006)? The subject matter at the centre of this book primarily concerns the second of these two main investigative questions: the question at the heart of every good crime novel: whodunnit? However, how do investigators actually strive to answer these two primary questions? Research (Nicol, Innes, Gee and Fiest, 2004) seems to suggest that it is not mere intuition as portrayed in fanciful works of fiction that gets to the root of the crime. Instead, it is believed, that systematic and methodical attention to detail through careful information-gathering processes and open-minded decision-making that helps our everyday police investigator solve crime (Savage and Milne, 2007; Shepherd and Milne, 2006; Investigative Doctrine, 2005).

Indeed, investigators have themselves noted that in order to seek answers to these core investigatory questions they invariably gather information from a number of different sources (Kebbell and Milne, 1998) and usually these sources of information are people: ie witnesses, victims, suspects, complainants, emergency services, experts, informants, or colleagues (eg first officer at the crime scene) (Milne and Bull, 2006). In the US, Sanders (1986) asked police officers: 'What is the central and most important feature of criminal investigations?'. The majority replied: 'witnesses'. A similar view is held in the UK where Kebbell and Milne (1998) asked 159 serving police officers for their perceptions of the utility of witnesses within investigations. It was found that witnesses/victims were perceived usually to provide the central leads in cases. Investigators also frequently have little or no other forensically relevant information to guide an investigation. Therefore the primary source of information and evidence for the investigator tends to be that which is gathered from the witness/victim. As a result information gained from witnesses/victims often forms the cornerstone of an investigation (Milne and Shaw, 1999; Milne and Bull, 1999; 2006).

Similarly but more specifically, Brown, Lloyd-Jones and Robinson (in submission) asked police officers the value of information about 'people' (or person information) within an investigation using a similar questionnaire to Kebbell and Milne (1998). It was found that 60% of the officers believed that person descriptions usually or almost always provided major leads in a case. However, it was also noted that witnesses rarely provided as many person descriptions as the investigator would like. Nevertheless, the officers believed the information that they did actually obtain to be accurate. This is a cause for concern as it will be seen as this chapter unfolds that witness memory is a very fragile and imperfect process and this is especially the case when we are talking about one's ability to remember people.

So the next question that needs to be examined is: 'How does information about people inform the investigative process, why is it so important?'. When examining investigative processes it can be seen that person information gleaned from witnesses/victims in the first instance often governs the initial direction of the investigation, helping the investigator(s) outline avenues of exploration and lines of enquiry to be pursued and helps to identify possible suspects (Milne and Bull, 2006). In the initial search for potential suspects, information obtained from victims and from witnesses present at the scene, from house-to-house enquiries, and gleaned from the emergency services who first attended the incident, all help the investigator to create a description of the person(s) who committed the offence, which in turn helps to outline potential suspects. CCTV images might even be released through the media in an attempt to trace possible suspects: 'Do you recognize this man seen on . . .?' (Valentine, 2006). Interestingly it seems that in the UK today, it is thought that few criminals use disguises when they carry out their offences, even in cases of serious interpersonal crimes (Silke, 2001).

When a suspect is apprehended and charged with an offence, information elicited from a well-conducted witness/victim interview can also be very helpful in the planning and preparation stage that should take place prior to the interview with the suspect (Milne and Bull, 1999; Kebbell and Daniels, 2005). This is because the more in-depth this stage of the interview process is the more skilled the resultant interview is likely to be (Griffiths and Milne, 2005). In addition, strength of evidence has been repeatedly shown to be associated with suspects giving an account (eg a valid confession) within an interview (see Gudjonsson, 2003, for a review). Thus, a detailed witness/victim account, including a clear and full description of the perpetrator(s) and a positive identification should help add weight to the strength of evidence disclosed to the suspect, prior to and during their interview and thus be at least partially responsible for attaining a full and faithful account/confession from a suspect (Milne and Bull, 2006; Soukara, Bull and Vrij, 2002). In addition, good witness testimony including description of perpetrators and positive identifications, and good congruence between the two, can also form part of the evidence against the defendant in court and thus person information also has an evidential use. It can be seen, therefore, that the elicitation of accurate and detailed person information through interview and identification procedures is crucial to effective crime investigation and the criminal justice system as a whole (Valentine, 2006).

However, obtaining the maximum quantity and quality of information from a witness and gaining an accurate identification is by no means an easy task (Milne and Bull, 1999; Valentine, 2006). The information about the incident and persons involved has to endure what we have termed an obstacle course that involves imperfect eyewitness memory processes (see Milne and Bull, 1999; Kebbell and Wagstaff, 1999 for a review), the difficulties associated with interviewing, the problems concerning the statement-taking process itself (Milne and Bull, 1999), and the fairness of any subsequent identification procedures (Valentine, 2006). The criminal justice system as a whole needs to be aware of the imperfection that is the eyewitness testimony process. This is because memory is incredibly fragile, it can be altered, changed, and manipulated and it is therefore imperative for investigators in the first instance (but anyone involved in the criminal justice system, from call handlers to judges) to learn how easily they can influence what interviewees/witnesses report (Milne and Bull, 2006).

In England and Wales, since 1976, judges have been required to inform the jury, in cases of person identification, about factors which have a marked effect on the quality of memory and these concern primarily viewing conditions at the scene (eg lighting and weather conditions). In the US in a landmark case (*Neil v Biggers* 409 US 188 (1972)), the US Supreme Court listed five factors that should be taken into consideration when examining whether an identification was deemed to be reliable: (i) viewing conditions (as in the UK); (ii) delay; (iii) level of witness certainty; (iv) degree of attention; and (v) the accuracy of the witness' prior description. (See later in this chapter and Chapter 4 for a discussion of whether these factors actually have an effect on the reliability of witness identification.)

As can be seen, information is the currency of the criminal justice process and it is, as a result, common sense to assume that the more information (ie *quantity* factor) that is gleaned which is of good *quality* the more likely a crime will be solved and successfully prosecuted (Milne and Bull, 2006). It then follows that the *way* in which the information is gathered about people within an investigation is *key* to successful crime solving. The methods used to find out the 'whodunnit' factor will in essence determine the quantity and quality of the information gained, and the success of the case as a whole. With regard to person information, within an investigation a witness (which includes anyone who may have information about people involved in the to-be-remembered (TBR) incident) is potentially interviewed a number of times throughout the inquiry before they are asked to go through one of a number of formal identification procedures. For example, a witness may be asked to help in the construction of facial composites and subsequently attend an identification parade.

Each of these information and evidence-gathering processes have a different impact on human memory and in turn on the resultant quality and quantity of information gained about 'the TBR people'. As a result the usefulness and reliability of the resulting information varies depending on the procedures used to elicit the information in the first place. Thus, what follows is an examination of each part of the investigative process and the relative effectiveness of each investigative tool used to gather person-related material.

When a crime has been committed there are a number of procedures and protocols that are immediately set in motion for the preservation of the crime scene(s) and any scenes related to the TBR event (eg location of murder weapon, victim's body if located away from where the event occurred). In addition, these protocols and procedures, underpinned by policy, have a scientific foundation informed by experts who have advised the police and criminal justice system as a whole regarding the optimal ways to avoid contamination (Wells and Loftus, 2001). Memory needs to be treated in the same way as physical trace evidence and is therefore also a crime scene needing to be protected. This is because research has consistently shown that memory is an incredibly fragile and malleable process (Loftus, 1979). Unfortunately, unlike physical trace evidence, eyewitness evidence does not yet have the same rigorous procedures (informed by memory experts) to provide the most optimal ways for collecting, preserving, recording, and interpreting such evidence. Nevertheless, here too there is a need for a robust scientific model (Wells and Loftus, 2001), as contaminated witness memory also can have devastating consequences on the investigation, subsequent court procedures and could result (and has done) in many miscarriages of justice (Savage and Milne, 2006).

INITIAL PHASE OF THE INVESTIGATION

CALL HANDLING

The majority of victims in the UK (and several other countries) report their crime via a phone call to a centralized police call handling centre (Ambler and Milne, 2006). The role of a call handler is primarily twofold: (i) to promptly determine the nature of the call; and (ii) to determine the most appropriate response to it. In order to do this the call handler questions/interviews the caller and at the same time records the information elicited. The effectiveness of this process in terms of the quality of the information obtained and the way in which the information is elicited is paramount as it is this initial interaction that is the starting point of many a criminal investigation. Unfortunately, to date there is limited knowledge as to what occurs at this vital stage of the investigation process (Ambler and Milne, 2006). Ambler and Milne (2006) conducted an examination of cases of undetected burglary at this initial investigation stage and found that not only was information given by witnesses/victims not recorded accurately, but that information, including that relating to perpetrators, was not passed on in full detail to investigators. For example, one victim clearly noted that the person who had just vacated her property after burgling it was suffering from a cold. This fact stood out to the victim as important and as something that could perhaps help a police officer to apprehend the perpetrator. However, this vital piece of information which could indeed have helped to identify the burglar was omitted from the description given to the attending officer. Furthermore, Ambler and Milne (2006) also found that the manner in which the information was elicited by the call handlers was highly interviewer-driven and included many leading questions. This undoubtedly causes concerns when examining the analogy given above with regards memory being akin to an uncontaminated crime scene and should thus be protected.

THE INITIAL DESCRIPTION

Generally, when initially interviewed, either by a call handler, or by an attending officer at the scene or later at a place of convenience, the witness is asked to recount what they remember about the event including a description of the perpetrator(s). What does this uninterrupted account (free recall) of a perpetrator usually consist of? What types of person details do witnesses provide? Police officers believe that the most often mentioned details about persons concern gender, followed by clothing, hair colour, age, ethnicity, height, and hair length (Brown, Lloyd-Jones and Robinson, 2008). The features least often thought to be noted were neck, cheeks, posture, lips, chin, forehead, hair texture and parting (Brown et al, 2008). Do police officer perceptions match actual witness descriptions?

Unfortunately, research seems to show that witness person descriptions are often very vague and as a result can apply to many people within the vicinity of the crime (Meissner, Sporer and Schooler, 2007; Fahsing, Ask and Granhag, 2004). Archival studies have examined the content of person descriptions in real cases and overall find that in general witnesses usually give between seven and nine pieces of person information (range 0 to 48 details; Kuehn, 1974; Sporer, 1996; Lindsay, Martin and Webber, 1994; Van Koppen and Lochun, 1997), but that these details tend to include more general characteristics, giving a more general impression of the person they were attempting to describe (eg gender, age, race, height, and build). Such impressions are not extremely helpful for directly locating and identifying an individual, but are only useful for narrowing down potential suspects within an enquiry. Characteristics that would be more helpful to identify specific individuals and those thought to be useful for identification were not frequently noted. When examining descriptions of facial features alone Sporer (1996) found that the upper half of the face, in particular the hair (an element that can be easily changed by a perpetrator) was referred to more frequently compared to the lower part of the face (see Ellis, Shepherd and Davies, 1980; Demarchi, Py and Ginet, 2003, for similar findings). Yuille and Cutshall (1986) conducted a case study and examined the descriptions given by 13 witnesses to a real life armed robbery. Overall, it was noted that the descriptions given were remarkably accurate, even some five months later. However, some person errors were made and these errors tended to concern height, weight, and age estimates (see more on this later). In addition, there were also mistakes made regarding style and colour of hair and clothing.

There are two primary problems with some of these archival studies. First, we do not always know the accuracy of the information obtained, as the 'ground truth' (ie exactly what occurred) is not known, thus only quantity of recall can be confidently examined. Indeed, Van Koppen and Lochun (1997) and Farrington and Lambert (1997) did attempt to estimate accuracy values by comparing witness descriptions to perpetrator appearance, but it is not an exact science. However, the above studies did find that the general characteristics were reported in a highly accurate manner (80% reliable). Fahsing, Ask and Granhag (2004) cleverly overcame the accuracy problem within archival studies by comparing witness descriptions to actual video footage of 48 real life bank robberies, which included a total of over 200 witness descriptions. They too found that over 65% of the details reported were completely accurate, with 23% being partly accurate, and only 13% being incorrect. (However, in all these robberies the robbers had covered their faces.)

So it seems that what we do know is that on the whole the majority of people give general characteristics within a description and these include height, weight, and age, and these values tend to be estimated in ranges (Fahsing et al, 2004). It is thought that people tend to use themselves as a comparison to estimate height and weight, and thus figures given are based on relative estimations. People also use population norms to help make these types of judgements. For example, shorter people tend to be over-estimated and taller people under-estimated (Flin and Shepherd, 1986).

Lee and Geiselman (1994) found that people use stereotypical expectations and ethnically related cognitive biases to estimate height. For example, white and Asian witnesses recalled an Asian perpetrator as shorter than a white perpetrator even though they were the same height. Similarly, age estimates are also thought to be accompanied by several biases: (i) young people tend to over-estimate the age of older people; and (ii) older people tend to under-estimate the age of younger people (George and Hole, 1995); (iii) the age of females under 18 years tend to be over-estimated compared to males within the same age bracket (George and Hole, 1995). In addition, people's age estimates of others of the same ethnic origin as themselves are more precise compared to estimates of people of a different ethnic background (Dehon and Bredart, 2001). Also a negative correlation has been found between perceived attractiveness and age estimates (Henss, 1991). Fahsing et al (2004) also found that there were systematic biases within the crime context where young offenders' age was over-estimated and older offenders' age was under-estimated. Thus, it seems that a description of the witness who is giving the description is also needed in order to interpret and estimate the accuracy of their general person descriptions, a suggestion noted many years ago (Clifford and Bull, 1978).

Speech was also found to be poorly reported within the archival studies (Van Koppen and Lochun, 1997). This is a problem as there are many crimes that are specifically related to language (eg bribery/abduction), where what was said becomes highly important. However, it tends to be the case that memory for conversation is in gist form as opposed to verbatim (Pezdek and Prull, 1993). Nevertheless interviewers often ask the impossible: 'Can you tell me what was said word for word?'. Such a request may render a witness feeling less than capable which in turn could lead to them being demotivated and even lead to a loss of rapport and cooperation.

It has also been found that witnesses actually use stereotypes to interpret incidents and predict behaviour (for more on this see Chapter 6). This is especially the case when the event happens quickly and unexpectedly (like a crime scenario) and when the witness' attention is divided (Macrae and Bodenhausen, 2001), for example doing another task (eg driving). Davies and Patel (2005) found that within a driving scenario car makes, gender and car colour were all linked with perceived aggressiveness of the driver, with young males driving red or black Ford Escorts or BMWs being judged to be more aggressive. Furthermore, when a group of raters evaluated two (made-up) accident statements which contained either the driver as fitting an aggressive or non-aggressive stereotype, they rated the aggressive stereotyped driver to be driving faster (than noted in the statement) and to be in the middle of the road, and gave him more blame for the accident than a non-aggressive stereotyped driver. Thus, it can be seen how stereotypes can have an influence on the initial interpretation and memory (of witnesses) of an incident, and probably on the subsequent memory of what occurred (at interview), and the final understanding of the event in a courtroom (eg by a jury, or judges in countries which don't have juries).

The second primary problem with archival studies, including Fahsing et al (2004) (who examined written summaries of police interviews—also known to be highly inaccurate: Baldwin and Bedward, 1991) is that we do not know *how* the information was elicited from the individuals. As has already been noted, and will be discussed more thoroughly throughout this chapter, memory is such a fragile process it can be easily modified and added to by inappropriate questioning. Thus, one needs to examine also the *process* used to elicit the person description.

There are, however, many factors which are thought to affect witness descriptions of people involved in an incident and these fall within three primary areas: (i) encoding-based factors which are present at the crime scene itself; (ii) factors concerning the 'rememberer' themselves; and (iii) factors at the retrieval of the event (ie the interview and recognition processes). Indeed, police officers themselves believe that the amount and quality of person information reported by witnesses are affected by a range of factors both internal and external to the rememberer. Brown et al (in submission) found that some factors were specifically noted by officers as affecting the resultant person description and these included the actual encoding conditions at the crime scene (eg weather and lighting conditions) and the stress levels of the rememberer both at encoding (crime scene) and retrieval (interview). It is to these factors that we now turn.

FACTORS AFFECTING THE INITIAL ENCODING OF PEOPLE IN AN EVENT (IE AT THE CRIME SCENE)

There are many factors at the crime scene itself thought to affect subsequent person descriptions and these are not mutually exclusive. Instead, each factor will combine (or not) depending on each different individual crime. For example, as the number of perpetrators involved in the crime increases, the ability of the witness to describe each individual diminishes (Newlands, George, Towl, Kemp and Clifford, 1999; Sporer, 1996; Van Koppen and Lochun, 1997; Fahsing, Ask and Granhag, 2004). This is because at the scene the witness' attention and encoding processes is subdivided between the individual perpetrators and thus less information about each is encoded into memory. In addition, the longer the actual event lasts, the greater the amount of recall as more information can be encoded during that time (Fahsing et al, 2004; Yarmey, Jacob and Porter, 2002).

SCENE CONDITIONS

As stated above, since 1976, judges in England and Wales have been required to inform the jury, in cases of person identification, about such factors as lighting conditions, duration of observation, and distance of the witness from the person, all of which can have a marked effect on the quality of memory (Deffenbacher, 1991). The US Supreme Court also considers viewing conditions to be one of the five factors (the other four being: (i) delay; (ii) level of certainty; (iii) degree of attention; and (iv) accuracy of witnesses prior description) that should be taken into consideration when evaluating the reliability of identification evidence (*Neil v Biggers*; Meissner, Sporer and Susa, 2008). Indeed, research would seem to substantiate these warnings with regard to scene conditions. For example (perhaps not surprisingly), Yarmey (1986) found that the accuracy of both the recall of the details of the incident/person and the recognition of the people involved was better in daytime and at the beginning of twilight than at the end of twilight or at night (see also Wagenaar and van der Schrier, 1994; Van Koppen and Lochun, 1997; Sporer, 1996 for similar findings). Indeed, colour vision is reduced in low levels of lighting (Meissner, Sporer and Schooler, 2007) and thus colour descriptions will be hindered.

STRESS LEVELS OF THE WITNESS/VICTIM

A witness' level of stress at the crime scene is also thought to have a bearing on how much is encoded and then later retrieved (eg at interview). Research examining real life witnesses seems to show that emotional events appear to be well retained and reported as long as the memories are elicited through appropriate interviewing procedures (the trauma superiority argument—Peace and Porter, 2004). (For an opposing view see the traumatic memory argument—Kihlstrom, 1996.) For example, Yuille and Cutshall (1986) found that witnesses to a homicide who indicated high stress levels had a mean recall accuracy of 93% when interviewed by the police two days after the event (ie little of what they reported was incorrect though, of course, they only recalled some of the information). Four to five months later researchers interviewed these witnesses again and found that even at this delay interval the witness reports had an average accuracy rate of 88%. Similarly, Christianson and Hubinette (1993) assessed the memory of bank tellers and customers who had been actual witnesses to an armed robbery. Their accounts too were very accurate. More recently, Peace and Porter (2004) asked people to recount positive and traumatic personal memories. It was found that the traumatic events were well remembered over time and were recollected in a vivid and detailed manner. For example, one of their participants reported: 'I remember his hands as he was choking me, I thought he was going to kill me. The whole event is just ingrained in my brain, I can remember it all so clearly' (Peace and Porter, 2004, 1153). This statement was made more than five months after a near fatal attack. The main problem with this research study, however, is that there is no accuracy measure as there is no knowing what actually occurred. Sporer (1996) in his archival study categorized people as victims, bystanders, and complainants and found a limited effect of stress on recall. Indeed the small effect that tended to emerge appeared to be a linear relationship where there was an increase in the number of details reported with increasing levels of stress. (See also, Wagstaff, MacVeigh, Boston, Scott, Brunas-Wagstaff and Cole, 2003 for similar effects, but see Van Koppen and Lochun, 1997 for the opposite effect).

Yuille and Cutshall (1989) proposed that the reason why people have good memories for emotionally charged events is because they have had practice in accessing and rehearsing these memories through 'remarking' on the incident to others. In addition, Howe, Courage and Peterson (1994) noted that stress is one factor which can make an event unique. In addition, real life traumatic events tend to force witnesses and victims to narrow their attention to core aspects of an incident (either internal feelings or external event factors) which are in turn stored and remembered for longer (especially central thematic event elements—Yuille and Tollestrup, 1992).

Another factor associated with stress and remembering is what has been termed 'weapon focus'. That is, the presence of a weapon at the crime scene may reduce the amount of correct recall reported by a witness, especially recall about the perpetrator holding the weapon (eg Kramer, Buckhout and Euginio, 1990; Loftus, Loftus and Messo, 1987; Maass and Köhnken, 1989). This effect is thought to occur because the witness who is experiencing the stressful event may respond by narrowing the scope of his/her attention to those aspects producing the stressful effects (ie the weapon). This in turn may reduce the amount of information about other aspects of the scene which are encoded and available for subsequent reporting (ie utilization theory—Easterbrook, 1959). Steblay (1992) conducted a meta-analysis of 12 studies examining weapon focus which involved 19 experiments. Six of these experiments found significant differences in the expected direction (ie less recall when a weapon is present). However, the remaining 13 did not. This was in part due to the fact that recognition procedures (eg an identification parade scenario) resulted in small weapon focus effects whereas much greater weapon focus effects were found for recall tasks (eg an interview scenario).

EVENT VIOLENCE

There is evidence that the violence associated with a crime may influence the encoding and subsequent storage of event information. Clifford and Hollin (1981) found that participants who viewed a violent episode were consistently less accurate about the appearance of the perpetrator in their subsequent answers to questions about the event. McLeod and Shepherd (1986) highlighted the importance of detail type when examining this relationship. They examined 135 actual cases of assault and their associated victim statements (379 statements in total). Cases were categorized into 'no injury' and 'physical injury' assaults. Where physical injury took place less information about the accused was given, but more information was provided about peripheral details (Milne and Bull, 1999).

WITNESS INVOLVEMENT

Another factor affecting the quantity and quality of witness testimony is witness involvement. The majority of witness research has examined the memories of bystanders who are not particularly involved in the event. But, the uninvolved bystander may not be that common a feature in forensic contexts (Yuille and Tollestrup, 1992). Studies have shown that events in which participants were involved were remembered better than those in which they were mere bystanders (eg Cohen and Faulkner, 1988; Yuille, Davies, Gibling, Marxen and Porter, 1994; Fahsing et al, 2004). This could be due to many factors. For example, because victims will be nearer and may have better viewing angles, their encoding conditions tend to be superior to bystanders.

ATTENTION

As stated above, to encode information we must attend to it (Milne and Bull, 1999). Within a crime scene it would be impossible to attend to everything. Thus, witnesses are selective about what they attend to and only attend to certain information. Importantly, only information which is attended to (at least to some extent) will be encoded and therefore may be available for later retrieval. As a consequence, much of what is in our environment never enters memory and so will not be available for later retrieval. Selective attention depends on a person's knowledge, expectancy, attitudes, past experience, interests, training, and what that particular person judges as the most important information at that point in time (Milne and Bull, 1999). Thus, different people will selectively attend to different parts of the same TBR event. Indeed, Fruzzetti, Toland, Teller and Loftus (1992) noted that if five different people witness an event five somewhat different versions of the event will result. Due to factors relating to attention, an interviewee has available only a limited amount of information about an event (Köhnken, 1995). The unavailability of information is not always due to retrieval or storage failure. Some of the information simply will not have been attended to. As a consequence, no interview technique, however sophisticated, will be able to elicit all that was part of an event, as it is impossible to recover information which was never stored in memory in the first place (Milne and Bull, 1999).

Think about the last time you went to a supermarket; can you remember the checkout person's eye colour? This is not because you have forgotten this information, but probably due to the fact that it was not attended to in the first place and did not enter memory. No interview technique will, therefore, ever be able to attain this information as it is not available in the person's memory. Instead, if an interviewer asks a direct question about eye colour the witness is more than likely to make a guess, especially if they have already reported the colour of the person's hair. As a result, sometimes it is better for questions to be left unsaid. This is because using closed specific questions (eg 'What colour were his eyes?') to elicit details about person information may result in inaccurate descriptions which bear little resemblance to a person that a witness may subsequently pick out of an identification procedure as the perpetrator (see more on interviewing and identification procedures later).

WITNESS FACTORS THOUGHT TO AFFECT PERSON DESCRIPTION

There are also a number of features relating to the individual witness themselves that may render them more or less likely to accurately and fully describe and identify a person they have witnessed. It is to these factors that we now turn.

Gender

Overall there are few differences between men and women and their ability to describe individuals. However, when differences do exist these tend to be due to women being more likely to attend to certain items at encoding (eg jewellery) but men have been found to be more confident in their responses (Yarmey, 2004). Sporer (1996) found that men provided longer descriptions but were not as precise as women.

Age

Children tend to be as accurate as adults but less complete when reporting incidents (Milne and Bull, 1999). Pozzulo and Warren (2003) found that 10 to 14 year olds were less complete compared to adults when giving person descriptions. Interestingly, the adults were more likely to report general characteristics (as already noted above), whereas the 10 to 14 year olds were more likely to describe accessories worn (eg belt and glasses). Thus, it could be that there exists an own-age bias in that individuals are better at describing their own age group (Lindholm, 2005). Children also have particular difficulty in estimating general characteristics such as age, height, and weight, and have difficulty describing colour. This problem is heightened by the fact that children also respond less accurately to specific questions which interviewers often use to try to elicit such information (Milne, 1999). (Chapter 8 covers the topic of children's person identification.)

Older adults (ie those above 65 years) are more likely to have vision deficits, especially at night and thus are less likely to be able to encode as much information compared to younger adults. Yarmey, Yarmey and Yarmey (1994) had two people approach individuals in public places and ask for directions. Two minutes later the individuals concerned were asked to describe and identify those who were seeking directions. The 18 to 29 year olds were superior to the 30 to 44 year olds who were in turn better than the 45 to 65 year olds in their ability to describe the individuals in respect of both completeness and accuracy (see also Searcy, Bartlett, Memon and Swanson, 2001 for similar findings). However, the targets were young adults and thus this could be due to an own-age bias effect (Sporer, 2001).

Ethnicity

Few studies have examined the so-called 'cross-race effect' on verbal descriptions. It seems that faces from a different ethnic grouping may be more difficult to identify

(Meissner and Brigham, 2001) but may not be as difficult to verbally recall (Fallshore and Schooler, 1995). However, when witnesses do describe people from ethnic groupings different from their own they tend to use features deemed relevant to their own ethnicity and thus use redundant descriptors (Meissner et al, 2007).

FACTORS AFFECTING THE RETRIEVAL OF MEMORY

The final area to be examined concerns the remembering process itself, and there are many factors at this stage in the obstacle course that affect how *much* information is retrieved and how *accurate* the elicited information actually is.

Memory is Constructive

What a person encodes is not recorded in memory ready to be played back like a video-recording. Instead the event is reconstructed using the information the person encoded about the event but also by using information that the person has about the world in general (Milne and Bull, 1999). For example, when presented with information regarding a person, people sometimes, often outside awareness, stereotype that person (eg 'he looks like a criminal') and then combine the information originally encoded with that in their stereotype. The resulting memory of that particular TBR person is therefore a combination of encoded information and stereotypical information. To the extent to which the stereotypical information does not match the TBR person, the resultant recall regarding the TBR person could be distorted (Milne and Bull, 1999). Hollin (1980) found that witnesses often used their stereotypes of known population norms regarding hair colour, eye colour, and complexion. Sometimes such gap filling is correct but often it is not. In Hollin's study the target person had blonde hair, green eyes, and a fair complexion. Of the 93% who correctly recalled the hair colour (blonde), nearly half erroneously reported blue eyes. (Yarmey (2004) found that people are not very accurate when describing eye colour.)

Time

Memory does depreciate over time (Kassin, Tubb, Hosch and Memon, 2001) but few studies have directly evaluated the impact of time between viewing the incident and giving a person description. Ellis, Shepherd and Davies (1980) examined person description either immediately, one hour, the next day, or a week following viewing and found that participants remembered fewer details after a week. Accuracy also declined after a week. Meissner (2002) also found significant decreases in quantity and quality of facial descriptions after a week compared to immediate retrieval. Archival studies also find that witnesses give fewer descriptions after longer delays (Van Koppen and Lochun, 1997). What needs to also be borne in mind is that the longer the delay between viewing an incident and being interviewed the greater the room for the contamination of memory from external sources (eg the media).

Another time problem inherent in eliciting initial person descriptions concerns the fact that interviewers are often under time pressures to obtain information quickly from people and thus resort to an interviewer-driven style of interview. Call handlers initially are needing to obtain information quickly for three primary reasons: (i) to determine the importance and severity of the call; (ii) to ascertain whether to send someone to the scene; and (iii) to deal with the call quickly. Like all call centres, performance is often measured by numbers of calls dealt with within a given timeframe and there are often devices highlighting to the handlers how many calls are waiting. An attending officer at the scene also needs to obtain information quickly (eg what did he/she look like, which way did they go?) Front-line interviewing needs to be quick and effective (Dando, Wilcock and Milne, 2008). Unfortunately, often officers resort to quick-fire questioning, peppered with inappropriate question types (eg leading questions), and often interrupt the witness to obtain the information they require (eg Wright and Allison, 2004). This again could contaminate the all-important fragile memory of the interviewee.

Witness Collaboration

Most police protocols outline that witnesses to an incident should be separated from each other as soon as possible and interviewed individually. Wanick and Sanders (1980) examined the influence of group discussion of a previously viewed event on individual witnesses' memory. Interestingly, it was found that individuals who had participated in the group discussion had superior memory with regard to both accuracy and completeness. Similarly Yarmey and Morris (1998) had a group provide a description together which was found to be more complete than one provided by an individual. This is what is termed 'collaborative' or 'pooled recall'. The downside to this is what is termed the 'conformity effect'. For example, Gabbert, Memon and Allan (2003) created a situation in which witnesses viewed events differing in several key features. Witnesses were then asked to discuss the event with each other before providing independent descriptions. It was found that 71% of participants incorporated erroneous details provided by a co-witnesses, a contamination of memory. As no two witnesses will ever have the exact same memory for an incident they have seen, pooling memory in this way will have the potential for contamination.

Questioning

For effective interviewing, open-ended questions (eg those often starting with 'Tell', 'Describe', 'Explain') should be asked after the free recall/narrative (and before other types of questions) to elicit a more detailed response (Milne and Bull, 1999). After this, interviewers can probe with closed-specific questions to cover omitted information. While the use of short-answer questions allows the investigator to control the interview and minimizes irrelevant information, it causes the interviewees to be passive, decreases their concentration, and therefore can result in less recall (Milne and Bull, 1999). Closed-specific questions (eg generally those referred to as the five WH questions: Who, What, Where, When, Why) also produce more incorrect responses compared to open-ended questions (eg Davis, McMahon and Greenwood, 2004) as they rely on an interviewee responding 'I don't know' to a question they do not know the answer to (eg What colour was his hair?). Unfortunately, even adult witnesses want to please and thus tend to guess an answer instead. Open-ended questions lend themselves to neutral rather than suggestive wording and with them the retrieval process is less influenced by external contamination (ie the interviewer) (Fisher, Falkner,

Trevisan and McCauley, 2000). Furthermore, when an interviewer asks a question it redirects an interviewee's attention from the important task of searching through memory to externally focusing on the interviewer asking the question (Powell, Fisher and Wright, 2005). What one is really therefore striving for is the questionless interview, as the fewer the questions that are asked during the course of the interview, the less likely that memory for the event will be contaminated (Fisher and Milne, 2006).

It is now well established that leading questions have a detrimental effect on memory, and indeed we are all susceptible to suggestive questions (Milne and Bull, 1999, for more on suggestibility). A leading question is a question that implies to the interviewee, in form or content, the desired interviewer response. For example, 'Tell me about the perpetrator's weapon?', would be an example of a leading question when no weapon has been mentioned by the interviewee within the prior phases of the interview. Such questioning is a particular problem when an interviewer develops a hypothesis or is party to the senior investigating officer's prime suspects and subsequently tries to prove rather than disprove the pre-existing views through the use of inappropriate questions (Shepherd and Milne, 1999; 2006; Savage and Milne, 2007). Unfortunately such leading questions have serious ramifications for witness memory as witnesses often incorporate such leading information into their own accounts and subsequently have difficulty discriminating the source of the information (ie whether information came from the incident—a true memory, or whether new information was embedded in question about the incident—the inserted information may be true or untrue). Witnesses can even be led into producing erroneous reports of events when words with an unanticipated implied content are used in a question. Since it is sometimes impossible to foretell the consequences of the use of a particular word or phrase, the sensible thing to do is to try and use the most neutral term (Milne and Bull, 1999). For example, Harris (1973) found that estimated height was 10 inches more when participants were asked 'How tall . . .?' as compared to 'How short . . .?'. Instead, the question 'What was the height of the individual?' is preferable. In addition, interviewees who do not provide distorted information in response to such questions are nevertheless likely to become irritated by questions that imply the intended answer, especially answers they know are incorrect. Interviewees may be more likely to succumb to suggestive questioning in a police interview as the officer may be seen as an authority figure who is an expert in criminal investigations (Smith and Ellsworth, 1987).

Brown et al (2008) asked UK officers which question types they thought they used when trying to gain a person description from a witness: 89% said that they used open-ended questions, 47% used specific-closed prompts to elicit details regarding physical characteristics (eg height, build, and age), and 48% used the phrase 'top to toe'. (See problems with this strategy in the discussion of the CI later in this chapter.) However, what people say they do and what they actually do are not ever one and the same. This can be seen by the discussion below.

Repeated Questioning

As has already been noted, witnesses are often interviewed many times within the course of an inquiry. Indeed, Brown et al (2008) asked officers how frequently witnesses were interviewed within an investigation for person information and 82% indicated more than once (ranged from two to six times). Persons were deemed to be asked for descriptions by one or more of the following people within the course of the investigation: (i) by the call handler, at the initial reporting of the crime (see discussion above); (ii) by the responding officer either at the scene or within the initial enquiries; (iii) by the investigating officer; and (iv) by a specialist (or other) interviewer, in a formal witness interview. What is the effect of this repeated questioning on witness memory?

It has been found that over repeated recall attempts witnesses provide a net increase in recall which is termed hypermnesia (ie the number of new items gained is greater than the number of items lost over successive attempts) (see Scrivner and Safer, 1988) and also an increase in total recall (eg Turtle and Yuille, 1994) which is termed reminiscence. Thus, repeated interviews can actually help to preserve memory and result in an increased number of details remembered about the incident and the persons involved. However, this initially depends on how the information was elicited across successive interviews. If the interviews are conducted appropriately using predominately free recall tasks and open-ended questions then there is less opportunity for the interviewer to unduly influence what the interviewee says. However, if the interviews involve a predominantly interviewer-driven questioning style, with large numbers of specific-closed questions and leading questions, then multiple interviews can render memory, for an incident and persons, increasingly less accurate and more contaminated across each interview (eg Meissner, 2002). Also, the effect of repeated interviewing on the preservation of memory depends on when the first interview is conducted (Ebbesen and Rienick, 1998). For example, it has been found that there is some protection of memory for persons when a witness is asked to describe a person one day after the event.

From the above discussion it can be seen that the *way* in which the interviewee is initially interviewed can affect the witness description both in quantity and quality. We now turn to the more formal interview process.

INTERVIEWING AND THE COGNITIVE INTERVIEW

The nature of the interview process is pivotal in understanding the quality and quantity of the information gained. This is because, as has been shown already in this chapter, the quality of the information gained is primarily governed by outside influences (eg interviewer ability). Thus, if interviewers interview witnesses appropriately and investigators use appropriate tools to elicit descriptions, then the primary problem that concerns witness memory is quantity of recall (ie they do not spontaneously report enough detail). Thus, it is up to psychologists to develop tools to help investigators increase the amount of information gained from witnesses without reducing the accuracy of the information.

In the UK, it was not until 1992 that the police service provided its officers with a standard training regime designed to improve the quality of its officers' witness and suspect interviewing skills. The training that was developed used the acronym PEACE:

- Planning and Preparation prior to the interview.
- Engaging with and Explaining the interview process to an interviewee.
- Account elicited from the interviewee (hopefully full and faithful).

- Closing the interview down appropriately.
- Evaluation of the interviewer's skill and the information attained within the interview as the final closure of the interview process.

Under the umbrella framework of PEACE, officers are trained in two primary styles of interviewing: (i) conversation management aimed at interviewing more resistant interviewees where the interviewer is primarily in control of the interview; and (ii) the cognitive interview (CI)—and enhanced cognitive interview (ECI)—used for interviewing more cooperative interviewees where the control of the interview is explicitly handed over to the interviewee (see Milne and Bull, 1999, for a full explanation of PEACE and of conversation management).

The CI/ECI was developed in the 1980s by two US psychologists Ed Geiselman and Ron Fisher in order to provide investigators with a tool to help them elicit a greater amount of accurate information from witnesses and victims of crime. The original CI comprised a set of four instructions given by the interviewer to the interviewee (Fisher, Geiselman and Amador, 1989). Each of the four techniques: (i) the report everything instruction; (ii) the mental reinstatement of context; (iii) the recalling of events in a variety of different orders; and (iv) the change perspective technique, were developed from research and theory concerning the retrieval of information from memory. (For a full description of the CI and ECI see Milne and Bull, 1999; Fisher and Geiselman, 1992). The 'report everything' instruction encourages interviewees to report *everything* they remember without any editing, even if the interviewees think the details are not important/trivial or cannot remember completely a particular aspect of the TBR event (Milne, 2004). The 'mental reinstatement of context' (CR) technique emanates from the research demonstrating that context can have a powerful effect on memory (eg Hammond, Wagstaff and Cole, 2006) and is thought by many to be the most important part of the CI (e. Davis, McMahon and Greenwood, 2004). The context reinstatement instruction asks interviewees to reconstruct in their minds the context, both physical (environmental) and personal (eg how they felt at the time) features of the witnessed event (Milne and Bull, 1999).

Once interviewees have (using free report) recounted the TBR event in their own order, the interviewer should now encourage the interviewee to recall the event using a variety of different orders; for example, from the end to the beginning of the TBR event (ie reverse order recall) and/or working backwards and forwards in time from the most memorable aspect of the event. This technique attempts to counter the constructive nature of memory where an event that is being remembered is influenced by a witness' prior knowledge, expectations, and the employment of scripts (eg what typically happens in an armed robbery), among numerous other factors (eg stereotype of a person associated with a particular gang) (Fisher Holst and Pezdek, 1992). When recalling people usually use their script knowledge of such events (eg what they think typically happens in a robbery) to help them recall this particular event. This results in the recall of information which is in line with the script. However, script-inconsistent information which did occur, may not be recalled (Geiselman, 1987).

People have a tendency to report events from their own psychological perspective (Fisher and Geiselman, 1992). The CI change perspective instruction asks the interviewee now to recall the event from a different perspective. For example, in an investigation, we heard about a secretary walking up the main street on her way to work and saw two men arguing. Later that day the police came to her office saying one of the men had killed the other. She could recall the murderer's hair colour but not its style or length. The interviewer then asked her to adopt the perspective of a hair stylist to search her memory. When doing this she recalled more.

There are also additional memory aids that can be used in conjunction with the four original CI techniques described above. These memory 'jogs' are used to help the reporting of specific details concerning people (eg names, faces, voices, clothing, appearance) and objects (eg vehicles, number sequences, weapons) whereas the four above techniques are directed toward improving recall overall (Milne and Bull, 1999). People are often unable to remember names (eg the tip-of-the-tongue phenomenon—Brown and McNeill, 1966). To assist with this the interviewer should ask the interviewee to think about the following: name frequency (ie common or unusual name), name length (ie short or long; number of syllables), and the first letter of the name (ie by conducting an alphabetical search). The 'first-letter' technique has been found to be successful approximately two-thirds of the time (Gruneberg and Monks, 1976).

Witnesses tend not to realize that the interviewer requires very detailed descriptions, specifically of the perpetrator, and instead tend to focus on the actions in the TBR event. Indeed, it was observed in a typical interview of a robbery victim that 64% of the details elicited concerned actions that took place and only 30% concerned people in the event (Fisher, Geiselman and Raymond, 1987a). Interviewers therefore need to instruct the witness to report *all* types of information and not just action information. Interviewees also often have difficulty reporting information about people (Clifford and Bull, 1978; Milne and Bull, 2006). This is because people tend to hold general impressions rather than specific mental images of people they know (Ede and Shepherd, 1997). When a mental image does exist, reporting information from that mental image involves a translation process from a visual to a verbal medium (see more on this later). This is a difficult task which requires concentration and assistance from the interviewer. This problem is compounded by the fact that most people have a limited vocabulary regarding person information. If asked to describe your own jaw structure, you would probably encounter difficulties due to a limited vocabulary (Milne and Bull, 1999). As already mentioned a result of this is that person descriptions tend to be short and incomplete. In an interview situation, however, police officers then try to help the interviewee by asking very narrow and focused questions in order to elicit a detailed description (Clarke and Milne, 2001). Unfortunately, as already noted, it is these types of questions that result in information that is less reliable than that attained from free recall and open-ended questions. Instead Fisher and Geiselman (1992) suggest that the following techniques may help in eliciting specific details about persons in the TBR event.

- *Physical appearance*
  Does the person remind you of someone you know and, if so, why? Are there any peculiarities?

- *Clothing*
  Did the clothing remind you of anyone and, if so, why? What was the general impression?
- *Speech characteristics and conversation*
  Did the voice remind you of anyone and, if so, why? Think of your reactions to the conversation.

Subsequently, the originators (Fisher et al, 1987) found that real-life police interviewing of witnesses lacked of what the psychology of interpersonal communication deemed important, including that anxious and inarticulate witnesses often seem unsure of their role in the interview (Fisher, Chin and McCauley, 1990). The enhanced cognitive interview (ECI) was therefore developed and represents an allegiance between two fields of study: cognition and communication (Stein and Memon, 2006; Fisher, 1999). The ECI constitutes a number of phases providing the interview with structure, from rapport building, through to explaining the aims of the interview (including report everything (RE) and context reinstatement (CR)), through questioning and probing topics using mental imagery and witness compatible questioning, through varied retrieval (including use of senses and reverse order instruction (RO) and change perspective instruction (CP)), through to closure (see Milne and Bull, 1999, for a full description of each of the phases).

A person properly trained in the ECI may demonstrate good skill, but how effective, in terms of recall, is this procedure, especially for person information? Over 65 empirical studies of the effectiveness of the CI have now been published (Stein and Memon, 2006) and the vast majority of these have found that the CI/ECI elicits more correct information than a comparison interview. However, the CI has also been found sometimes to increase slightly the reporting of incorrect details (for a meta-analysis of 42 CI/ECI investigations see Köhnken, Milne, Memon and Bull, 1999). However, the accuracy of the information (proportion of correct details relative to the total amount of details reported) obtained with CI/ECIs and with comparison interviews is usually almost identical (eg average accuracy for the CI was 85% and average accuracy for the comparison interview was 82%; Köhnken et al, 1999). The CI has been found to increase the reporting of all types of information, specifically information relating to *persons* and actions (Milne et al, 1999) and information concerning conversations, both gist and verbatim (Campos and Alonso-Quecuty, in press, 2008). The increase in correct recall with the CI has also been found with different types of interviewees; that is adults in the general population, adults with a learning disability (eg Milne, Clare and Bull, 1997), adults with low socio-economic backgrounds (Stein and Memon, 2006), the elderly (Mello and Fisher, 1996; Wright and Holliday, 2007), and children, including those with a learning disability (Milne, Clare and Bull, 1999; Holliday, 2003). Kebbell, Milne and Wagstaff (1999) also found that police officers perceived the CI to be useful, but their respondents noted that time was a major problem in applying this technique in the field. It could be that a shortened and less complex version of the CI may be more realistic for day-to-day police interviewers (Kebbell et al, 1999; Dando, Wilcock and Milne, 2008). Indeed, researchers have begun to create a shortened CI for front-line officers where time is of the essence (Davis, McMahon and Greenwood,

2005; Dando, Wilcock, Milne and Daniels, under review, 2008). Brown et al (2008) also found that a number of the CI mnemonics were perceived to be effective for eliciting person information and thus also believed to be used frequently by officers (these were RE, CR, and imagery). Thus, with regard to person information the CI/ECI has been found to help in increasing the accurate reporting of this type of information. One area in which the CI does not seem to enhance performance is for a visual recognition task, such as an identification parade (Clifford and Gwyer, 1999).

Another hurdle in the investigation process concerns the way in which the information is recorded. In most countries adult witness interviews are not routinely electronically recorded. As a result, at interview, what the interviewee communicates verbally and non-verbally has to be fully encoded by the interviewer (Milne and Bull, 2005). However, the multitude of tasks required in a witness interview setting puts a lot of cognitive demands on the interviewer, especially so when there is no recording of the interview (eg the interviewer has to conduct an appropriate interview and also write down everything that the interviewee is saying). As a result the quality of the interview might suffer (Clarke and Milne, 2001) and there will be incomplete encoding of the available information (ie what the witness is reporting). The information that is encoded may be stored in the interviewer's memory but this later has to be recalled (eg to produce a written statement or report). Unless the interview is electronically recorded the interviewer's written report/statement will be involve further loss of information (Milne and Bull, 2005). (The information reported by the interviewee must now travel through the memory processes of the interviewer, as well as those of the interviewee.) Research has found that even if a police report is written immediately after the interview phase, the report contains only two-thirds of the relevant information reported by the interviewee (Koehnken, Thurer and Zoberbier, 1994). A third of the relevant information reported by the interviewee is therefore missing! Lamb, Orbach, Sternberg, Hershkowitz and Horowitz (2000) found that even when investigators took notes within an interview, 25% of the forensically relevant details provided by a child interviewee were not included in them (17.8% of these details were considered to be central to the investigation). Lamb et al concluded that 'interviewers cannot be expected to provide complete accounts of their interviews without electronic assistance' (2000, 705).

Even before an interview begins interviewers form judgements about the event and persons that may be involved in it (Shepherd and Milne, 1999). For police investigators these primarily arise from the crime category to which the alleged offence belongs, what typically occurs in such offences, and who the usual suspects are (ie offence knowledge) (Shepherd and Milne, 1999; 2006). In an investigation investigators will, wittingly or unwittingly, utilize this information to guide the direction of the case (Ask and Granhag, 2005). Most interview training around the globe advocates that interviewers need to plan adequately and prepare for the interview, thus part of this process will concern pre-interview judgements (eg topic areas to be covered). If, however, interviewers are guided too much by their own views of the event then relevant and vital information may be (wittingly or unwittingly) overlooked, screened out, ignored, forgotten, disposed of, or deleted, even at this pre-interview stage (for full discussion of these processes see Shepherd and Milne, 1999; Ask and Granhag, 2005). In the interview itself interviewers are also influenced by these judgements and they guide the informa-tion processing systems acting as filters, with the interviewer attending to the (pre-sumed) 'important' points of the information reported by the interviewee (Milne and Bull, 1999). The interviewer may hold certain hypotheses about the event in question and who they believe has committed the offence (especially if they have a suspect in custody) and as a consequence information which is consistent with the interviewer's pre-existing view will receive preferential treatment while inconsistent details may be distorted or even filtered out completely (Milne and Shaw, 1998). Interviewers may also filter information in accordance with their awareness of the particular case (Shepherd and Milne, 1999; McLean, 1995). It is this process which often compels interviewers to confirm what they already know or think they know (ie enter the interview room with a confirmatory bias), and to close the interview prematurely (ie once they have attained the information that they sought without exploring all avenues of questioning). This may result in vital information never being sought and/or being lost. It is, therefore, imperative to at least tape-record interviews with witnesses/victims, so that everything that is reported to the interviewer can be preserved (Milne and Shaw, 1998).

After the interview process witnesses are sometimes asked to help to construct a facial composite of the perpetrator(s) involved in the event they have witnessed. It is to this part of the investigation that we now turn. (For new developments in identifi-cation procedures see Chapter 9).

FACIAL COMPOSITES

A facial composite is an image constructed by a witness working with a police opera-tor which represents a 'type-likeness' of the perpetrator (Brace, Pike, Kemp, Turner and Bennett, 2006). Unfortunately, research tends to show that composite images produced by mock witnesses bear little resemblance to the target being constructed (eg Davies, van der Willik and Morrison, 2000). This is thought to be for a number of reasons. The first potential problem is with the system itself. In the UK the old systems, Identikit and Photofit (see similar problems in the US with Mac-a-Mug and FACES—Wells, Charman and Olson, 2005) were problematic because they asked the witness to piece together each individual feature of the face (eg eyes, then nose shape, etc) whereas faces are processed holistically (see Chapter 2). This presents a witness with a piecemeal task of face construction that goes against the usual cognitive opera-tions involved in facial processing and as a result renders the already difficult task even more difficult (Ellis, Davies and Shepherd, 1978).

Three relatively new computer systems are now in use in the UK at present: (i) E-fit; (ii) CD-fit; and (iii) PROfit, which try to take into account the past criticisms and allow the witness to construct the face holistically using a much more expan-sive database of facial features (Brace et al, 2006). With these systems the witness is initially interviewed, the description is then entered into the computer, and exem-plars are generated to create the initial whole face. This is then shown to the witness who then works on this whole face in conjunction with the operator to modify it until it is the best likeness possible. However, research has found that these systems still produce poor likenesses (eg Davies et al, 2000). This is probably due to the fact that witnesses have to translate a mental image into words and then back into visual images again, a three-pronged problem (Brace et al, 2006). However, more recent research is finding that part of the problem could be due to having only one composite. It is suggested that if the witness produces four composites of the same individual (which are either shown together or morphed into a prototype) better likenesses are being produced (Bruce, Ness, Hancock, Newman and Rarity, 2002; Brace et al, 2006). As a result, UK police now allow the use of multiple composites within an enquiry if it concerns serial offences and the suspect is linked to the crime by other compelling evidence (eg DNA).

Does the process of producing a composite help the witness in a subsequent identification procedure? Research concerning this issue is mixed, with some saying that it helps slightly (eg Wells et al, 2005, Expt 2), whilst other research shows the opposite effect (eg Wells et al, 2005, Expt 1). The whole issue depends on the procedure used to elicit the composite in the first place (ie the interview). If this is conducted inappropriately and the resultant facial image bears little resemblance to the perpetrator in the witness' mind's eye, then this composite could act as misinformation and distort the actual image of the perpetrators face in the witness memory rendering any subsequent identification very difficult. Much more research is warranted in this vital area of the investigation process. (See Chapter 9 for more details of composites.)

PERSON DESCRIPTION AND IDENTIFICATION EVIDENCE

As already noted within a real life investigation typically a witness/victim is interviewed one or more times (see above) before attempting an identification. It is estimated by officers themselves in the UK that witnesses may be put before an identification parade between one and six weeks after the incident (Brown et al, 2008). It would be common sense to assume that first describing an individual should help in any subsequent identification procedure. Furthermore, it would also be natural to assume that the better at describing the perpetrator the witness was, the more likely they would be able to accurately identify him/her from a subsequent identification parade (ie the quantity and quality of a person's initial verbal description will have a direct bearing on the quality of their subsequent identification). In addition, this view is also at the centre of examination within a courtroom where a witness' initial description of the perpetrator does not match partially or completely whom they then select from an identification parade and who may be standing in the courtroom as the accused (Sporer and Cutler, 2003). These inconsistencies are dwelled upon and often render the witness' testimony as unreliable in the face of the judge and jury. However, the research examining this very issue is not so clear-cut.

It has been found that for distinctive faces there is a positive relationship between description recall ability and subsequent recognition tasks (Wells, 1985). However, that is where the relationship seems to end, as a meta-analysis including 33 studies with over 4,000 participants (Meissner, Sporer and Susa, 2008) has recently found that there is a very weak and often non-existent relationship between *accuracy* of (person) recall and subsequent identification performance. In the real world we do not know the ground truth and thus it is very difficult to assess what details are accurate and inaccurate. Thus, one can only realistically use *quantity* of details recalled as a measure but unfortunately the meta-analysis demonstrated that there is at best a very weak relationship here. Indeed, the meta-analysis found that when witnesses have not had long to view the face and when there is a delay between the interview and the subsequent identification procedure the relationship between the amount of (descriptive/verbal) information recalled and accuracy of identification is negative. Where more complete, descriptions tend to be less accurate.

The reason for this poor correlation between recall and identification performance is that in a recall task, when a person is asked to verbally describe a face, they have to break down the visual image into its constituent parts, and then attempt to describe these individual parts. This is a very difficult process. The recognition task, however, is a very different task, as it is a more holistic configural process and recognition in essence requires more of a matching process. Thus, as a result of the psychological differences between the two types of tasks, the ability of a witness to be able to do one has no relationship to their ability to do the other (Diamond and Carey, 1986; Farah et al, 1998). Indeed, the recall task is also highly dependent on the ability of the interviewer and it can be seen from the prior discussion that the interview process itself is of great importance in determining the quantity and quality of the description gained from the interviewee. Unfortunately, this all-important interview process, in the majority of countries, is not routinely recorded in order to preserve the nature of the process to enable people (investigator or courts) at a later date to determine the actual quality of a particular description. This seems unbelievable especially in light of the fact that the US courts determine the reliability of a witness identification based on the accuracy of his/her prior description. The interview process, which is so pivotal in determining reliability of information, is unknown.

Verbal Overshadowing

Some believe and have demonstrated that verbally describing an individual can have a detrimental effect on subsequent identifications due to a process termed the 'verbal overshadowing effect' (Schooler, 2002). In one of the first demonstrations of this effect Schooler and Engstler-Schooler (1990) showed a group of participants a video recording of a bank robbery. Some of the participants then verbally described the facial features of the robber whilst others, the control group, did not. Then all participants had to try and identify the said robber seen in the video-clip. It was found that those who gave a prior verbal description of the robber were less likely to pick him out. Differences of up to 30% in identification accuracy have been found (eg Brandimonte, Schooler and Gabbino, 1997) and the effect is seen to be heightened the more elaborate the retrieval task (eg Meissner and Brigham, 2001). This is a worrying finding in practical investigative terms. This is because the typical order of investigation procedures is that a witness is first interviewed to obtain a verbal recall or account of the perpetrator(s), then witnesses are sometimes asked to help construct a facial composite, and sometimes they are also asked to attend a formal identification procedure (a recognition task). As a result of the practical and theoretical implications of the verbal overshadowing effect, a large body of research has now been conducted to examine the extent of these findings. A meta-analysis including over 2,000 participants from

29 comparisons indeed found that participants who first described a face were more likely to misidentify someone from a following identification parade (Meissner and Brigham, 2001) but this effect was largely due to descriptions that involved incorrect details.

The mechanisms underpinning the verbal overshadowing effect are thought to be due to one of three processes: (i) 'recoding interference' account where it is thought that the act of verbally describing a face and the output of that task (a verbal description) interferes with access to the original visual memory of the face and may even change/recode the memory of the original face required for the matching identification task (eg Schooler and Engstler-Schooler, 1990; Meissner, Brigham and Kelley, 2001); (ii) the 'transfer-inappropriate processing shift/retrieval' account notes that the act of verbally describing a face is a featural process (ie when describing a face, an individual describes each facial feature separately) and as a result this interferes with the subsequent identification recognition task which necessitates a more global holistic matching exercise (Schooler, Fiore and Brandimonte, 1997; Schooler, 2002). This is a type of retrieval-induced forgetting (Anderson et al, 2000); and (iii) the 'criterion-shift' explanation determines that witnesses who give a description regardless of the accuracy of the information are less likely to make a positive identification because they lower their level of judgement through the description and any inaccurate descriptions, made perhaps through guessing features, may affect the actual memory for the face and then hinder subsequent identification.

However, it seems that the verbal overshadowing effect is short-lived in time. For example, Finger and Pezdek (1999) found that although using the CI to enhance verbal description of a face reduced subsequent identification accuracy, this negative effect was markedly reduced when a delay of 24 minutes was inserted. Thus, it was concluded that giving a verbal account does not overwrite the original memory of the face it just makes it less accessible for a short period of time. Luckily it is very unlikely that an identification procedure will be conducted within 24 minutes of the interview and therefore the theory of verbal overshadowing may well have limited practical implications. In addition, it has been found that the verbal over-shadowing effect does not occur when the TBR event has multiple perpetrators/faces (more like a real crime), where those faces that were verbalized after viewing were actually later more likely to be accurately identified (Ryan and Schooler, 1994). Furthermore, it has been found recently that when the description of the target face is not elaborated upon using forced recall (eg specific-closed type questions: the five WHs), and instead a description is gained through the use of free recall and the resultant description is short in duration a prior description actually has what has been termed a verbal facilitation effect on memory (ie enhances the subsequent identification process) (Brown and Lloyd-Jones, 2005, 2006; Meissner et al, 2001). It also depends on the type of questions being asked within the interview, as Brown and Lloyd-Jones (2006) found that when witnesses gave personality trait judgements (eg niceness) about the target, subsequent recognition performance was enhanced compared to when giving judgements about physical characteristics (eg gender). This is thought to be in part due to the fact that people use more global impressions of the face when judging traits. In conclusion, it seems that the verbal overshadowing effect is fragile, only exists for very short periods of time, and thus is likely to have limited or no effects in real world investigations. Interestingly, however, the effect is heightened when an interviewer-driven questioning style is used which is characterized by a predominance of closed-specific questions. This questioning style is the very one that researchers are trying to dissuade investigators from using. However, it is the very one which investigators also find very difficult to steer clear of (Griffiths and Milne, 2006; Powell, Fisher, and Wright, 2005).

Overall, it can be seen that answering the basic investigative question of 'Whodunnit?' involves a very difficult path and the outcome can have devastating effects on the criminal justice system if there are not enough safeguards in place.

FURTHER READING

MEISSNER, C., SPORER, S., and SCHOOLER, J. (2007). Person Descriptions as Eyewitness Evidence. In R.C.L. Lindsay, D.F. Ross, J.D. Read, and M.P. Toglia (eds) *Handbook of Eyewitness Psychology Volume 11*. Mahwah, NJ: Lawrence Erlbaum Associates, 1–34.

MILNE, R. and BULL, R. (1999). *Investigative Interviewing: Psychology and Practice*. Chichester: Wiley.

REFERENCES

ACPO (2005). *Practice Advice on Core Investigative Doctrine*. Cambridgeshire: Centrex.

AMBLER, C. and MILNE, R. (2006). *Call Handling Centres—An Evidential Opportunity or Threat?* Paper presented at the Second International Investigative Interviewing Conference, Portsmouth, July.

ASK, K. and GRANHAG, P. A. (2005). Motivational sources of confirmation bias in criminal investigations: The need for cognitive closure. *Journal of Investigative Psychology and Offender Profiling, 2*, 43–63.

BALDWIN, J. and BEDWARD, J. (1991). Summarising tape recordings of police interviews. *Criminal Law Review, 671–679*.

BRACE, N., PIKE, G., KEMP, R., TURNER, J. and BENNETT, P. (2006). Does the presentation of multiple facial composites improve suspect identification? *Applied Cognitive Psychology, 20*, 213–226.

BRANDIMONTE, M., HITCH, G. and BISHOP, D. (1992). Influence of short-term memory codes on visual image processing: Evidence from image transformation tasks. *Journal of Experimental Psychology: Learning, Memory and Cognition, 18*, 157–165.

BROWN, C. and LLOYD-JONES, T. (2005). Verbal facilitation of face recognition. *Memory and Cognition, 33*, 1442–1456.

—— and —— (2006). Beneficial effects of verbalization and visual distinctiveness on remembering and knowing faces. *Memory and Cognition, 34*, 277–286.

——, —— and ROBINSON, M. (2008). Eliciting person descriptions from eyewitnesses: A survey of police perceptions of eyewitness performance and use of interview techniques. *Special Edition European Journal of Cognitive Psychology*.

Brown, R. and McNeill, D. (1966). The 'Tip-of-the-Tongue' phenomenon. *Journal of Verbal Learning and Verbal Behavior, 5*, 325–337.

Bruce, V., Ness, H., Hancock, P.J.B., Newman, C. and Rarity, J. (2002). Four heads are better than one: Combining face composites yields improvements in face likeness. *Journal of Applied Psychology, 87*, 894–902.

Campos, L. and Alonso-Quecuty, M. (in press, 2008). Language crimes and the cognitive interview: Testing its efficacy in retrieving a conversational event. *Applied Cognitive Psychology.*

Christianson, S. A. and Hubinette, B. (1993). Hands up! A study of witness emotional reactions and memories associated with bank robberies. *Applied Cognitive Psychology, 7*, 365–379.

Clarke, C. and Milne, R. (2001). *National Evaluation of the PEACE Investigative Interviewing Course.* Police Research Award Scheme, PRAS/149. London: Home Office.

Clifford, B.R. and Bull, R. (1978). *The Psychology of Person Identification.* London: Routledge and Kegan Paul.

—— and Gwyer, P. (1999). The effects of the cognitive interview and other methods of context reinstatement on identification. *Psychology, Crime and Law, 5*, 61–80.

—— and Hollin, C. (1981). Effects of type of incident and the number of perpetrators on eyewitness memory. *Journal of Applied Psychology, 66*, 364–370.

Cohen, N.J. and Faulkner, D. (1988). Life Span Changes in Autobiographical Memory. In M. Gruneberg, P. Morris and R.N. Sykes (eds) *Practical Aspects of Memory: Current Research and Issues.* Chichester: Wiley.

Dando, C., Wilcock, R. and Milne, R. (2008). The Cognitive Interview: Inexperienced Police Officers' Perceptions of Their Witness/Victim Interviewing Practices. *Legal and Criminological Psychology, 13*, 59–70.

——, ——, —— and Henry, L. (in submission, 2008). A modified cognitive interview procedure for frontline police investigators. *Psychology, Crime and Law.*

Davies, G.M. and Patel, D. (2005). The influence of car and driver stereotypes on attributions of vehicle speed, position on the road and culpability in a road accident scenario. *Legal and Criminological Psychology, 10*, 45–62.

——, van der Willik, P. and Morrison, L.J. (2000). Facial composite production: A comparison of mechanical and computer-driven systems. *Journal of Applied Psychology, 85*, 119–124.

Davis, M.R., McMahon, M. and Greenwood, K. (2004). The role of visual imagery in the enhanced cognitive interview: Guided questioning techniques and individual differences. *Journal of Investigative Psychology and Offender Profiling, 1*, 33–51.

——, —— and —— (2005). The efficacy of mnemonic components of the cognitive interview: Towards a shortened variant for time-critical investigations. *Applied Cognitive Psychology, 19*, 75–93.

Deffenbacher, K.A. (1991). A maturing of research on the behaviour of eyewitnesses. *Applied Cognitive Psychology, 5*, 377–402.

Dehon, H. and Brédart, S. (2001). An 'other-race' effect in age estimation from faces. *Perception, 30*, 1107–1113.

Diamond, R. and Carey, S. (1986). Why faces are and are not special: An effect of expertise. *Journal of Experimental Psychology: General, 115*, 107–117.

Easterbrook, J.A. (1959). The effect of emotion on cue utilisation and the organisation of behaviour. *Psychological Review, 66*, 183–201.

Ebbesen, E. and Rienick, C. (1998). Retention interval and eyewitness memory for events and personal identifying attributes. *Journal of Applied Psychology, 83*, 745–762.

EDE, R. and SHEPHERD, E. (1997). *Active Defence: A Solicitor's Guide to Police and Defence Investigation and Prosecution and Defence Disclosure in Criminal Cases*. London: The Law Society.

ELLIS, H.D., DAVIES, G.M. and SHEPHERD, J.W. (1978). A critical examination of the PhotoFIT system for recalling faces. *Ergonomics, 21*, 297–307.

FAHSING, I., ASK, K. and GRANHAG, P-A. (2004). The man behind the mask: Accuracy and predictors of eyewitness offender descriptions. *Journal of Applied Psychology, 89*, XX.

FALLSHORE, M. and SCHOOLER, J. (1995). The verbal vulnerability of perceptual expertise. *Journal of Experimental Psychology: Learning, Memory, and Cognition, 21*, 1608–1623.

FARAH, M., WILSON, K., DRAIN, M. and TANAKA, J. (1998). What is 'Special' about face perception? *Psychological Review, 105*, 482–498.

FARRINGTON, D. and LAMBERT, S. (1997). Predicting Offender Profiles From Victim and Witness Descriptions. In J. Jackson and D.A. Bekerian (eds) *Offender Profiling: Theory, Research, and Practice*. Chichester: Wiley.

FINGER, K. and PEZDEK, K. (1999). The effect of the cognitive interview on face identification accuracy: Release from verbal overshadowing. *Journal of Applied Psychology, 84*, 340–348.

FISHER, R.P. (1999). Probing Knowledge. In D. Gopher and A. Koriat (eds) *Attention and Performance: XVII*. Cambridge, MA: The MIT Press, 537–556.

——, CHIN, D.M. and McCAULEY, M.R. (1990). Enhancing Eyewitness Recollection With the Cognitive Interview. *National Police Research Unit Review, 6*, 3–11.

——, FALKNER, K., TREVISAN, M. and McCAULEY, M. (2000). Adapting the cognitive interview to enhance long-term (35 years) recall of physical activities. *Journal of Applied Psychology, 85*, 180–189.

—— and GEISELMAN, R.E. (1992). *Memory-enhancing Techniques for Investigative Interviewing: The Cognitive Interview*. Springfield, IL: Charles Thomas.

——, —— and AMADOR, M. (1989). Field test of the cognitive interview: Enhancing the recollection of actual victims and witness of crime. *Journal of Applied Psychology, 74*, 722–727.

——, —— and RAYMOND, D.S. (1987a). Critical analysis of police interviewing techniques. *Journal of Police Science and Administration, 15*, 177–185.

——, ——, ——, JURKEVICH, L. and WARHAFTIG, M.L. (1987b). Enhancing eyewitness memory: Refining the cognitive interview. *Journal of Police Science and Administration, 15*, 291–297.

—— and MILNE, R. (2006). *The Cognitive Interview: The Basics*. Workshop presented at the Second International conference on Investigative Interviewing, Portsmouth, July.

FISHER HOLST, V. and PEZDEK, K. (1992). Scripts for typical crimes and their effects on memory for eyewitness testimony. *Applied Cognitive Psychology, 6*, 573–587.

FLIN, R. and SHEPHERD, J. (1986). Tall Stories: Eyewitnesses' Ability to Estimate Height and Weight Characteristics. *Human Learning, 5*, 29–38.

FRUZZETTI, A.E., TOLAND, K., TELLER, S.A. and LOFTUS, E.F. (1992). Memory and Eyewitness Testimony. In M. Gruneberg and P. Morris (eds) *Aspects of Memory, Vol. 1: The Practical Aspects*. New York: Routledge.

GABBERT, F., MEMON, A. and ALLAN, K. (2003). Memory conformity: Can eyewitnesses influence each other's memories for an event?. *Applied Cognitive Psychology, 17*, 533–543.

GEISELMAN, R.E. (1987). The Cognitive Interview Technique for Interviewing Victims and Witnesses of Crime. *The National Sheriff, October-November*, 54–56.

GEORGE, P. and HOLE, G. (1995). Factors influencing the accuracy of age estimates of unfamiliar faces. *Perception, 24*, 1059–1073.

GINET, M. and PY, J. (2002). *A Technique for Enhancing Memory in Eyewitness Testimonies for Use by Police Officers and Judicial Officials: The Cognitive Interview.* Unpublished manuscript.

GRIFFITHS, A. and MILNE, R. (2005). Will it All End in Tiers? Police Interview With Suspects in Britain. In T. Williamson (ed.) *Investigative Interviewing: Rights, Research, Regulation.* Cullompton: Willan Publishing.

——, RETFORD, A. and MILNE, R. (2006). *Is All Training Good Training? A Comparison of Two Different Witness Interview Training Programmes.* Paper presented at the Second International Conference on Investigative Interviewing, Portsmouth, July.

GUDJONSSON, G.H. (2003). *The Psychology of Interrogations and Confessions.* Chichester: Wiley.

HAMMOND, L., WAGSTAFF, G.F. and COLE, J. (2006). Facilitating eyewitness memory in adults and children with context reinstatement and focused meditation. *Journal of Investigative Psychology and Offender Profiling, 3,* 117–130.

HARRIS, R.J. (1973). Answering questions containing marked and unmarked adjectives and adverbs. *Journal of Experimental Psychology, 97,* 399–401.

HENSS, R. (1991). Perceiving age and attractiveness in facial photographs. *Journal of Applied Psychology, 21,* 933–946.

HOLLIDAY, R. (2003). Reducing misinformation effects in children with cognitive interviews: Dissociating recollection and familiarity. *Child Development, 74,* 728–751.

HOLLIN, C. (1980). *An investigation of certain social, situational and individual factors in eyewitness memory.* Unpublished doctoral thesis, North East London Polytechnic.

HOWE, M.L., COURAGE, M.L. and PETERSON, C. (1994). How can I remember when I wasn't there: long-term retention of traumatic experiences and convergence of the cognitive self. *Consciousness and Cognition, 3,* 327–355.

KASSIN, S., TUBB, V., HOSCH, H. and MEMON, A. (2001). On the 'general acceptance' of eyewitness testimony research. *American Psychologist, 56,* 405–416.

KEBBELL, M.R. and DANIELS, T. (2005). Mock suspects decisions to confess: the influence of eyewitness statements and identifications. Paper presented at the 15th European Psychology and Law conference, Vilnius, Lithuania, July.

—— and MILNE, R (1998). Police officers' perception of eyewitness factors in forensic investigations. *Journal of Social Psychology, 138,* 323–330.

——, —— and WAGSTAFF, G. (1999). The cognitive interview: A survey of its forensic effectiveness. *Psychology, Crime and Law, 5,* 101–116.

—— and WAGSTAFF, G. (1999). *Face value? Evaluating the accuracy of eyewitness information.* Police Research Series Paper 102. London: Home Office.

KIHLSTROM, J.F. (1996). The trauma-memory argument and recovered memory theory. In K. Pezdek and W.P. Banks (eds) *The Recovered/False Memory Debate.* San Diego, CA: Academic Press.

KÖHNKEN, G. (1995). Interviewing adults. In R. Bull and D. Carson (eds) *Handbook of Psychology in Legal Contexts.* Chichester: Wiley.

——, MILNE, R., MEMON, A. and BULL, R. (1999). The cognitive interview: A meta-analysis. *Psychology, Crime and Law, 5,* 3–28.

——, THÜRER, C. and ZOBERBIER, D. (1994). The cognitive interview: Are the interviewers' memories enhanced too? *Applied Cognitive Psychology, 8,* 13–24.

KRAMER, H.T., BUCKHOUT, R. and EUGINIO, P. (1990). Weapon focus, arousal and eyewitness memory. *Law and Human Behavior, 14,* 167–184.

KUEHN, L. (1974). Looking down a gun barrel: person perception and violent crime. *Perceptual and Motor Skills, 39,* 1159–1164.

LAMB, M.E., ORBACH, Y., STERNBERG, K., HERSHKOWITZ, I. and HOROWITZ, D. (2000). Accuracy of investigators' verbatim notes of their forensic interviews with alleged child abuse victims. *Law and Human Behavior, 24,* 699–708.

LEE, T. and GEISELMAN, E. (1994). Recall of perpetrator height as a function of eyewitness and perpetrator ethnicity. *Psychology, Crime and Law, 1,* 11–19.

LINDHOLM, T. (2005). Own-age biases in verbal person memory. *Memory, 13,* 21–30.

LINDSAY, R., MARTION, R. and WEBBER, L. (1994). Default values in eyewitness descriptions: A problem for the match-to-description lineup foil selection strategy. *Law and Human Behavior, 18,* 527–541.

LOFTUS, E.F. (1979). *Eyewitness Testimony.* Cambridge, Mass: Harvard University Press.

——, LOFTUS, G.R. and MESSO, J. (1987). Some facts about weapon focus. *Law and Human Behavior, 11,* 55–62.

MAASS, A. and KÖHNKEN, G. (1989). Eyewitness identification: Simulating the 'weapon effect'. *Law and Human Behavior, 13,* 397–408.

MACRAE, C.N. and BODENHAUSEN, G.V. (2001). Social cognition: Categorical person perception. *British Journal of Psychology, 92,* 239–256.

McLEAN, M. (1995). Quality investigation? Police interviewing of witnesses. *Medicine, Science and the Law, 35,* 116–122

McLEOD, M.D. and SHEPHERD, J.W. (1986). Sex differences in eyewitness reports of criminal assaults. *Medicine, Science and the Law, 26,* 311–318.

MELLO, E. and FISHER, R.P. (1996). Enhancing older adult eyewitness memory with the cognitive interview. *Applied Cognitive Psychology, 10,* 403–417.

MEISSNER, C. (2002). Applied aspects of the instructional bias effect in verbal overshadowing. *Applied Cognitive Psychology, 16,* 295–305.

—— and BRIGHAM, J. (2001). A meta-analysis of the verbal overshadowing effect in face identification. *Applied Cognitive Psychology, 15,* 603–616.

——, —— and KELLEY, C. (2001). The influence of retrieval processes in verbal overshadowing. *Memory and Cognition, 29,* 176–186.

——, SPORER, S. and SCHOOLER, J. (2007). Person descriptions as eyewitness evidence. In R.C.L. Lindsay, D.F. Ross, J.D. Read and M.P. Toglia (eds) *Handbook of Eyewitness Psychology Volume 11.* Mahwah, NJ: Lawrence Erlbaum Associates, 1–34.

——, —— and SUSA, K. (2008). A theoretical review and meta-analysis of the description-identification relationship in memory for faces. *European Journal of Cognitive Psychology, 20,* 414–455.

MILNE, R. (1999). Interviewing children with learning disabilities. In A. Memon and R. Bull (eds), *Handbook of the Psychology of Interviewing.* Chichester: Wiley.

—— (2004). *The Cognitive Interview: A Step-By-Step Guide.* Unpublished training manual.

—— and BULL, R. (1999). *Investigative Interviewing: Psychology and Practice.* Chichester: Wiley.

—— and —— (2006). Interviewing victims of crime, including children and people with intellectual difficulties. In M.R. Kebbell and G.M. Davies (eds) *Practical Psychology for Forensic Investigations.* Chichester: Wiley.

——, CLARE, I.C.H. and BULL, R. (1999). Interviewing adults with learning disability with the cognitive interview. *Psychology, Crime and Law, 5,* 81–100.

—— and SHAW, G. (1999). Obtaining witness statements: Best practice and proposals for innovation. *Medicine, Science and the Law, 39,* 127–138.

NICOL, C., INNES, M., GEE, D. and FEIST, A. (2004). *Reviewing Murder Investigations: An Analysis of Progress From Six Police Forces.* London: HMSO.

PEACE, K. and PORTER, S. (2004). A longitudinal investigation of the reliability of memories for trauma and other emotional experiences. *Applied Cognitive Psychology, 18,* 1143–1159.

PEZDEK, K. and PRULL, M. (1993). Fallacies in memory for conversations: Reflections on Clarence Thomas, Anita Hall and the like. *Applied Cognitive Psychology, 7,* 299–310.

POWELL, M.B., FISHER, R.P. and WRIGHT, R. (2005). Investigative interviewing. In N. Brewer and K. Williams (eds) *Psychology and Law: An Empirical Perspective.* New York: Guildford, 11–42.

POZZULO, J. and WARREN, K. (2003). Descriptions and identifications of strangers by youth and adult eyewitnesses. *Journal of Applied Psychology, 88,* 315–323.

PRYKE, S., LINDSAY, R.C.L. and POZZULO, J.D. (2000). Sorting mug shots: Methodological issues. *Applied Cognitive Psychology, 14,* 81–96.

RYAN, R. and SCHOOLER, J. (1998). Whom do words hurt?: Individual differences in susceptibility to verbal overshadowing. *Applied Cognitive Psychology, 12,* 105–126.

SANDERS, G.S. (1986). The usefulness of eyewitness research from the perspective of police investigators. Unpublished manuscript, State University of New York. In R. Fisher, R.E. Geiselman and M. Armador. (1989). Field test of the cognitive interview: Enhancing the recollection of actual victims and witnesses of crime. *Journal of Applied Psychology, 74,* 722–727.

SAVAGE, S. and MILNE, R. (2007). Miscarriages of justice—the role of the investigative process. In T. Newburn, T. Williamson and A. Wright (eds) *Handbook of Criminal Investigation.* Cullompton: Willan.

SCHOOLER, J. (2002). Verbalization produces a transfer inappropriate processing shift. *Applied Cognitive Psychology, 16,* 989–997.

—— and ENGSTLER-SCHOOLER, T. (1990). Verbal overshadowing of visual memories: Some things are better left unsaid. *Cognitive Psychology, 22,* 36–71.

——, FIORE, S. and BRANDIMONTE, M. (1997). At a loss from words: Verbal overshadowing of perceptual memories. In D. Medin (ed.) *Handbook of Learning and Motivation* (Vol. 37). Orlando, FL: Academic Press.

SCRIVNER, E. and SAFER, M.A. (1988). Eyewitness show hypermnesia for details about a violent event. *Journal of Applied Psychology, 73,* 371–377.

SEARCY, J., BARTLETT, J., MEMON, A. and SWANSON, K. (2001). Aging and lineup performance at long retention intervals: Effects of metamemory and context reinstatement. *Journal of Applied Psychology, 86,* 207–214.

SHEPHERD, E. (1986). Conversational core of policing. *Policing, 2,* 294–303.

—— and MILNE, R. (1999). Full and faithful: Ensuring quality practice and integrity of outcome in witness interviews. In A. Heaton-Armstrong, D. Wolchover and E. Shepherd (eds) *Analysing witness testimony.* Blackstone Press.

—— and —— (2006). Have you told management about this?: Bringing witness interviewing into the twenty-first century. In A. Heaton-Armstrong, E. Shepherd, G. Gudjonsson, and D. Wolchover (eds) *Witness Testimony: Psychological, Investigative, and Evidential Perspectives.* Oxford: Oxford University Press.

SHEPHERD, J.W. and ELLIS, H.D. (1996). Face recall methods and problems. In S.L. Sporer, R.S. Malpass and G. Kohneken (eds) *Psychological Issues in Eyewitness Identification.* Hillsdale, NJ: Erlbaum.

——, —— and DAVIES, G. (1982). *Identification Evidence: A Psychological Examination.* Aberdeen: Aberdeen University Press.

SILKE, A. (2001). Behind the mask. *Police review, September,* 20–21.

SMITH, V.L. and ELLSWORTH, P.C. (1987). The social psychology of eyewitness accuracy: Misleading questions and communicator expertise. *Journal of Applied Psychology, 72,* 294–300.

SOUKARA, R., BULL, R. and VRIJ, A. (2002). Police detectives' aims regarding their interviews with suspects: Any change at the turn of the millennium? *International Journal of Police Science and Management, 4,* 101–114.

SPORER, S. (1996). Psychological aspects of person descriptions. In S. Sporer, R. Malpass and G, Köhnken (eds) *Psychological issues in eyewitness identification.* Mahaw, NJ: Erlbaum.

—— (2001). Recognizing faces of other ethnic groups: An integration of theories. *Psychology, Public Policy and Law, 7,* 36–97.

—— and CUTLER, B. (2003). Identification evidence in Germany: Commonsense assumptions, empirical evidence, guidelines, and judicial practices. In P.J. van Koppen and S.D. Penrod (eds) *Adversarial vs. inquisitorial justice: Psychological perspectives on criminal justice systems.* New York: Plenum.

STEBLAY, N.M. (1992). A meta-analytic review of the weapon focus effect. *Law and Human Behavior, 16,* 413–424.

STEIN, L. M. and MEMON, A. (2006). Testing the efficacy of the cognitive interview in a developing country. *Applied Cognitive Psychology, 20,* 597–605.

TURTLE, J. and YUILLE, J. (1994). Lost but not forgotten details: Repeated eyewitness recall leads to reminiscence but not hypermnesia. *Journal of Applied Psychology, 79,* 260–271.

VALENTINE, T. (2006). Forensic facial identification. In A. Heaton-Armstrong, E. Shepherd, G. Gudjonsson, and D. Wolchover (eds) *Witness Testimony: Psychological, Investigative, and Evidential Perspectives.* Oxford: Oxford University Press.

VAN KOPPEN, P. and LOCHUN, S. (1997). Portraying perpetrators: the validity of offender descriptions by witnesses. *Law and Human Behavior, 21,* 661–685.

WAGENAAR, W.A. and VAN DER SCHRIER, J. (1994). *Face recognition as a function of distance and illumination: A practical test for use in the court-room.* Paper presented at the Fourth European Conference on Law and Psychology, Barcelona, April.

WAGSTAFF, G., MACVEIGH, J., BOSTON, R., SCOTT, L., BRUNAS-WAGSTAFF, J. and COLE, J. (2003). Can laboratory findings on eyewitness testimony be generalized to the real world? An archival analysis of the influence of violence, weapon presence, and age on eyewitness accuracy. *Journal of Psychology: Interdisciplinary and Applied, 137,* 17–28.

WARNICK, D. and SANDERS, G. (1980). Why do witnesses make so many mistakes?. *Journal of Applied Social Psychology, 10,* 362–367.

WELLS, G.L. (1985). Verbal descriptions of faces from memory: Are they diagnostic of identification accuracy. *Journal of Applied Psychology, 70,* 619–626.

——, CHARMAN, S.D. and OLSON, E.A. (2005). Building face composites can harm lineup identification performance. *Journal of Experimental Psychology: Applied, 11,* 147–156.

WICKHAM, L.H.V. and SWIFT, M.A. (2004). Articulatory suppression attenuates the verbal overshadowing effect: A role for verbal encoding in face identification. *Applied Cognitive Psychology, 20,* 157–169.

WRIGHT, A. and ALISON, L. (2004). Questioning sequences in Canadian police interviews: Constructing and confirming the course of events. *Psychology, Crime and Law, 10,* 137–154.

—— and HOLLIDAY, R. (2007). Enhancing the recall of young, young-old, and old-old adults with cognitive interviews. *Applied Cognitive Psychology, 21,* 19–43.

YARMEY, A.D. (1986). Verbal, visual, and voice identification of a rape suspect under different conditions of illumination. *Journal of Applied Psychology, 71,* 363–370.

—— (2004). Eyewitness recall and photo identification: A field experiment. *Psychology, Crime and Law, 10,* 53–68.

——, JACOB, J. and PORTER, A. (2002). Person recall in field settings. *Journal of Applied Social Psychology, 32,* 2354–2367.

—— and MORRIS, S. (1998). The effects of discussion on eyewitness memory. *Journal of Applied Social Psychology, 28*, 1637–1648.

——, YARMEY, A.L. and YARMEY, M.J. (1994). Face and voice identification in showups and lineups. *Applied Cognitive Psychology, 8*, 453–464.

YUILLE, J.C. and CUTSHALL, J. (1986). A case study of eyewitness memory for a crime. *Journal of Applied Psychology, 71*, 291–301.

—— and —— (1989). Analysis of the statements of victims, witnesses and suspects. In J.C. Yuille (ed.) *Credibility Assessment*. Dordrecht, The Netherlands: Kluwer Academic.

——, DAVIES, G., GIBLING, F., MARXSEN, D. and PORTER, S. (1994). Eyewitness memory of police trainees for realistic role plays. *Journal of Applied Psychology, 79*, 931–936.

—— and TOLLESTRUP, P.A. (1992). A model of the diverse effects of emotion on eyewitness memory. In S.A. Christianson (ed.) *The Handbook of Emotion and Memory*. Hillsdale, NJ: Lawrence Erlbaum.

4

FACTORS AFFECTING THE ACCURACY OF EYEWITNESS IDENTIFICATIONS

INTRODUCTION

Many different factors affect the accuracy of eyewitness identification evidence. In 1978, Wells divided these factors into *estimator variables* and *system variables*. *Estimator variables* can be viewed as factors that the police and the Criminal Justice System have little control over. Examples of *estimator variables* include age of the witness and the circumstances in which the crime occurred, such as poor visibility of the perpetrator because the crime was committed at night in a poorly lit area. The Criminal Justice System cannot control who witnesses a crime and the age of that witness, neither can it control the circumstances in which a crime occurs. The effect of these variables on subsequent identification accuracy can only be estimated after the crime has occurred. Conversely, *system variables* are factors that are under the control of the police and the Criminal Justice System. Examples of *system variables* include instructions given to the witness prior to a line-up and the number of members included in a line-up. Chapter 7 provides an in-depth discussion of research that has examined system variables and the extent to which that research has guided current recommendations for conducting line-ups. This chapter will examine the effect of estimator variables on identification accuracy.

ESTIMATOR VARIABLES

Research examining the effect of estimator variables on eyewitness identification performance has generally used three different research methodologies: (i) face recognition studies where participants view many faces and after a delay are asked to respond to a test set of faces containing some of the faces they saw earlier along with some new faces not seen before. Using this method allows researchers to look at factors affecting accuracy across many different faces in a highly controlled manner; (ii) a mock witness identification paradigm where participants (ie mock witnesses) view a simulated crime event and after a delay view an identification parade/line-up or a photo-spread.

The line-up can be either target present (TP) which simulates a situation in which the police suspect is the perpetrator, or the line-up can be target absent (TA) which simulates a situation in which the police suspect is innocent. This mock witness identification paradigm is closer to real world conditions than a face recognition study and therefore has more ecological validity but generally researchers only use one line-up and therefore it may be difficult to generalize findings from one target face to other examples (Wells and Windschitl, 1999); (iii) field studies where researchers examine police records of witness performance on line-ups and can investigate whether certain factors lead to greater or fewer suspect identifications. Whilst this method has the greatest ecological validity, researchers do not have the control they have in mock witness and face recognition studies conducted in a laboratory setting. They may not know for sure whether the suspect is the perpetrator or whether there may be other estimator variables operating in addition to the specific factor(s) they are investigating. Studies using all three methodologies will be discussed in this chapter.

Shapiro and Penrod (1986) conducted a meta-analysis (a procedure of combining data from multiple studies to find out the most likely effect of one or several factors) examining 128 mock eyewitness identification and facial recognition studies to investigate factors that affect the accuracy of eyewitness identifications. This meta-analysis is the most comprehensive published meta-analysis to examine factors affecting identification performance and it will be referred to later in this chapter along with several other meta-analyses that examine more specific factors. Since this early meta-analysis, Narby, Cutler and Penrod (1996) reviewed the effect of estimator variables on identification accuracy and they divided them into three groups: (i) those estimator variables that relate to the witness such as age of the witness; (ii) those that relate to the perpetrator such as whether the perpetrator wore a disguise; and (iii) those that are situational variables such as how long the crime lasted (see Table 4.1 for a list of estimator variables

Table 4.1 Estimator variables according to witness, perpetrator, and situational factors

Witness Factors	Perpetrator Factors	Situational Factors
Age	Race	Stress and arousal
Race	Gender	Weapon presence
Gender	Distinctiveness	Alcohol
Intelligence	Disguise	Own race identification
Face recognition ability	Change of appearance	Own gender identification
Visual memory		Own age identification
Personality traits		View of the perpetrator
Occupation		Verbal overshadowing
Expectancies and stereotypes		Production of composite
Quality of description		Exposure to mug shots
Confidence		
Response latency		
Judgement strategy		

broken down by witness, perpetrator, and situation). Further investigations of the effect of estimator variables have been conducted since the overview by Narby et al, and it is to this research we now turn.

WITNESS FACTORS

AGE OF WITNESS

A considerable amount of research has been conducted which examines the performance of both child witnesses and older adult witnesses (over 60 years) on identification line-ups. There is clear evidence, especially regarding TA line-ups, that children (Pozzulo and Lindsay, 1998) and older adults (Searcy, Bartlett and Memon, 1999) perform less well than younger adults. Valentine, Pickering and Darling (2003) in a field study looked at the effect of age of witness on the likelihood of suspect identifications from 314 identification parades conducted by the Metropolitan Police Service. Across 640 attempts made by witnesses, the suspect was more likely to be identified if the witness was 30 years or younger. From age 31 onwards there was with age a slow decline in the number of suspect identifications made. Whilst these findings are of interest both from a theoretical and applied perspective, research has also begun to address how we may be able to aid the performance of such witnesses. For children the use of elimination line-ups (Pozzulo and Lindsay, 1999) and practice line-ups (Schwartz-Kenney, Bottoms and Goodman, 1996) has been investigated. For older adults, the use of context reinstatement (Wilcock, Bull and Vrij, 2007) and enhanced line-up instructions (Wilcock, Bull and Vrij, 2005) has been examined. Such research with children and older adults will be discussed at length in Chapter 8.

RACE OF WITNESS

Research on this factor is included in investigations of the 'own race bias' which we will consider later in this chapter.

GENDER OF WITNESS

Similarly to race of witness, research on this factor has developed into investigations of an 'own gender bias' which will be considered later in the chapter.

INTELLIGENCE OF WITNESS

There has been very little research on whether intelligence of a witness relates to line-up performance. One study dating back to 1932 found a significant correlation between face recognition and intelligence (Howells, 1938). However, a more recent study showed that intelligence was not associated with identification performance (Wojcikiewisz, 1990). On the basis of these findings it is difficult to draw a reliable conclusion as to the nature of the relationship between intelligence and identification performance.

FACE RECOGNITION ABILITY

Researchers have been interested to see if performance on tests of facial recognition ability relates to how successful a witness will be on a later identification line-up. Hosch (1994) reviewed five studies where the Benton Face Recognition Test (BFRT) was used to assess face recognition.

> NOTE: The Benton Face Recognition Test (BFRT) is a booklet containing a series of single (target) faces shown on one page and shown on the opposite page are linked arrays of six highly similar faces which have been manipulated to show faces in differing profiles and degrees of shade. People are asked to carefully examine the target face and then select it from the array of six similar faces. As one proceeds through the booklet it get progressively more difficult to select the target face from the array. When people complete the BFRT it is likely that they rely on similar perceptual processes as they would use were they viewing a line-up.

Four out of the five studies found a positive correlation between face recognition performance and identification accuracy, indicating that higher scores on the BFRT were associated with line-up accuracy. Geiselman et al (2001) showed participants two different crime scenarios and found that the BFRT was predictive of performance for one scenario but not for the other. These authors hypothesized that face recognition ability may only be important when an identification situation is difficult (eg if a witness viewed the perpetrator only briefly). A follow-up study investigated whether difficulty of the line-up moderated the predictive effect of the BFRT and found that BFRT scores were predictive of line-up performance for participants viewing the medium and difficult line-ups but not for participants viewing the easy line-up. Thus, research suggests that face recognition ability may be associated with line-up performance particularly when the line-up task may be difficult.

Further research on the relationship between face recognition and line-up performance has focused on people's self-reported ability at face recognition and their subsequent performance on an actual face recognition task. Olsson and Juslin (1999) found a small but significant correlation between self-reported recognition ability and identification performance. Those participants who stated they were good at remembering faces were more likely to make a correct identification compared to those who reported they were poor. Olsson and Juslin (1999) also found that participants who reported using a holistic strategy when viewing the face (ie looking at the face as a whole) were more likely to be accurate on the line-up than those participants who reported using an analytic strategy (focusing on certain features of the face such as eye colour).

VISUAL MEMORY ABILITY

Similar to face recognition, memory for visual images may also be an indicator of identification accuracy. Slone, Brigham and Meissner (2000) used the Rey-Osterreith Complex Figure Test to examine the relationship between visual memory and identification performance. This is a measure where people are asked to look at a large drawing of a shape containing different sections with different details in each section. The drawing is then taken away and people are asked to draw as much of it as possible from memory. Scores on this test correlated with overall performance on the line-ups and recognition accuracy. This suggests that assessing visual memory could be a good indicator for witness performance on identification line-ups.

PERSONALITY

Snyder (1979) identified a personality construct called self-monitoring which refers to the extent to which an individual looks to others in a social situation to guide their own behaviour. People who constantly monitor how they will be perceived are high self-monitors. Hosch and Platz (1984) hypothesized that high self-monitors would be more accurate on identification line-ups because they are constantly looking at others, and may therefore be better at recognizing faces. The results indicated a significant positive correlation between the self-monitoring score and identification accuracy. Hosch (1994) concluded, after reviewing five identification studies which included self-monitoring as a variable, that high self-monitors are better able to remember faces of people they have met because they process information differently from low self-monitors.

Field dependence/independence is a cognitive personality style that refers to the ability to discriminate fine detail from the background in which it is embedded. Witkin, Dyk, Faterson, Goodenough and Karp (1962) suggested that this personality style could be relevant for eyewitness identification because people who are field dependent may be better at recognizing faces (than people who are field independent) because they are likely to be more attentive to their environment (which may include crime perpetrators). Field dependence/independence is measured using the Group Embedded Figures Test where people view a page of different small complex shapes and are asked to identify the same simple geometric figure within each complex shape. The task is timed and people who have the ability to quickly identify the simple geometric figure without being distracted by the complex shape are said to be field independent. Conversely, people who are slower on the task are more likely to get distracted by the complex shape and are said to be field dependent. Evidence that field dependent people are better at identifying faces than field independent people is mixed. Messick and Damarin (1964) found participants who were field dependent were more likely to remember faces previously seen. However, Clifford and Bull (1978) found little evidence that people who are field dependent are likely to be better at identifying faces. Hosch (1994) reviewed the literature on field dependence/independence and concluded that the evidence in support of this construct being related to face recognition performance was conflicting.

More recent research has examined whether field dependent/independent people are likely to benefit from using context reinstatement (CR) when trying to remember an event. Emmett, Clifford and Gwyer (2003) found that field dependent participants benefited from CR probably because the to-be-remembered (TBR) event was encoded (taken into memory) within the context that it was viewed in, whereas field independent participants did not benefit from CR possibly because they only encoded key central elements of the event and not contextual details. Applied to a line-up situation, field dependent people may be more likely to benefit from CR to aid their memory and performance on a line-up compared to field independent people. Emmett et al (2003) also found that giving retrieval cues (specific relevant pieces of key information about an event to help people remember) was helpful for field independent participants, possibly because when they viewed the event they only encoded the key central elements of it. Again, applied to a line-up situation, one could argue that there will be no difference in performance between field dependent and field independent people on a TP line-up because the face of the perpetrator provides field independent people with a powerful retrieval cue to memory and, as per the original field dependence/independence hypothesis, field dependent people should be able to identify the perpetrator because they have been attentive to their environment (Witkin et al, 1964). This could explain why we see the mixed findings regarding field dependence/independence reported above.

NOTE: *Context Reinstatement* (CR) is based on Tulving and Thomson's (1973) encoding specificity hypothesis which suggests that the more overlap there is between the time of encoding an event and the subsequent retrieval cues, the more a person will remember. When mental CR is used witnesses are encouraged to mentally picture the environment they were in immediately prior to witnessing the crime. They will be encouraged to focus on all senses: visual, auditory, olfactory, and environmental conditions such as dampness. Mental CR has been used very successfully as part of the Cognitive Interview (CI) which increases the amount of accurate information given by witnesses compared to a structured interview or standard police interview (Köhnken, Milne, Memon and Bull, 1999). CR has also been used to aid the performance of witnesses on identification line-ups (Cutler, Penrod and Martens, 1987; Malpass and Devine, 1981; O'Rourke, Penrod, Cutler and Stuve, 1989; Wilcock, Bull and Vrij, 2007).

Other personality traits that have been studied in the past include neuroticism and extraversion. For example, Bothwell, Brigham and Pigott (1987) assigned participants to different levels of arousal (arousal refers to physiological responses such as heart rate, blood pressure, and muscle tone which vary according to the levels of stress or anxiety we are feeling. If we are very anxious there will be an increase in arousal, ie an increase in heart rate, blood pressure, and muscle tone). Participants experienced either low, moderate, or high levels of arousal and the authors found that high arousal levels were beneficial for participants classed as emotionally stable but led to poorer identification performance for participants classed as neurotic. The effect of arousal on a measure of state anxiety (measurement of anxiety at a specific point in time) indicated that participants classed as either stable or neurotic showed similar levels of anxiety which led these authors to suggest that differences in performance between the two groups could be explained using optimal level theory. That is, participants classed as neurotic possibly reached their optimal level of performance (on the line-up) before the participants classed as emotionally stable did so, hence higher levels of arousal led to poorer performance in the neurotic group but good performance in the stable group (who did not actually reach their optimal level of performance). Bothwell et al found no relationship between extraversion/introversion and identification performance.

Additional personality traits and their relationship with identification performance have been studied but on the whole personality of the witness is not viewed as a reliable predictor for identification performance.

OCCUPATION OF WITNESS

One may assume that people who have a certain job may make better witnesses, for example, police officers who deal with crime on a day-to-day basis may be more observant and this may mean they make better witnesses than civilians. Lindholm, Christianson and Karlsson (1997) found that although police officers remembered significantly more information about the perpetrator than did civilians, there were no significant differences between police officers and civilians on a TP line-up. Interestingly, these authors did find that police officers were significantly better than civilians at identifying the knife that was used in the mock crime event from a selection of eight knives. These authors suggested that the reason there were no differences between officers' and civilians' performance on the line-up could be because identification rates of the perpetrator were very low in both groups possibly because the photo of the perpetrator used in the line-up differed from his appearance in the mock crime event (something that could happen in real life). In a further study investigating police officers' performance as witnesses, Christianson, Karlsson and Persson (1998) compared police recruits, experienced police officers, teachers, and university students on their memory for a violent crime. Experienced police officers were significantly better at remembering information about the crime compared to the other groups (including the new police recruits) and they were also somewhat more likely to correctly identify the perpetrator, although this effect failed to reach significance. These authors concluded that police officers, through their experience of dealing with criminal events, are better able to organize key elements of a crime that are important for investigative purposes and this means they may make better witnesses to crime.

WITNESS EXPECTATIONS AND STEREOTYPES

Research has questioned whether expectations and stereotypes held by witnesses are likely to affect their accuracy as a witness. Kassin, Tubb, Hosch and Memon (2001) found that 92% of experts in the eyewitness field would be happy to testify in court about the effect of stereotypes and expectations on accuracy. (Chapter 6 will provide an in-depth discussion on this topic.)

QUALITY OF DESCRIPTIONS

There has been much debate over the relationship between descriptions given by witnesses and their line-up accuracy. There is some evidence that verbal descriptions can harm identification accuracy (Schooler and Engster-Schooler, 1990), equally there is some evidence that witnesses re-reading the description of the perpetrator prior to viewing a line-up can be of benefit (Sporer, 2007). Valentine et al (2003) in their field study using real identification parades conducted by the Metropolitan Police Service found that 66% of witnesses who gave a detailed description identified the suspect, compared to 40% of the witnesses who gave average descriptions, and just 14% of those who gave poor descriptions. (Chapter 3 contained an in-depth discussion on the relationship between the quality of a description given by a witness and their subsequent performance on an identification task).

CONFIDENCE OF WITNESSES

There are a number of measures that can be taken during or after a witness has made an identification which researchers have investigated to see if they 'postdict' the accuracy of a witnesses line-up decision. One such postdictor is how confident a witness is that their line-up decision was correct. The relationship between how confident a witness is and the accuracy of their line-up decision has provoked considerable debate among psychologists and has led to large amounts of research being conducted. The relationship between confidence and accuracy is considered to be very important because evidence given by a confident witness is more likely to be believed by jurors than evidence given by a less confident witness (Wells, Lindsay and Ferguson, 1979). Using a mock jury study Cutler, Penrod and Stuve (1988) found that witness confidence was the only factor that significantly affected (i) jurors' belief that the witness had made an accurate identification and (ii) the verdict they gave. These results have more recently been replicated by Brewer and Burke (2002).

Brewer (2006) suggests that there are factors *prior* to the line-up that could affect both the likelihood that a witness will make an identification from the line-up and also their confidence surrounding their line-up decision. For example, the strength of a witness' memory for the offender may be strong because they had a long time to view the offender under good viewing conditions, therefore, the witness may well expect that they would be able to correctly identify the offender. However, Busey, Tunnicliff, Loftus and Loftus (2000) have demonstrated that people are not always good at monitoring their own memory ability which may lead them to express higher levels of confidence regardless of the accuracy of their memory. Thus far, research on the relationship between pre-identification confidence and accuracy is limited.

There is, however, a vast amount of research on the relationship between confidence and accuracy when confidence is measured immediately *after* an identification has been made. Early reviews of the confidence-accuracy relationship suggested that there was no significant positive correlation between confidence and accuracy, that is, more confident witnesses were *not* more likely to be correct on a line-up than less confident witnesses (eg Bothwell, Defenbacher and Brigham, 1987; Deffenbacher, 1980; Wells and Murray, 1984). Since then some research has found stronger confidence-accuracy correlations under particular circumstances. Sporer, Penrod, Read and Cutler (1995) conducted a meta-analysis involving 30 studies involving 4,036 participants and found that the relationship between confidence and accuracy differed for participants who made a choice from the line-up versus participants who did not make a choice from the line-up. For participants who made a choice from the line-up, confidence was more likely to be associated with accuracy (the correlation value was $r = .41$, where 1 would be a perfect correlation and 0 would mean there is no correlation) whereas for participants who did not make a choice from the line-up confidence and accuracy were less likely to be associated ($r = .12$). This suggests that for witnesses who identify a member of the line-up, confidence may be a stronger predictor of accuracy than previously thought.

Additional support that confidence may be linked to accuracy comes from data collected in a field study conducted by Behrman and Richards (2005). They examined cases where there was substantial evidence in addition to the line-up evidence, for example, confessions and/or fingerprint evidence. The data showed that 43% of suspect identifications were made with high confidence whereas just 10% of foil identifications were made with high confidence.

Possible reasons why we see differences in findings between studies examining the confidence-accuracy relationship could be due to differences in the methodology used in the research. For example, whether the correlations are 'across' participants (ie each participant sees only one line-up) or are 'within' participants (ie each participant sees several different line-ups, each time for a different target). Read, Lindsay and Nicholls (1998) investigated the confidence-accuracy relationship in participants who made decisions for 40 line-ups containing public figures as the targets and compared each participant's performance across the 40 line-ups. They found that 72% of participants produced confidence-accuracy correlations in excess of $r = .50$ regardless of whether they had made a choice or not from the line-up; and 81% of participants who made a choice from the line-up achieved confidence-accuracy correlations in excess of $r = .50$. However, these findings relate to line-ups of 'familiar' faces rather than to line-ups for a once seen face, as in a real crime.

In a further study which adopted another slightly different methodology, Lindsay, Read and Sharma (1998) manipulated the witnessing conditions. Participants were assigned to one of four witnessing conditions: (i) *worst*, participants focused on location rather than people shown in a ten-second video event; (ii) *medium*, participants told to focus on the person's appearance in the ten-second video event; (iii) *good*, participants told to focus on the person's appearance in a one-minute video event and; (iv) *best*, participants told to focus on the person's appearance in a three-minute video event. Line-up accuracy improved across viewing conditions, furthermore witnesses confidence increased across viewing conditions. Of importance here is that the confidence-accuracy correlation when examining participant's performance across all viewing conditions was higher than the confidence-accuracy correlation for each separate viewing condition. These findings suggest that the relationship between confidence and accuracy may be reliable when there are differences in participants' memory for the perpetrator. In a related study Lindsay, Nilsen and Read (2000) replicated the findings of Lindsay et al (1998) regarding differences in viewing conditions. However, they also assessed the ability of line-up administrators to distinguish between accurate and inaccurate witnesses. Interestingly, line-up administrators were able to distinguish between accurate and inaccurate witnesses but witnesses' own ratings of confidence were more predictive of accuracy than the investigators' decisions. Thus, it would appear that witnesses' level of confidence may be a better predictor of accuracy than line-up administrators' judgements of witness accuracy.

A Different Approach to Measuring Confidence Accuracy

Despite positive confidence-accuracy correlations being found in certain situations, other researchers have looked at a different way in which to assess the relationship between confidence and accuracy. Juslin, Olsson and Winman (1996) suggested that a calibration approach may be a more informative way to assess the relationship between confidence and accuracy in eyewitness identification. Calibration involves asking participants about their subjective confidence that the person they identified is the perpetrator and plotting that against the objective measure of accurate identifications. (In a fictitious example of a perfectly calibrated witness they will be 90% confident when they have 90% correct identifications, 80% confident when they have 80% correct identifications and so on, known as a positive linear calibration curve.) Researchers using the calibration approach in assessing the relationship between confidence and accuracy in identification want to know how far the confidence-accuracy calibrations obtained in research differ from perfect calibration (Brewer, 2006).

Research using the face recognition paradigm (explained above, that is involving many faces) has revealed that positive linear calibration curves exist when participants judge that a face has been seen before (Weber and Brewer, 2003; 2004). More relevant research has considered whether a linear calibration curve exists when using the mock witness paradigm. Juslin et al (1996) asked participants to view two eight-person line-ups and then asked participants to rate their confidence using a 1 to 11 scale (equating to 0%, 10%, 20%, through to 100% confidence). Results revealed generally positive linear calibration curves suggesting that witnesses making identifications may be well calibrated in confidence and accuracy. The procedures and photos used to compose the line-ups in this study are those used by Swedish Police in real crime investigations and so the results can be viewed as relatively ecologically valid. In a more recent, larger study (N = 1,200) investigating how well confidence and accuracy are calibrated in an eyewitness identification situation Brewer and Wells (2006) asked participants to view two eight-person line-ups and rate their confidence using a 1 to 11 scale (equating to 0%, 10%, 20%, through to 100% confidence). The findings indicated that confidence and accuracy were well calibrated for witnesses who made a choice from the line-up but not for witnesses who failed to make a choice. (Witnesses who do not make a choice from a line-up could be very confident that the line-up does not contain the perpetrator and therefore not choosing any one is the correct decision).

Both the above studies investigating calibration of confidence and accuracy in identification situations have used simultaneous line-ups. Sauer, Brewer and Wells (2008) investigated calibration of confidence and accuracy using sequential line-ups and found similar linear calibration curves for sequential line-ups as have been found for simultaneous line-ups for people who made a choice from the line-up (see Chapter 7 for an explanation of simultaneous versus sequential line-up presentation).

From the vast amount of research that has been conducted looking at the relationship between confidence and accuracy measured immediately *after* viewing a line-up we now know that in some settings confidence may be related to accuracy if an identification is made. However, Kassin et al (2001) found that 95% of experts were willing to testify in court that confidence is malleable and can be affected by factors other than accuracy. There is still much research to do before psychologists can be confident about making statements as to whether confidence should be taken as an indicator of a witnesses' accuracy on a line-up.

Post-Identification Feedback and Confidence Ratings

One key issue that researchers have focused on within the confidence-accuracy area is the effect of feedback being given to a witness after they have made a line-up decision and the effect of that feedback on their subsequent confidence. Wells and Bradfield (1998) found that if a line-up administrator told mock witnesses who had made false identifications (after viewing a TA line-up) 'Good, you identified the actual suspect' they were significantly more certain that their identification was accurate compared to those who had received no feedback. This post-identification feedback effect, sometimes known as 'bolstering' has been replicated and extended for witnesses who make not only false identifications from TA line-ups, but also for witnesses viewing TP line-ups who make correct identifications, false identifications, and incorrect rejections, and for witnesses viewing TA line-ups who make correct rejections (Semmler, Brewer and Wells, 2004). Inflation in witness confidence after receiving confirming feedback has also been found when witnesses have been told that a co-witness also identified the same line-up member as they did (Luus and Wells, 1994).

More recently, a meta-analysis examining 20 studies involving over 2,400 participants demonstrates a robust effect of confirming feedback ('Good, you identified the suspect') increasing witnesses' estimation of confidence that their identification is accurate (Bradfield Douglas and Steblay, 2006). On the basis of these findings researchers have stressed the importance of asking witnesses to rate their confidence in the accuracy of their line-up decision immediately *after* the line-up and without line-up administrator influence. Furthermore, it is this initial confidence rating that should be used as evidence in court rather than any subsequent expressions of confidence (Bradfield Douglas and Steblay 2006; Brewer, 2006).

Additional recent research has focused on possible circumstances where the effects of confirmatory feedback may be moderated. For example, Bradfield Douglas and McQuiston-Surrett (2006) investigated whether sequential line-ups and witness expectation of a line-up task would moderate the post-identification feedback effect. The authors found that neither sequential line-ups or witness expectation of a line-up task moderated the post-identification feedback effect. Lampinen, Scott, Pratt, Leding and Arnal (2007) found post-identification feedback effects could be eliminated when participants were warned that the feedback they had received had been randomly generated by a computer. However, when they adapted the warning to be more forensically relevant by asking witnesses to ignore any feedback they had received, as they would be instructed to do in a real courtroom, and rely entirely on their independent recollection of the event, the results demonstrated a post-identification feedback effect. For now, it seems safest to assume that taking a confidence rating immediately after the line-up and using that rating is the best way to avoid the influence of post-identification feedback on confidence ratings.

RESPONSE LATENCY

A further postdictor of line-up accuracy investigated by researchers is the length of time it takes for a witness to make and report their line-up decision. Sporer (1993) examined response latency by studying mock witnesses who made a choice from the line-up versus mock witnesses who did not make a choice. The results revealed that the witnesses were significantly faster when making correct identifications than false identifications. For those who did not make a choice from the line-up, it took longer to make a correct rejection than an incorrect rejection, though this effect was not statistically significant. Since 1993 other studies have found that accurate identifications are made in a shorter period of time than are inaccurate identifications (Smith, Lindsay and Pryke, 2000; Smith, Lindsay, Pryke and Dysart, 2001). Smith et al (2000) examined the time it took mock witnesses to make a decision by dividing participants into three groups: those that made a decision in between 1 to 15 seconds, 16 to 30 seconds, and over 30 seconds. Those who were in the 1 to 15 seconds group were significantly more likely to be accurate than those in the 16 to 30 seconds group who in turn were more accurate than the over 30 seconds group. Dunning and Perretta (2002) went further and stated (on the basis of four studies) that mock witnesses making identifications in a timeframe of between 10 and 12 seconds were most likely to be accurate. Mock witnesses making their identification faster than 10 to 12 seconds were likely to be 90% accurate whereas accuracy of mock witnesses who took over 10 to 12 seconds dropped to 50%. However, more recent research suggests that the 10 to 12 second rule proposed by Dunning and Perretta (2002) may be moderated by various factors such as how memorable a perpetrator, the degree of line-up similarity and, age of witness (Weber, Brewer, Wells, Semmler and Kreast, 2004), line-up size, and retention interval (Brewer, Caon, Todd and Weber, 2006). Furthermore, Weber et al (2004) found that across four experiments, the timeframe in which witnesses were most likely to be accurate was highly variable (between 5 and 29 seconds) and also even in that timeframe the proportion of accurate witnesses was relatively poor. However, the authors note that when response latency (10-second timeframe) and confidence of the witness (90% to 100%) are used together as postdictors of line-up accuracy, the probability of an accurate identification rose to nearly 90% and higher (than when using response latency or confidence independently). Response latency has also been examined in real cases by Valentine et al (2003) and results support those found in the laboratory: 87% of witnesses making a fast decision identified the suspect, compared to 38% and 31% of witnesses who made average or slow decisions, respectively. Thus the time it takes a witness to make an identification on a line-up could give some guide to their likely accuracy.

JUDGEMENT STRATEGY

The final postdictor related to decision latency is the judgement strategy used by the witness. (See Chapter 2 for full discussion regarding judgement strategies involved in recognition.) Dunning and Perretta (2002) suggested that witnesses who are accurate are more likely (than inaccurate witnesses) to make an automatic recognition without effortful processing and hence make their decision quickly. Dunning and Stern (1994) found that accurate witnesses reported statements, such as 'His face just "popped out" at me', indicative of automatic recognition. Conversely, those witnesses who made false identifications reported statements, such as 'I compared the photos to each other to narrow the choices', indicative of a process of elimination strategy. Furthermore, witnesses reporting statements associated with automatic recognitions were significantly faster at making their line-up decisions compared to witnesses reporting statements associated with an elimination strategy. In a more recent investigation, Behrman and Richards (2005) examined police reports of actual crimes where witnesses viewed a line-up. They identified witnesses who appeared to have chosen a line-up member rapidly without deliberative thought and also looked for any statements made by witnesses at the time that would be indicative of an elimination strategy being used. Few witnesses spontaneously reported statements indicative of an elimination strategy. Witnesses who responded rapidly and who did not make statements indicative of an elimination strategy were more likely to choose the suspect than a foil. A follow-up laboratory study replicated the findings from the field study.

The research reported above indicates the large number of factors relating to witnesses that may affect accuracy of their identification. Some are likely to have a greater impact such as age of the witness, while others will have a lesser impact such as personality of the witness. Despite the large amounts of research examining witness factors, there is still much to do before we fully understand their effect on accuracy and furthermore how they may interact with one another. In particular the postdictor variables identified (confidence, decision latency, and reported judgement strategies) are likely to guide much of the future research relating to witness factors in an attempt to understand how witnesses make their choices when viewing a line-up.

PERPETRATOR FACTORS

Surprisingly small amounts of research have been concerned with factors relating to the perpetrator, though some factors have been subsumed within research looking at situational factors.

RACE OF FACE

Evidence from Shapiro and Penrod's (1986) meta-analysis found that white targets were identified more easily that black targets. However, 81% of studies had used white targets compared to 6% that had used black targets (13% involved black and white targets). The results could therefore be due to the large proportion of studies that used white targets and white participants reflecting more 'own race bias' than an effect of race of perpetrator per se. (See discussion of 'own race bias' later in this chapter under situational factors.)

GENDER OF PERPETRATOR

Shapiro and Penrod (1986) found that female targets are more likely to be recognized than male targets, however, this should be viewed more widely in terms of a possible 'own gender bias' (see discussion under situational factors in this chapter).

DISTINCTIVENESS OF FACE

Research looking at the effect of facial distinctiveness has largely utilized the face recognition paradigm rather than a mock witness identification paradigm. Findings generally show that faces judged to be distinctive are more likely to be correctly identified compared with faces judged to be typical (Valentine, 1991). This could be due to distinctive faces being encoded in a different way from typical faces (Valentine, 1991). Further research has asked participants to classify their positive recognition decisions as either 'Remember' (where a participant is able to recall details of the situation when they saw the item) or 'Know' (where a participant simply has a feeling of familiarity for the item rather than being able to specifically remember the circumstances when they originally saw it). Using this procedure Dewhurst, Hay and Wickham (2005) found results that suggest the more distinctive a face is the more likely it will be recognized and classified as a 'remember' response than a 'know' response. When considering the effect of distinctiveness it is important to bear in mind problems of measuring what constitutes a distinctive face (Wickham, Morris and Fritz, 2000). Possibly a more pressing question for police officers than the effect of distinctiveness on recognition ability is what is the best way to construct a line-up if the suspect is judged to be distinctive looking? At present research is lacking to inform the police as to how best go forward in this situation.

DISGUISE AND CHANGE OF APPEARANCE

If a perpetrator wears a disguise at the time of the crime which conceals his or her face and/or appearance then the witness may not be able to encode the perpetrator therefore making an identification much harder or impossible. For example, Cutler et al (1987) found that participants who viewed a perpetrator wearing a hat which fully covered his hair were less likely to be accurate on a subsequent line-up compared to participants who viewed the perpetrator without a hat. Sometimes a perpetrator will change their appearance between the crime and a line-up, either unconsciously through ageing or consciously by, for example, changing their hairstyle. Patterson and Baddeley (1977) looked at the effect of changing hair, facial hair, and glasses. They found that if the target looked identical at encoding and recognition participants could fairly easily recognize the person. If all three things had changed correct identifications dropped significantly. Pozzulo and Marciniak (2006) found that participants who viewed a perpetrator who changed his hairstyle between viewing the mock crime and seeing the line-up were less likely to make correct identifications for simultaneous and sequential line-ups than participants who did not see a change in hairstyle. However, correct rejections from TA line-ups were unaffected by the change in hairstyle. On the basis of this research we know that perpetrator disguise or change of appearance can severely affect the likelihood of a witness making an accurate identification.

SITUATIONAL FACTORS

STRESS AND AROUSAL

For many years researchers have examined the effect of varied levels of stress on eyewitness memory. Deffenbacher, Bornstein, Penrod and McGorty (2004) reviewed the literature and included 27 studies which examined the effect of heightened stress on eyewitness identification performance in a meta-analysis. The results demonstrated that participants who experienced high levels of stress were less likely to correctly identify the perpetrator (compared to participants who experienced lower levels of stress). The high levels of stress were more likely to lead to false identifications from TP line-ups. Performance on TA line-ups appeared to be unaffected. The results were moderated by study methodology in that stress was most likely to detrimentally affect accuracy in studies employing an eyewitness identification paradigm rather than a face recognition paradigm. This leads us to the main problem with research investigating the effect of stress on identification accuracy. How best to replicate the real life situation of a crime and the stress and anxiety and associated rise in arousal felt by some witnesses? For example, in a laboratory test of the effect of stress on eyewitness memory the researchers may ask mock witnesses to look at film of a somewhat gruesome accident. Two studies have made attempts to overcome the problems with this sort of test.

Morgan et al (2004) examined eyewitness accuracy of recruits attending military survival school who were exposed to a mock prisoner of war camp and experienced isolation followed by interrogation (as part of their training): 509 active duty military personnel participated in the study and they experienced high stress interrogation (which included physical confrontation) and low stress interrogation (without physical confrontation but tricking the participant to give away information). Each interrogation lasted for 40 minutes, the room was illuminated and participants could see and hear the interrogators. Participants then viewed either a live line-up, a simultaneous photo line-up, or a sequential photo line-up to try to identify their interrogators (from the low and high stress interrogations). Participants were significantly more likely to be able to identify the interrogator from the low stress interrogation than the high stress interrogation. These results provide evidence to suggest that eyewitness memory for events which are realistic and highly stressful is likely to be error prone.

In a more recent study Valentine and Mesout (2007) asked members of the public visiting the London Dungeon to take part in a study assessing the effect of state anxiety on identification accuracy. It was arranged that participants encountered an actor whilst in the 'Horror Labyrinth'. (A pilot study had shown that the heart rate of visitors was elevated whilst in the labyrinth.) Participants who measured high on a measure of state anxiety demonstrated fewer correct identifications from a target present photograph line-up than those participants who were classified as low. The findings of this study together with those of Morgan et al (2004) provide us with ecologically valid data which support data found in laboratory studies (eg Deffenbacher et al, 2004) suggesting stress and anxiety are likely to lead to a decrease in accuracy of eyewitness identifications. More realistic ecologically valid studies are required to further our understanding of the role stress plays in eyewitness performance. One question still to be answered is whether individual differences in people's experience of stress affects the relationship between stress and eyewitness identification accuracy.

WEAPON FOCUS EFFECT

Related to research considering the effect of stress involved in crimes is research examining the effect of weapon presence on eyewitness identification accuracy. Loftus, Loftus and Messo (1987) found that participants who watched a series of slides depicting a perpetrator holding a gun were less likely to correctly identify the perpetrator than participants who watched the same event and perpetrator but instead of holding a gun he held a personal cheque. Witnesses viewing the gun were also observed to fixate on it for longer than participants viewing the personal cheque. This has become known as the 'weapon focus effect'. Steblay (1992) conducted a meta-analysis on the weapon focus effect examining 19 sets of data which used different methodologies including real life enactments. Results revealed poorer line-up accuracy when a weapon was present (compared to when a weapon was absent). Research since this time has largely focused on trying to explain why the weapon focus effect occurs. One school of thought is that the weapon is a threat and, therefore, in line with Easterbrook's (1959) cue utilization hypothesis, attention becomes focused on the weapon (which is accurately encoded compared to the face of the perpetrator which is not attended to), hence leading to a reduced likelihood of the witness subsequently being able to accurately identify the perpetrator. An alternative explanation centres on the unusualness or unexpectedness of a weapon. Pickel (1998) found that witnesses' memory for a target was poorer if he held an object rated as unusual regardless of whether it was a weapon or not. In a further study Pickel (1999) found witnesses demonstrated poorer performance recognizing a vicar who held a gun compared to recognizing a police officer who held a gun, suggesting that the context in which a weapon is viewed may also be important.

The most recent research has focused on the role of attention in the weapon focus effect. Hope and Wright (2007) found that participants shown a threatening object (a gun) or an unusual object (a feather duster) during a slide presentation whilst also attending to a reaction time test demonstrated slower reaction times on the reaction time test compared to participants shown an in-context neutral object (a wallet). Also, participants in the weapon condition demonstrated poorer recognition performance on a number or questions relating to the culprit's description compared to participants in the unusual object condition and the in-context neutral condition. These authors suggested on the basis of these results that unusual or threatening objects command more of our attention than neutral (in-context) objects, but also that the further deficit shown only by participants viewing a weapon could be explained by a 'significance factor' (because we know that a weapon can harm us and we generally associate weapons with negative emotions such as fear).

In a further study looking at the role of attention Pickel, Ross and Truelove (2006) investigated whether weapons automatically capture attention or if people can be instructed to overcome the weapon focus effect. They gave half their participants a lecture about the weapon focus effect in which they were told that in order to give the police a good description of a culprit one should focus on the culprit rather than the gun (educated condition). The other half of participants received a lecture unrelated to the weapon focus effect on confidence-accuracy (control condition). Participants did not realize they would have to act on the lecture content they had received. Regarding a subsequent staged event 'educated' witnesses were able to give more description details about a culprit than 'control' witnesses. Conversely, for participants who viewed the culprit carrying a book instead of a gun there was no significant difference in the amount of details given by educated witnesses or control witnesses. A second study replicated these findings using a different culprit and using mock witnesses with raised anxiety levels. Data from these two studies suggest that witnesses even when anxious, can direct their attention away from a weapon to focus on the culprit's face.

As with research examining the effect of stress on identification accuracy, when examining the weapon focus effect we should bear in mind how findings gained in laboratory studies may or may not translate to real crimes where a weapon has been involved. Three field studies have revealed different findings regarding the weapon focus effect in real life cases. Tollestrup, Turtle and Yuille (1994) found evidence of the weapon focus effect with fewer suspect identifications when a weapon was present. Valentine et al (2003) found that weapon presence had no effect on suspect identifications. Behrman and Davey (2001) also failed to find support for the weapon focus effect and furthermore, found weapon presence in some situations led to increased choosing of the suspect. From these field studies it is difficult to draw a reliable conclusion about the weapon focus effect. However, taken together with the findings from laboratory studies that have used live staged events, weapon presence is an important factor to consider when judging eyewitness accuracy.

EFFECTS OF ALCOHOL

The 2005/06 British Crime Survey found that victims of violent incidents believed the perpetrator was under the influence of alcohol in 48% of incidents reported. However, we also need to be aware that witnesses to crime may also be under the influence of alcohol. Indeed Kassin et al (2001) found that 90% of experts were willing to testify in court that alcohol impairs eyewitness performance. Dysart, Lindsay, MacDonald and Wicke (2002) examined the effects of alcohol on identification accuracy from show-ups (show-ups refer to a line-up where only the suspect is seen). For TP show-ups blood alcohol level had no significant effect on accuracy. However, for TA show-ups participants with higher blood alcohol levels were less likely to make a correct rejection (than participants with lower blood alcohol levels). These authors suggested that, in accordance with alcohol myopia theory which suggests that alcohol has the effect of decreasing our cognitive capacity, intoxicated witnesses will encode only salient cues which will be sufficient for identifying a perpetrator from a TP line-up. However, unlike sober witnesses, they will not have encoded subtle cues necessary for correctly rejecting a TA line-up. Bearing in mind the high proportion of crimes that involve alcohol surprisingly little research has examined the effect of alcohol on witness performance on line-ups.

OWN RACE BIAS

The 'own race bias' also referred as the 'cross race effect' relates to evidence gained in laboratory studies utilizing both a face recognition paradigm and a mock witness identification paradigm that adults are more likely to successfully recognize a person of their own race than another race (Meissner and Brigham, 2001). The number of studies that have demonstrated the existence of such a cross race effect is great and Kassin et al (2001) found that 90% of experts were willing to testify in court that eyewitnesses find it more difficult to identify members of a different race than their own race. Meissner and Brigham (2001) conducted a meta-analysis to examine the extent of the cross race effect and analysed data from nearly 5,000 participants across 39 studies spanning three decades. The data revealed that own race faces were 1.4 times more likely to be correctly identified than other race faces, and that other race faces were 1.56 times more likely to be falsely identified than own race faces. Data from mock witness identification studies revealed a greater proportion of hits in own race recognitions than data from face recognition studies, whilst there was no difference in rate of false identifications between the two methodologies.

Essentially, it is clear that the cross race effect exists in studies that utilize both a face recognition paradigm and a mock witness identification paradigm. The majority of research examining the cross race effect has focused on just black and white participants. However, some research has confirmed the existence of this effect in other racial groups including Hispanic participants (MacLin, MacLin and Malpass, 2001) and Asian participants (Ng and Lindsay, 1994). As mentioned above, most of the research has been conducted in a laboratory setting utilizing either a face recognition paradigm or mock witness identification paradigm. However, two field studies have also examined the existence of an own race bias in real world identifications and have found mixed results. Valentine at al (2003) found no evidence of a cross race effect, whilst Beherman and Davey (2001) found that there were significantly more suspect identifications in same race cases (60%) than cross race cases (45%). In light of the field data it would seem important that the existence of the cross race effect in real world data be confirmed.

Various theories have been offered to explain the existence of the cross race effect focusing on both social and cognitive explanations. Some researchers have investigated whether there is an effect of racial attitudes on memory for faces. Whilst there appears to be no direct relationship between racial attitudes and the cross race effect (Meissner and Brigham, 2001), racial attitudes may moderate the degree of interracial contact. Meissner and Brigham (2001) found that self-reported interracial contact plays a small but reliable role in mediating the cross race effect. Other theories as to why the cross race effect exists focus more on cognitive explanations concerned with how we encode faces. Brigham, Brooke Bennett, Meissner and Mitchell (2007) put forward several possible hypotheses concerned with how we encode other race faces. For example, we may focus on facial features that may be useful for distinguishing between own races faces but those same features are less helpful for distinguishing between other race faces, that is, white people may use eye colour to distinguish between own race faces but eye colour may not be as helpful for distinguishing between black faces (see Shepherd and Deregowski, 1981). Possibly we encode own race faces at a deeper level and other race faces at a more shallow level (see MacLin, Van Sickler, MacLin and Li, 2004). An alternative explanation may be that other race faces are not represented in our memory as efficiently as own race faces (Valentine, 1991, see explanation in Chapter 2). Sporer (2001) has attempted to bring all these explanations together in an In Group/Out Group Model of the cross race effect.

Whilst researchers may not yet fully understand why the cross race effect occurs, some have begun to put forward suggestions for good practice in collecting cross racial eyewitness identifications. Many of the suggestions reiterate those made by Wells, Small, Penrod, Malpass, Fulero and Brimacombe (1998) such as use of non-biased line-up instructions and ensuring the officer conducting the line-up does not know the identity of the suspect (these factors will be discussed at length in Chapter 7). However, one recommendation pertains specifically to constructing line-ups in cases of cross-race identification. Brigham and Ready (1985) found evidence to suggest that people constructing line-ups for suspects of a different race selected foils who were less similar looking to the suspect than did people constructing line-ups for suspects of their own race. On the basis of these findings Wells and Olson (2001) have recommended that line-ups be constructed by people of the same race as the line-up suspect.

OWN GENDER BIAS

Researchers have not only been interested in the own race bias but also an own gender bias and own age bias (see below). In terms of own gender bias Cross, Cross and Daly (1971) found no differences between females and males on a face recognition task containing male faces. However, females were better at recognizing female faces (compared to male faces). More recent research has shown similar findings in that females are more likely to be accurate when recognizing female faces than male faces (Lewin and Herlitz, 2002; Slone et al, 2000). In the most recent investigation of the own gender bias Wright and Sladden (2003) found that an own gender bias existed for both male and female participants on a face recognition task. The authors of this research also manipulated presence or absence of hair and found that hair was more important in own gender recognition than cross gender recognition suggesting that hair is a contributing factor in the own gender bias. In the real world of course, hair presence or absence and hairstyle can be changed. All of the research on own gender bias has used a face recognition paradigm, it would be useful to confirm whether an own gender bias exists using a more ecologically valid test.

OWN AGE BIAS

Some evidence shows that an own age bias exists where adults are more accurate at recognizing people of their own age than a different age. This has been found in research using a face recognition paradigm (Anastasi and Rhodes, 2006) and using a mock witness identification paradigm (List, 1986; Wright and Stroud, 2002). The own age bias has been found across a range of different ages including 18 to 25 years and 35 to 55 years (Wright and Stroud, 2002) and 20 to 24 years and 65 to 80 years (Perfect and Moon, 2005). However, other tests of own age bias have not always found such clear results. Memon, Barlett, Rose and Gray (2003) found no evidence of an own age bias in either a young (16 to 33 years) or old (60 to 82 years) participant group. Similarly Wilcock et al (2007) found no existence of an own age bias in old participants (64 to 86 years) but found that young participants (16 to 30 years) were more likely to make a choice, regardless of accuracy, from the old line-up rather than the young line-up. Further research is required to fully test the existence of an own age bias.

VIEW OF PERPETRATOR

When considering situational factors which may affect the accuracy of a crime, it is important to examine the crime viewing conditions experienced by the witness. According to English and Welsh law in court cases where identification evidence is disputed judges should instruct the jury about the 'Turnbull Guidelines'. The guidelines ask the jury when examining identification evidence to consider the following questions: How long was the witness viewing the perpetrator for? How far away were they from the perpetrator? Was the crime committed in good visibility (eg daylight opposed to darkness)? Was there anything in the way of the witness observing the crime (eg passing traffic)? Did they know the perpetrator? If they did not, was there any reason for them to remember the perpetrator? What length of delay was there between the witness viewing the perpetrator and them making an identification? Were there substantial differences in the description of the perpetrator given by the witness compared with the suspect's appearance? Having considered these questions, jurors should be in a better position to assess the reliability of a witness' identification evidence.

Research has considered the effect of some of these factors on identification accuracy. In a field study Valentine et al (2003) found that crimes viewed under good light quality, with an unobstructed view, and where the witness viewed the perpetrator from less than two metres led to more identifications of the suspect, however, the effects were not statistically significant. The only factor that was significant was crime duration, in that witnesses who viewed the perpetrator for over a minute were more likely to make an identification of the suspect. Evidence from a laboratory study using a mock witness paradigm also found that witnesses were more likely to correctly identify the perpetrator and make fewer false identifications after viewing the perpetrator for 45 seconds compared to participants who had viewed the perpetrator for just 12 seconds (Memon, Hope and Bull, 2003). Shapiro and Penrod (1986) in their meta-analysis also found evidence to suggest that the longer the period of time a person has to view a target face the more likely they will be to recognize it later.

Research has also investigated the effect of delay between viewing a crime and attending a line-up. Two field studies reveal similar findings that the rate of suspect identifications falls after one week (Behrman and Davey, 2001; Valentine et al, 2003). Shepherd (1983) investigated the effect of delay using a mock witness paradigm. Participants viewed a live staged event and were then asked to return to view a TP line-up one week, one month, three months, or 11 months later. The results demonstrated that there was a significant decrease in correct identifications after the 11-month delay compared to the other delay conditions. However, there were no significant differences in correct identifications between the one week, one month, and three month delay conditions. Dysart and Lindsay (2007) points out that surprisingly little research has been conducted on the effect of delay and whilst it is likely that delay leads to a decline in accuracy there needs to be a systematic investigation to look at the precise circumstances in which delay is likely to be most detrimental.

Verbal Overshadowing

Some researchers are not concerned so much about the length of delay between a crime and line-up but are more concerned about what may occur during the delay. Prior to a witness viewing a line-up they will typically have been asked for a description of the perpetrator. As mentioned above there is some evidence that verbal descriptions can harm identification accuracy. Schooler and Engster-Schooler (1990) referred to this as 'verbal overshadowing' where a verbal description of the perpetrator interferes with subsequent visual memory of the perpetrator and reduces the chance of an accurate identification. (This was discussed in-depth in Chapter 3.)

Production of a Composite

When witnesses give a description of a perpetrator, but the police have no suspect, sometimes they will request that a facial composite be constructed. Wells, Charman and Olson (2005) investigated the effect of building a facial composite and viewing another witness' facial composite on identification accuracy. They found that participants who built facial composites were significantly less likely to identify the perpetrator from a subsequent line-up compared with participants who had viewed a composite built by another participant and with control participants. In a second more ecologically valid study that employed a simulated crime event shown on videotape such findings were replicated. However, for TA line-ups there was no significant effect on accuracy of composite building. These authors suggest that for cases in which there are multiple witnesses it may be wise for one witness to build a facial composite and the other witnesses be saved to view a subsequent line-up. There are different methods of constructing facial composites which may moderate the results found by Wells et al (2005). (For a full discussion of facial composites please see Chapter 9.)

Exposure to Mug Shots

A recent meta-analysis has found evidence to suggest that if witnesses view mug shots prior to a line-up they may be less accurate on the line-up both in terms of a reduction in hit rates and increase in false alarm rates (Deffenbacher, Bornstein and Penrod,

2006). These findings were moderated by the presence of a commitment effect in that if a witness had chosen a mug shot and that mug shot was then included in the subsequent line-up witnesses were highly likely to choose that mug shot, particularly if it was a TA line-up. If witnesses failed to identify any mug shots but were then exposed again to the same mug shots in a line-up, they were more likely to make false alarms to the previously seen mug shots. Exposure to mug shots, none of which were included in a subsequent line-up, did not impair correct identifications of the perpetrator. The number of mug shots shown to witnesses prior to a line-up also moderated the detrimental effect of mug shot exposure on line-up accuracy. Smaller numbers of mug shots were more likely to affect accuracy on the line-up compared to exposure to large numbers of mug shots, possibly because smaller numbers are easier to encode successfully than large numbers. Kassin et al (2001) found that 95% of experts would be willing to give expert testimony in court that exposure to mug shots of a suspect leads to a greater chance of the suspect being identified in a subsequent line-up. This could be a problem when the suspect is actually not the perpetrator. The safest way forward for police would be to exclude from a line-up any faces that have been seen by a witness prior to the line-up (Deffenbacher et al, 2006).

From this overview of situational factors and how they may affect identification accuracy it is clear, as with witness factors, that some may be more likely to affect witness performance than others. In particular, substantial amounts of research have shown that the weapon focus effect, the cross race effect, and showing mug shots of a suspect prior to a line-up have a clear effect on line-up accuracy. However, with each of these factors there is more work to be done until we can fully understand why they affect line-up performance.

CONCLUSION

In this chapter we have reviewed many factors relating to the witness, the perpetrator, and the crime situation that may to a lesser or greater extent affect witness performance on an identification parade/line-up, photo spread etc. When considering how the findings of this research may be applied in the real world there are at least two points that must be borne in mind. First, how well will estimator variables studied largely in a laboratory situation translate to the real world? Second, in real cases it is likely that there will be multiple estimator variables interacting together, some may be more likely to affect line-up performance while others may be less likely to, thus making it difficult to verify the true impact of each estimator variable on identification performance. Nevertheless research does give us an insight into factors that may affect line-up accuracy which should allow people working in the police and Criminal Justice System to make more informed decisions than they otherwise would be able to. Additionally, knowledge about estimator variables can lead to new research concerned with developing line-up procedures to reduce the impact of some estimator variables.

FURTHER READING

BREWER, N. (2006). Use and abuses of eyewitness identification confidence. *Legal and Criminological Psychology, 11*, 3–23.

BRIGHAM, J.C., BROOKE BENNETT, L.B., MEISSNER, C.A. and MITCHELL, T.L. (2007). The influence of race on eyewitness memory. In R.C.L. Lindsay, D.F. Ross, J.D. Read and M.P. Toglia. *The Handbook of Eyewitness Psychology: Memory for People.*

KASSIN, S.M., TUBB, V.A., HOSCH, H.M. and MEMON, A. (2001). On the 'General acceptance' of eyewitness testimony research. *American Psychologist, 56*, 405–416.

VALENTINE, T., PICKERING, A. and DARLING, S. (2003). Characteristics of eyewitness identifications that predict the outcome of real lineups. *Applied Cognitive Psychology, 17*, 969–993.

REFERENCES

ANASTASI, J.S. and RHODES, M.G. (2006). Evidence for an own age bias in face recognition. *North American Journal of Psychology, 8*, 237–252.

BEHRMAN, B.W. and DAVEY, S.L. (2001). Eyewitness identification in actual criminal cases: An archival analysis. *Law and Human Behavior, 25*, 475–491.

—— and RICHARDS, R.E. (2005). Suspect/foil identification in actual crimes and in the laboratory: A reality monitoring analysis. *Law and Human Behaviour, 29*, 279–301.

BOTHWELL, R.K., BRIGHAM, J.C. and PIGOTT, M.A. (1987). An exploratory study of personality differences in eyewitness memory. *Journal of Social Behavior and Personality, 2*, 335–343.

——, DEFFENBACHER, K.A. and BRIGHAM, J.C. (1987). Correlation of eyewitness accuracy and confidence: Optimality hypothesis revisited. *Journal of Applied Psychology, 72*, 691–695.

BRADFIELD DOUGLASS, A. and McQUISTON-SURRETT, D. (2006). Post-identification feedback: Exploring the effects of sequential photospreads and eyewitnesses' awareness of the identification task. *Applied Cognitive Psychology, 20*, 991–1117.

—— and STEBLAY, N. (2006). Memory distortion in eyewitnesses: A meta-analysis of the post identification feedback effect. *Applied Cognitive Psychology, 20*, 859–869.

BREWER, N. (2006). Use and abuses of eyewitness identification confidence. *Legal and Criminological Psychology, 11*, 3–23.

—— and BURKE, A. (2002). Effects of testimonial inconsistencies and eyewitness confidence on mock-juror judgements. *Law and Human Behavior, 26*, 353–364.

——, CAON, A., TODD, C. and WEBER, N. (2006). Eyewitness identification accuracy and response latency. *Law and Human Behavior, 30*, 31–50.

—— and WELLS, G.L. (2006). The confidence-accuracy relationship in eyewitness identification: Effects of lineup instructions, foil similarity and target absent base rates. *Journal of Experimental Psychology: Applied, 12*, 11–30.

BRIGHAM, J.C., BROOKE BENNETT, L.B., MEISSNER, C.A. and MITCHELL, T.L. (2007). The influence of race on eyewitness memory. In R.C.L. Lindsay, D.F. Ross, J.D. Read and M.P. Toglia (eds) *The Handbook of Eyewitness Psychology: Memory for People*. Mahwah, NJ: Lawrence Erlbaum Associates, 257–282.

—— and READY, D.J. (1985). Own race bias in lineup construction. *Law and Human Behavior, 9,* 415–424.

BUSSEY, T.A., TUNNICLIFF, J., LOFTUS, G.R. and LOFTUS, E.F. (2000). Accounts of the confidence-accuracy relation in recognition memory. *Psychonomic Bulletin and Review, 7,* 26–48.

CHRISTIANSON, S-A, KARLSSON, I. and PERSSON, L.G.W. (1998). Police personnel as eyewitnesses to a violent crime. *Legal and Criminological Psychology, 3,* 59–72.

CLIFFORD, B.R. and BULL, R. (1978). *The Psychology of Person Identification.* London: Routledge and Kegan Paul.

CROSS, J.F., CROSS, J. and DALY, J. (1971). Sex, race, age, and beauty as factors in recognition of faces. *Perception and Psychophysics, 10,* 393–396.

CUTLER, B.L., PENROD, S.D. and MARTENS, T.K. (1987). Improving the reliability of eye-witness identifications: Putting context into context. *Journal of Applied Psychology, 72,* 629–637.

——, —— and STUVE, T.E. (1988). Juror decision making in eyewitness identification cases. *Law and Human Behavior, 12,* 41–55.

DEFFENBACHER, K.A. (1980). Eyewitness accuracy and confidence. Can we infer anything about their relationship? *Law and Human Behavior, 4,* 243–260.

——, BORNSTEIN, B.H. and PENROD, S.D. (2006). Mugshot exposure effects: Retroactive interference, mugshot commitment, source confusion, and unconscious transference. *Law and Human Behavior, 30,* 287–307.

——, ——, —— and MCGORTY, E.K. (2004). A meta-analytic review of the effects of high stress on eyewitness memory. *Law and Human Behavior, 28,* 987–706.

DEWHURST, S.A., HAY, D.C. and WICKHAM, L.H. (2005). Distinctiveness, typicality, and rec-ollective experience in face recognition: A principal components analysis. *Psychonomic Bulletin and Review, 12,* 1032–1037.

DUNNING, D. and PERRETTA, S. (2002). Automaticity and eyewitness accuracy: A 10 to 12-second rule for distinguishing accurate from inaccurate positive identifications. *Journal of Applied Psychology, 87,* 951–962.

—— and STERN, L.B. (1994). Distinguishing accurate from inaccurate eyewitness identifica-tions via enquiries about decision processes. *Journal of Personality and Social Psychology, 67,* 818–835.

DYSART, J.E. and LINDSAY, R.C.L. (2007). The effects of delay on eyewitness identification accuracy: Should we be concerned? In R.C.L. Lindsay, D.F. Ross, J.D. Read and M.P. Toglia (eds) *Handbook of Eyewitness Psychology Volume 11.* Mahwah, NJ: Lawrence Erlbaum Asso-ciates, 361–376.

——, ——, MACDONALD, T.K. and WICKE, C. (2002). The intoxicated witness: Effects of alco-hol on identification accuracy from showups. *Journal of Applied Psychology, 87,* 170–175.

EASTERBROOK, J.A. (1959). The effect of emotion on the utilization and organization of behaviour. *Psychological Review, 66,* 183–201.

EMMETT, D., CLIFFORD, B. and GWYER, P. (2003). The influence of field dependency on eyewitness accuracy in free and cued recall. In M. Vanderhallen, G. Vervaeke, P.J. Van Koppen and J. Goethals. *Much Ado About Crime: Chapters on Psychology and Law.* Belgium: Politeria.

GEISELMAN, R.E., TUBRIDY, A., BLUMKIN, R., SCHROPPEL, T., TURNER, L., YOAKUM, K. and YOUNG, N. (2001). Benton Facial Recognition Test scores: Index of eyewitness accuracy. *American Journal of Forensic Psychology, 19,* 77–88.

HOME OFFICE (2006). *Crime in England and Wales.* London: Statistical Bulletin.

HOPE, L. and WRIGHT, D. (2007). Beyond unusual? Examining the role of attention in the weapon focus effect. *Applied Cognitive Psychology, 21,* 951–961.

HOSCH, H. (1994). Individual differences in personality and eyewitness identification. In J.D. Read, D.F. Ross and M.P. Toglia (eds) *Adult Eyewitness Testimony: Current Trends and Developments*. New York: Cambridge University Press, 328–347.

—— and PLATZ, S.J. (1984). Self-monitoring and eyewitness accuracy. *Personality and Social Psychology Bulletin, 10,* 289–292.

HOWELLS, T.H. (1938). A study of ability to recognise faces. *Journal of Abnormal Social Psychology, 33,* 124–127.

JUSLIN, P., OLSSON, N. and WINMAN, A. (1996). Calibration and diagnosticity of confidence in eyewitness identification: Comments on what can be inferred from the low confidence-accuracy correlation. *Journal of Experimental Psychology: Learning, Memory, and Cognition, 22,* 1304–1316.

KASSIN, S.M., TUBB, V.A., HOSCH, H.M. and MEMON, A. (2001). On the 'general acceptance' of eyewitness testimony research. *American Psychologist, 56,* 405–416.

KÖHNKEN, G., MILNE, R., MEMON, A. and BULL, R. (1999). The cognitive interview: A meta-analysis. *Psychology, Crime, and Law, 5,* 3–27.

LAMPINEN, J.M., SCOTT, J., PRATT, D., LEDING, J.K. and ARNAL, J.D. (2007). 'Good, you identified the suspect . . . But please ignore this feedback': Can warnings eliminate the effects of post identification feedback. *Applied Cognitive Psychology, 21,* 1037–1056.

LEWIN, C. and HERLITZ, A. (2002). Sex differences in face recognition: Women's faces make the difference. *Brain and Cognition, 50,* 121–128.

LINDHOLM, T., CHRISTIANSON, S-A. and KARLSSON, I. (1997). Police officers and civilians as witnesses: Intergroup biases and memory performance. *Applied Cognitive Psychology, 11,* 431–444.

LINDSAY, D.S., NILSEN, E. and READ, J.D. (2000). Witnessing-condition heterogeneity and witnesses' versus investigators' confidence in the accuracy of witnesses' identification decisions. *Law and Human Behavior, 24,* 685–697.

——, READ, J.D. and SHARMA, K. (1998). Accuracy and confidence in person identification: The relationship is strong when witnessing conditions vary widely. *Psychological Science, 9,* 215–218.

LIST, J.A. (1986). Age and schematic differences in the reliability of eyewitness testimony. *Developmental Psychology, 22,* 50–57.

LOFTUS, E.F., LOFTUS, G.R. and MESSO, J. (1987). Some facts about 'weapon focus'. *Law and Human Behavior, 11,* 55–62.

LUUS, C.A.E. and WELLS, G.L. (1994). The malleability of eyewitness confidence: Co-witness and perseverance effects. *Journal of Applied Psychology, 79,* 714–723.

MACLIN, O.H., MACLIN, M.K. and MALPASS, R.S. (2001). Race, arousal, attention, exposure, and delay: An examination of factors moderating face recognition. *Psychology, Public Policy and Law, 7,* 134–152.

——, VAN SICKLER, B.R., MACLIN, M.K. and LI, A. (2004). A Re-examination of the cross-race effect: The role of race, inversion and basketball trivia. *North American Journal of Psychology, 6,* 189–204.

MALPASS, R.S. and DEVINE, P.G. (1981). Guided memory in eyewitness identification. *Journal of Applied Psychology, 66,* 343–350.

MEISSNER, C.A. and BRIGHAM, J.C. (2001). Thirty years of investigating the own race bias in memory for faces. *Psychology, Public Policy and Law, 7,* 3–35.

MEMON, A., BARTLETT, J.C., ROSE, R.A. and GRAY, C. (2003). The aging eyewitness: Effects of age of face, delay and source memory. *Journal of Genrontology: Psychological Sciences, 58,* 338–345.

——, HOPE, L. and BULL, R. (2003). Exposure duration: Effects on eyewitness accuracy and confidence. *British Journal of Psychology, 94,* 339–354.

MESSICK, S. and DAMARIN, F. (1964). Cognitive styles and memory for faces. *Journal of Abnormal and Social Psychology, 69,* 313–318.

MORGAN, C.A., HAZLETT, G., DORAN, A., GARRETT, S., HOYT, G., THOMAS, P., BARANOSKI, M. and SOUTHWICK, S.M. (2004). The accuracy of eyewitness memory for persons encountered during exposure to highly intense stress. *International Journal of Law and Psychiatry, 27,* 265–279.

NARBY, D.J., CUTLER, B.L. and PENROD, S.D. (1996). The effects of witness, target, and situational factors on eyewitness identifications. In S.L. Sporer, R.S. Malpass and G. Koehnken (eds) *Psychological Issues in Eyewitness Identification.* Mawah, NJ: Lawrence Erlbaum Associates, 23–52.

NG, W. and LINDSAY, R.C.L. (1994). Cross-race facial recognition: Failure of the contact hypothesis. *Journal of Cross Cultural Psychology, 25,* 217–232.

OLSSON, N. and JUSLIN, P. (1999). Can self-reported encoding strategy and recognition skills be diagnostic of performance in eyewitness identifications? *Journal of Applied Psychology, 84,* 42–49.

O'ROURKE, T.E., PENROD, S.D., CUTLER, B.L. and STUVE, T.E. (1989). The external validity of eyewitness research: Generalizing across subject populations. *Law and Human Behavior, 13,* 385–395.

PATTERSON, K.E. and BADDELEY, A.D. (1977). When face recognition fails. *Journal of Experimental Psychology: Human Learning and Memory, 3,* 406–417.

PERFECT, T.J. and MOON, H.C. (2005). The own age effect in face recognition. In J. Duncan, L. Phillips, and P. McLeod (eds) *Measuring the mind.* Oxford: Oxford University Press, 317–337.

PICKEL, K.L. (1998). Unusualness and threat as possible causes of 'weapon focus'. *Memory, 6,* 277–295.

—— (1999). The influence of context on the 'weapon focus effect'. *Law and Human Behaviour, 299–311.*

——, ROSS, S.J. and TRUELOVE, R.S. (2006). Do weapons automatically capture attention? *Applied Cognitive Psychology, 20,* 871–893.

POZZULO, J.D. and LINDSAY, R.C.L. (1998). Identification accuracy of children versus adults: A meta-analysis. *Law and Human Behavior, 22,* 549–570.

—— and —— (1999). Elimination lineups: An improved procedure for child eyewitnesses. *Journal of Applied Psychology, 84,* 167 –176.

—— and MARCINIAK, S. (2006). Comparing identification procedures when the perpetrator has changed appearance. *Psychology, Crime and Law, 12,* 429–438.

READ, J.D., LINDSAY, D.S. and NICHOLLS, T. (1998). The relation between confidence and accuracy in eyewitness identification studies: Is the conclusion changing? In C.P. Thompson, D.J. Herrmann, J.D. Read, D. Bruce, D.G. Payne and M.P. Toglia (eds) *Eyewitness Memory: Theoretical and Applied Perspectives.* Mawah, NJ: Lawrence Earlbaum Associates, 107–130.

SAUER, J.D., BREWER, N. and WELLS, G. (2008). Is there a magical time boundary for diagnosing eyewitness identification accuracy in sequential line-ups? *Legal and Criminological Psychology, 13,* 123–135.

SCHOOLER, J.W. and ENGSTER-SCHOOLER, T.Y. (1990). Verbal overshadowing of visual memories: Some things are better left unsaid. *Cognitive Psychology, 22,* 36–71.

SCHWARTZ-KENNEY, B.M., BOTTOMS, B.L. and GOODMAN, G.S. (1996). Improving children's person identification. *Child Maltreatment, 1,* 121–133.

SEARCY, J.H., BARTLETT, J.C. and MEMON, A. (1999). Age differences in accuracy and choosing in eyewitness identification and face recognition. *Memory and Cognition, 27,* 538–552.

SEMMLER, C., BREWER, N. and WELLS, G.L. (2004). Effects of postidentification feedback on eyewitness identification and nonidentification confidence. *Journal of Applied Psychology, 89*, 334–346.

SHAPIRO, P.N. and PENROD, S. (1986). Meta-analysis of facial identification studies. *Psychological Bulletin, 100*, 139–156.

SHEPHERD, J.W. (1983). Identification after long delays. In S.M.A. Lloyd-Bostock and B.R. Clifford. *Evaluating Witness Evidence.* John Wiley and Sons.

—— and DEREGOWSKI, J.B. (1981). Races and faces: A comparison of the responses of Africans and Europeans to faces of the same and different races. *British Journal of Social Psychology, 20*, 125–133.

SLONE, A.E., BRIGHAM, J.C. and MEISSNER, C.A. (2000). Social and cognitive factors affecting the own race bias in whites. *Basic and Applied Social Psychology, 22*, 71–84.

SMITH, S.M., LINDSAY, R.C.L. and PRYKE, S. (2000). Postdictors of eyewitness errors: Can false identifications be diagnosed? *Journal of Applied Psychology, 85*, 542–550.

——, ——, —— and DYSART, J.E. (2001). Postdictors of eyewitness errors: Can false identifications be diagnosed in the cross-race situation? *Psychology, Public Policy and Law, 7*, 153–169.

SNYDER, M. (1979). Self-monitoring processes. In L. Berkowitz (ed.) *Advances in Experimental Social Psychology (Vol 12)*. New York: Academic Press.

SPORER, S.L. (1993). Eyewitness identification accuracy, confidence, and decision times in simultaneous and sequential lineups. *Journal of Applied Psychology, 78*, 22–33.

—— (2001). Recognizing faces of other ethnic groups: An integration of theories. *Psychology, Public, Policy and Law, 7*, 36–97.

—— (2007). Person descriptions as retrieval cues: Do they really help? *Psychology, Crime and Law, 13*, 611–625.

——, PENROD, S., READ, D. and CUTLER, B. (1995). Choosing, Confidence, and Accuracy: A meta-analysis of the confidence-accuracy relation in eyewitness identification studies. *Psychological Bulletin, 118*, 315–327.

STEBLAY, N.M. (1992). A meta-analytic review of the weapon focus effect. *Law and Human Behavior, 16*, 413–424.

TOLLESTRUP, P.A., TURTLE, J.W. and YUILLE, J.C. (1994). Actual victims and witnesses to robbery and fraud: An archival analysis. In J.D. Read, D.F. Ross and M.P. Toglia (eds) *Adult Eyewitness Testimony: Current Trends and Developments.* New York: Cambridge University Press, 144–162.

TULVING, E. and THOMSON, D.M. (1973). Encoding specificity and retrieval processes in episodic memory. *Psychological Review, 80*, 352–373.

VALENTINE, T. (1991). A unified account of the effects of distinctiveness, inversion, and race in face recognition. *The Quarterly Journal of Experimental Psychology, 43A*, 161–204.

—— and MESOUT, J. (2007). *Eyewitness Identification Under Stress in the London Dungeon.* Unpublished manuscript.

——, PICKERING, A. and DARLING, S. (2003). Characteristics of eyewitness identifications that predict the outcome of real lineups. *Applied Cognitive Psychology, 17*, 969–993.

WEBER, N. and BREWER, N. (2003). The effect of judgment type and confidence scale on confidence-accuracy calibration in face recognition. *Journal of Applied Psychology, 88*, 490–499.

—— and —— (2004). Confidence-accuracy calibration in absolute and relative face recognition judgements. *Journal of Experimental Psychology: Applied, 10*, 156–172.

——, ——, WELLS, G.L., SEMMLER, C. and KREAST, A. (2004). Eyewitness identification accuracy and response latency: The unruly 10–12 second rule. *Journal of Experimental Psychology: Applied, 10*, 139–147.

WELLS, G.L. (1978). Applied eyewitness testimony research: System variables and estimator variables. *Journal of Personality and Social Psychology, 36,* 1546–1557.

—— and BRADFIELD, A.L. (1998). 'Good you identified the suspect': Feedback to eyewitnesses distorts their reports of the witnessing experience. *Journal of Applied Psychology, 83,* 360–376.

——, CHARMAN, S.D. and OLSON, E.A. (2005). Building face composites can harm lineup identification performance. *Journal of Experimental Psychology: Applied, 11,* 147–156.

——, LINDSAY, R.C.L. and FERGUSON, T.J. (1979). Accuracy, confidence, and juror perception in eyewitness identification. *Journal of Applied Psychology, 64,* 440–448.

—— and MURRAY, D.M. (1984). Eyewitness confidence. In G.L. Wells and E.F. Loftus (eds) *Eyewitness testimony: Psychological Perspectives.* New York: Cambridge University Press, 155–170.

—— and OLSON, E.A. (2001). The other race effect in eyewitness identification: What do we do about it? *Psychology, Public Policy and Law, 7,* 230–246.

——, SMALL, M., PENROD, S., MALPASS, R.S., FULERO, S.M. and BRIMACOMBE, C.A.E. (1998). Eyewitness identification procedures: Recommendations for lineups and photospreads. *Law and Human Behavior, 22,* 603–647.

—— and WINDSCHITL, P.D. (1999). Stimulus sampling and social psychological experimentation. *Personality and Social Psychology Bulletin, 25,* 1115–1125.

WICKHAM, L.H.V., MORRIS, P.E. and FRITZ, C.O. (2000). Facial distinctiveness: Its measurement, distribution and influence on immediate and delayed recognition. *British Journal of Psychology, 91,* 99–123.

WILCOCK, R.A., BULL, R. and VRIJ, A. (2005). Aiding the performance of older eyewitnesses: Enhanced non-biased lineup instructions and presentation. *Psychiatry, Psychology, and Law, 12,* 129 –140.

——, —— and —— (2007). Are older witnesses always poorer witnesses? Identification accuracy, context reinstatement, own age bias. *Psychology, Crime, and Law, 13,* 305–316.

WITKIN, H.A., DYK, R.B., FATERSON, H.F., GOODENOUGH, D.R. and KARP, S.A. (1962). *Psychological differentiation: Studies in Development.* New York: Wiley.

WOJCIKIEWICZ, J. (1990). Decoding of memory traces as a function of witness' intelligence. *Forensic Science International, 46,* 83–85.

WRIGHT, D.B. and SLADDEN, B. (2003). An own gender bias and the importance of hair in face recognition. *Acta Psychologia, 114,* 101–114.

—— and STROUD, J.N. (2002). Age differences in line-up identification accuracy: People are better with their own age. *Law and Human Behavior, 26,* 641–654.

5

IDENTIFICATION BY VOICE OR BY GAIT

VOICE IDENTIFICATION

In 1994 one of the authors of the present book (Ray Bull) was contacted by the solicitor (ie lawyer) representing a man who had been remanded in custody suspected of rape. The man was in prison awaiting trial. The main evidence against him came from the rape victim who had identified his voice from a set of recorded voices played to her by the police. At that time in England there existed no 'official' guidance that the police could use on the conducting of voice parades/line-ups, so they tried to follow the official guidance on visual identification parades (as far as it was relevant). The woman listened (twice) to each of the voices in the parade/line-up and then selected the numbered voice that was, in fact, that of the suspect. The police (sensibly) video recorded the whole procedure. The video recording was made available to the suspect and his solicitor. The suspect then expressed concern that his voice sample was different from the others in the set and requested an expert report. A small-scale study was therefore conducted in which a number of participants listened to the voice line-up and then independently indicated 'which, if any, of the voices was edited from an interview with the police'. Almost all of the participants chose the voice that was, in fact, that of the suspect. All of the other voices were not edited but spoke in monologue. Thus, while these voice samples (i) spoke for a similar time duration to the suspect's, (ii) had fairly similar accents, and (iii) were of men of somewhat similar ages to the suspect, they differed from the suspect's in a forensically relevant way.

At the trial expert witness testimony was given regarding this difference between the suspect's voice sample and the others in the line-up. After a considerable time period spent trying to agree upon a verdict, the members of the jury could not agree, even upon a 'majority' verdict. Thus a re-trial was ordered at which (one year later) the same evidence/testimony was provided. This time the suspect was convicted.

A few years later, another English police force conducted a voice line-up that the suspect's solicitor was concerned about and he also contacted the co-author of the present book. A witness to the serious crime in this case described the perpetrator as having a strong Irish accent. Although the police had taken the trouble to have in the voice line-up only voices that had an Irish accent, a simple study involving people rating the voices revealed that the suspect had the strongest Irish accent of the voices in the line-up.

Communication among the police forces in England and Wales (on some matters) can be good and they gradually became aware via cases such as those above that guidance on voice parades was necessary. They then drafted a document and invited expert comments upon it. The resultant 'unofficial' guidance was in place for a few years until December 2003 when the government published 'official' guidance entitled 'Advice on the use of voice identification parades'. (The relevant contents of this government advisory document will be described later in this chapter.) The 'unofficial' guidance strongly suggested that the voice samples that would be in the line-up should be selected by an independent forensic phonetics/linguistics expert from a much larger set of voice samples provided by the police. Other important aspects of this guidance included:

- that the victim/witness provide a description of the perpetrator's voice;
- that all of the voice samples were to be speaking naturally (ie not reading from a prepared text) and contain no content relevant to the offence;
- that the samples be from persons of the same age and same ethnic, regional, and social group as the suspect;
- that the resultant line-up consist of nine voices (including the suspect's); and
- that 'mock witness' tests be conducted to check that uninvolved people cannot identify which voice is that of the suspect.

(For a fuller account of the 'unofficial' guidance see the appendix in Nolan, 2003.)

In a landmark case (*R v Khan & Bains*—Central Criminal Court, December 2002) the police to a large extent successfully followed their own guidance. For example, all of the voice samples were edited from police interviews. In his 2003 journal article, the prosecution expert witness Dr Francis Nolan provided a comprehensive account of the many steps that he took at the request of the police to try to ensure that the voice parade contained similar voices. A co-author of the present book was asked by the defence to produce an expert report. The identification evidence in this murder case was provided by a lodger who claimed to have overheard a highly relevant conversation from outside a room in a lodging house (the door of which was closed) and who claimed that one of the voices was of someone whom had once visited the lodging house and spoken to him. In one of his statements to the police this witness had said that the voice was 'high pitched'. However, when listening to the voice line-up the defence expert noticed that the suspect's voice seemed to be higher pitched than the other voices. (It seems that the prosecution expert had not been made aware of the witness statement mentioned above.) A small scale study was therefore conducted in which participants were asked to rate each voice in the parade regarding its pitch. Over 80% of participants rated the suspect's voice as the highest pitched (and the remainder rated his voice and one other as both being the highest pitched).

During the trial in which the voice identification evidence was to be the main evidence both the prosecution and the defence experts described the strengths and limitations of this voice parade (for a worthwhile account see Nolan, 2003). However, in an unexpected development, the co-accused (the other man in the overheard conversation) then admitted his part in the crime and implicated the suspect/co-defendant. Both men were found guilty.

In his account of this case the prosecution expert concluded that:

the success of the prosecution should not be taken as a green light to press ahead with cases where there is little other hard evidence to complement an identification of a voice parade or a claimed recognition. The general uncertainties over the reliability of lay voice identification, and the enormous practical difficulties in the construction of fair parades, remain. (Nolan, 2003, 288)

Readers of the current book will by now be aware that eyewitness testimony can be error prone. However, it would be interesting to know why this prosecution expert should recommend great caution and that 'commissioning a voice parade should not be undertaken lightly. The well known constraints of voice memory already place a serious limit on the weight which can be attached to a positive identification' (Nolan, 2003, 287).

One probable reason was his likely awareness of research (largely by psychologists) on people's voice identification abilities. This research has consistently found performance to be poor. Indeed, in his 2007 review of the literature Yarmey noted that overall the level of correct performance when the target voice is present in the line-up is lower than the rate of incorrect choosing when the target is not present in the line-up.

A CALL FOR RESEARCH

One of the major calls for research on voice identification came from a committee set up by the government in England and Wales in 1974 to try to understand why honest eyewitnesses can be mistaken. This 'Devlin Committee' (named after its chairperson) noted that while, even then, some worthwhile psychological research had been published regarding visual identification (Bull and Clifford, 1976), there seemed to exist very little research on voice identification (for reviews of the available research see Bull, 1981, 1982.) In its report (Devlin, 1976) the committee made the point that research should proceed as rapidly as possible into the practicality of voice parades. As part of its response to the committee's recommendations the government funded a research project that examined some basic yet possibly key factors that might influence voice identification such as: (i) the delays between first hearing a voice and later attempting to identify it in a voice parade (Clifford, Rathborn and Bull, 1981); (ii) hearing the voice over the telephone (Rathborn, Clifford and Bull, 1981); (iii) whether the listener was blind (Bull, Rathborn and Clifford, 1983); and (iv) the length of the voice samples, the number of voices in the parade, and voice disguise (Bull and Clifford, 1984). In summarizing the outcomes of our research studies we concluded that:

we recommend that prosecutions based solely on a witness' identification of a suspect's voice (if the suspect is a stranger) ought not to proceed. We say this because we are of the opinion that earwitnessing and eyewitnessing are similarly and considerably error prone. (Bull and Clifford, 1984, 123)

Indeed, even though aspects of our research studies had examined voice identification performance under rather optimal conditions, performance was generally poor.

OVERVIEWS OF THE RESEARCH

A few years later an overview of the then available research written by several North American psychologists came to a very similar conclusion (Deffenbacher et al, 1989). In 1995, Yarmey reviewed 32 publications on the topic (including 12 of his own). He concluded that 'identification for unfamiliar voices must be treated with caution' (1995, 270). In 1998 an overview paper presented to the British Academy of Forensic Sciences (summarized in Bull and Clifford, 1999) noted that the growing body of relevant research consistently seemed to lead to the conclusion that voice identifications are often incorrect. Then in 1999 the National Court of Appeal in London, when quashing a conviction that had largely rested on earwitness testimony, noted that the defence had supplied it with a copy of the 1998 overview paper mentioned above. In two other cases in 1998 and 1999 the Court of Appeal suggested that from then on an appropriately adapted version of the 'Turnbull warning' given to jurors about possible limitations in eyewitness testimony (see Chapter 4 of the present book) should be given (ie by the judge) in all cases involving voice identification.

Soon after that, in the 'Criminal Law Review', Ormerod commented that 'voice identification has been largely ignored in the legal literature' (2001, 596). In his extensive review this law professor noted that it 'is now well-recognised to be extremely unlikely that people can identify with any accuracy voices of strangers which they have heard only once before for a short period' (2001, 622).

By 'well-recognised' Ormerod probably meant by relevant researchers (mostly psychologists) and by some members of the legal world. A more recent publication by Philippon, Cherryman, Bull and Vrij (2007a) examined police officers' and potential jurors' beliefs concerning voice identification and found that only a third of them believed that earwitness testimony is generally an unreliable source of evidence.

THE RESEARCH FINDINGS

The previously published reviews of the relevant research findings concerning voice identification have organized these in a variety of ways but usually under the major headings of: (i) aspects of the voice heard; (ii) factors relating to the witness; and (iii) how best to conduct the voice identification task (eg a voice line-up).

Aspects of the Voice Heard

Duration

In optimal testing conditions Bull and Clifford (1984) found in a series of studies that an initial voice sample of a sentence was sufficient for correct identification performance to be at above chance level. In his more recent review of the relevant research Yarmey (2007) concluded that correct identification is more likely the longer the opportunity the witness had to listen to the perpetrator.

As stated in previous chapters in the present book, sometimes the police suspect is not the perpetrator (ie the line-up is target absent (TA)). The few published studies that have examined whether perpetrator voice sample length/duration affects performance on TA line-ups have produced contradictory findings in that while Kerstholt, Jansen, Van Amelsvoort and Broeders (2004) found fewer choices from TA line-ups when the initial voice duration was 70 seconds than 30 seconds, Orchard and Yarmey (1995) did not find an effect. A further complication is that for some crimes the information about the length of the perpetrators' voice sample can only come from the witness, who could be in error concerning this (Orchard and Yarmey, 1995).

Use of the Telephone

Some crimes involve use of the telephone which could degrade the voice sample. Rathborn et al (1981) found that if a telephone was initially used this reduced subsequent line-up performance. However, recording the line-up voices over the telephone did not increase performance if the initial voice was over the telephone, nor did it decrease performance if the initial hearing of the voice did not involve the telephone. Both Yarmey (2003a) and Kersthold, Jansen, Amelsvoort and Broeders (2006) found no effect of telephone usage.

Disguise

A thinking criminal may decide at the time of the crime to distort/disguise his/her voice. (Doing this at the time of the line-up would obviously risk it being noticed by the police.) Several research studies (see Yarmey, 2007) have supported Bull and Clifford's (1984) finding that voice disguise substantially reduces the likelihood of correct identification.

Accent/Language

In his 2007 review of the limited number of relevant studies Yarmey (2007) concluded that if the perpetrator speaks with a strong but unfamiliar accent or in a language that the witness does not understand then later identification will be impaired. This conclusion is partly supported by the findings of a study by Philippon, Cherryman, Bull and Vrij (2007b) in which English speakers heard a target voice speaking either English or French (a language that they were not familiar with). In this study the participants saw and heard a man speaking (clearly for 45 seconds) into a telephone to a crime accomplice. This man was either a 'native speaker' of English or a 'native speaker' of French. (In fact three English and three French men were used, their voices having been matched for distinctiveness.) At test 30 minutes later the line-ups consisted of speakers of French or English (that had been evaluated by French and English speakers not to have any unusual characteristics), one language per line-up. The individual speech samples each lasted for 30 seconds and all said the same thing (translated into French where appropriate.) For some participants the line-up contained the target voice, for others it did not.

For the target present (TP) line-ups, whether the target initially spoke French (and therefore the line-up was all in French) or English did not affect correct performance (at 47%) but did affect false choosing of an incorrect voice (47% versus 20%) and, the frequency of saying that the target was not in the line-up (6% versus 33%, for French and English, respectively.) For the TA line-ups the rates of incorrect choosing of a voice were 93% and 67% (for French and English respectively). Thus, what this study reveals is that significantly more French voices were incorrectly chosen than were English voices (though the rate of correct identification of French and English voices did not differ).

Voice Already Known

One of the probable explanations of why Philippon et al (2007a) found that most people did not agree that earwitness testimony (regarding strangers' voices) can be an unreliable source of evidence is their awareness that they are good at recognizing the voices of people they know well and assume that this applies also to once-heard voices. Indeed, Yarmey, Yarmey, Yarmey and Parliament (2001) found, as had others, that correct identification of familiar voices is usually good. However, as familiarity decreases so does correct identification. Furthermore, research has found that strangers' voices can often be mis-identified as being of familiar people (Goldstein and Chance, 1985). Such research can be highly relevant to cases in which a witness claims to have recognized (ie at the time of the crime) the voice of the perpetrator (eg who was not visible). In two criminal cases in which a co-author of the present book was involved, a crucial issue involved the extent to which the findings of psychological research could allow the Court to decide whether there was any merit in the claim of the defence, that the witness had mistakenly decided via voice that the perpetrator was known to him.

Presence of a Weapon

In one of these two court cases a shopkeeper had been approached from behind and a knife put to his throat. Does the so-called 'weapon focus effect' (see Chapter 4 of this book) apply to voice identification? The very few studies that have examined this question found no such effect (Yarmey, 2007), though one study did find that the presence of a weapon decreased how much witnesses could remember of what the 'perpetrator' said (Pickel, French and Betts, 2003), possibly due to high levels of stress experienced by the witnesses.

Factor Relating to the Witness

Stress

Research on the effect of stress/fear upon people's ability to identify voices is currently lacking. However, given the complex relationships that research has found for eyewitnessing, the picture is likely to be similarly complex for earwitnesing.

Age

Also needed is more research on the possible effects of age on voice identification performance. At the present time we know that the performance of children can be as poor as that of adults (Clifford and Toplis, 1996) and that of people of 40 years of age is poorer than that of younger adults (Bull and Clifford, 1984).

Gender

There exist many more studies on the effect of witness gender and these have consistently found no general effect, though women may be better at identifying a female voice (Wilding and Cook, 2000).

Blindness

Being blind might possibly result in a greater ability to identify voices, including those heard only once (eg of a crime perpetrator). However, while one study found that blind earwitnesses performed better than sighted people (Bull et al, 1983), two others did not (Elaad, Seger and Tobin, 1998; Winograd, Kerr and Spence, 1984).

Witness Confidence

Witnesses who are highly confident about their voice identifications could have a greater impact upon the courts and the police than witnesses who are less confident. However, research has found that, as for eyewitnessing (see Chapter 4), the confidence-accuracy relationship for earwitnessing is complex. For example, Yarmey and Matthys (1992) found that while confidence and accuracy were positively related for long voice sample durations (ie two to six minutes) they were negatively related for short voice samples (18 seconds). A fairly consistent finding is that participants' degree of confidence is noticeably higher than their accuracy (Olsson, Juslin and Winman, 1998), which usually is poor. More research is needed to see whether the factors (reviewed in Chapter 4) influencing the confidence-accuracy relationship for eyewitnessing have the same effect for earwitnessing. Yarmey concluded that 'witnesses' confidence in their identification decisions for unfamiliar speakers are not reliable predictors of accuracy of identification' (2007, 111). This conclusion was based on studies that have compared people high in confidence with those lower in confidence. Rarely would a witness be involved in several line-ups in the same police investigation. However, when this occurs, it might be important to note that Bull and Clifford (1984) found for such witnesses that their confidence in their decision for each separate line-up was significantly related to their accuracy, but only for line-ups that did actually contain the target.

How Best to Conduct the Line-up

Delay

Almost everyone assumes that retrieving information from memory becomes more difficult the longer the time interval between initially encoding it and later trying to retrieve it. While, in general, this is a sensible assumption, psychological research on the topic of person identification has for decades demonstrated that the effects of such delays are not straightforward (Clifford and Bull, 1978; Yarmey, 2007). In our 1994 overview we noted that while the first two published research studies on this topic (McGehee, 1937, 1944) were in agreement that voice identification performance is poorer after a two-week delay interval than after a few days, the effect of longer delays was present in one study but not in the other. In our own study (Clifford, et al, 1981) we found for 'easy-to-recognize voices' no significant differences in performance among delays of one, seven or 14 days but a difference between those three delay intervals and a delay of only ten minutes. For 'difficult-to-recognize' voices the effects of delays were more straightforward in that performance progressively became poorer the longer the delay (ie up to 14 days). The results of these studies would suggest that effort should be made to conduct the voice identification task within a few days of the earwitnessed event. Somewhat similarly, Kersholt et al (2006) found for TP line-ups that correct performance declined with delays (of one, three, and eight weeks). However, such increasing delays did not reduce performance for TA line-ups.

However, the possible effect of shorter delays (eg two hours versus two to three days versus up to seven days) seems to depend on whether the target is actually in the voice line-up. Furthermore, at least one study has found delay (up to two weeks) to be associated with an improvement in performance (Hollein, Bennett and Gelfer, 1983). Perhaps an important issue is what happens during the delay interval (eg in terms of practising retrieving the voice from memory). The various published studies have employed rather different voice durations, testing procedures, and so on (Bull and Clifford, 1999) and so it is not surprising that the findings of the studies differ to some extent.

The Number and Duration of the Voices in the Line-ups

We found (Bull and Clifford, 1984) that increasing the number of voices (in target present line-ups) from four to six voices improved correct performance but that a further increase to eight voices led to no extra improvement. However, others (eg Hammersley and Read, 1996) have contended that more than six voices should be used. Very few studies have examined the effects of the duration of the voices in the line-up. In our studies we used utterances that were one sentence in length. However, as stated above, our own studies were largely designed to find out how good/poor voice identification performance would be in fairly optimal conditions. Official government guidance in England and Wales distributed at the end of 2003 (see below) states that each sample in the voice parade should be about 60 seconds long.

What Should the Line-up Voices Say?

If the non-suspect voices in the line-up (and the suspect's) were required all to say the same thing then the voice samples would not truly be of spontaneous speech because it is likely that they could be reading from a script. Yarmey (2007) recommends that samples of spontaneous speech be used.

GUIDELINES FOR CONDUCTING VOICE LINE-UPS

In England and Wales in December 2003 the government published 'Advice on the use of voice identification parades' (available from <http://www.circulars.homeoffice. gov.uk>). This circular advises that:

1. as much descriptive detail as possible should be obtained about the voice from the witness;
2. a representative sample of the suspect's voice should be obtained which contains spontaneous speech;
3. no less than 20 samples of similar speakers to the suspect should be obtained to be passed to a recognized expert for final selection to be in the line-up;
4. in the line-up there should be a total of nine speakers (each speaking for about one minute);

5. nothing in what is said should identify the suspect;
6. a 'mock witness' evaluation be conducted to ensure that the suspect's voice does not unduly stand out;
7. the witness must be instructed that the actual perpetrator's voice may or may not be present; and
8. the witness listening to the line-up and his/her selecting (or not) of a voice should be video-recorded.

Guidance such as this indicates a fruitful liaison between psychological research and police practice with the aim of securing reliable witness evidence.

However, while the volume of research on voice identification/how a person talked has become sufficient to result in official guidance, this is not yet the case for other sources of non-facial person information, such as witness' memory for how a person walked.

IDENTIFICATION VIA WALK/GAIT

In 1978 we pointed out that '[p]erson recognition by visual, non-facial cues is a topic which has largely been ignored' (Clifford and Bull, 1978, 111). This section presents a review of work published on the topic of person identification by their walk/gait.

Over 70 years ago Kreezer and Glanville (1937) noted that while a verbal description of how a person walks (ie her/his gait) is difficult, partly because of the limited vocabulary available for this, visual recognition via gait may be easier. Allport and Vernon (1933) had noted that people do reliably differ in stride length and walking speed, as did Borg, Edgnen and Markland (1973). However, in an early study Wolff (1933) found that people were unable to recognize their wives or friends (all wearing the same 'trousers') from films (from the waist down) of them walking. Nevertheless, more recently in a UK national newspaper ('Aiming to catch criminals red-footed', *The Times*, 10 July 2006) it was stated that 'one thing will always identify criminals—their walk . . . scientists now believe that an individual's gait can give the game away'.

In 1977 Cutting and Kozlowski conducted a study involving three male and three female students who all were known to each other. Light sources were attached to each of their joints and they were filmed (in darkness) while walking five strides (ie for 2.7 seconds). (This point-light technique involves individuals in tight-fitting black clothing with reflectors or lights on their joints so that only the movements of the lights/reflectors can be seen.) Two months later the participants were shown the film clips and had to try to identify who of the six was shown moving in each clip. In all 60 clips were shown and the overall correct recognition rate was 38%. Performance improved as more clips were shown (ie from 27% near to the beginning to 59% near to the end) even though no 'feedback' was given after each recognition attempt. Recognition of others was not significantly better than of self (36% and 43%). For recognition decisions that the participants were very confident about the accuracy was significantly better than for their low confidence decisions. When asked how they recognized the walkers, the participants mentioned speed, rhythm, step length, and arm swing.

The correct recognition rate of nearly 60% toward the end of the study does suggest that there are aspects of a person's gait that might assist their recognition/identification (as suggested in the 2006 article in *The Times*). However, if, in general, men walk in a way different from women, then this could have greatly assisted the participants in the study reported in the previous paragraph because only three male and three female walkers were involved.

Indeed, a set of studies by the same authors published in the following year (Barclay, Cutting and Kozlowski, 1978) found that gender could be to some extent identified from gait. In their first study the gait of seven males and seven females was filmed using lights on the joints. Gender was correctly identified by other students at a rate of 66% (better than at chance level, which is 50%) only for the longer film clips that had a duration of 4.4 seconds. For shorter film clips (ie 1.6, 0.8, and 0.4 seconds) performance was not better than chance. For the longest film clips the women were better at gender recognition than were the men (71% and 61%). In their second study these researchers found a similar correct gender recognition rate of 64% for the 4.4 second film clips. However, if the film speed was slowed down to a third of the normal rate, gender recognition was at chance level. In a recent overview of studies on the recognition of gender from gait Pollick, Kay, Heim and Stringer (2003) noted average performance levels of between 66% and 71% (when chance is 50%).

Whether people can identify their friends, themselves, and strangers from moving point-light displays was studied by Loula, Prasad, Harber and Shiffrar (2005). Initially the participants (involving some pairs of friends) were filmed performing each of ten actions (eg walking, jumping, dancing, running). A few months later these participants were shown a series of clips from the films and for each had to say whether it was of a friend or a stranger or of themselves. For the clips of strangers, identifying them as such was close to chance level (which equals 33%). However, for friends performance was 47% and for self was 69%. With regard to the ten actions, identification of the type of person (ie friend, stranger, self) was best for dancing but was poorest for running or walking (which were at chance levels). Loula et al concluded that the identities of walking people are not well recognized. Their second experiment produced very similar results.

Somewhat more encouraging results were found by Stevenage, Nixon and Vince (1999). They filmed six people (three male, three female) of similar height and build walking wearing the same clothing (ie loose-fitting black polo-neck jumper, black track-suit bottoms, black balaclava). The walkers were filmed in simulated daylight, in simulated dusk conditions, and using point-light displays in darkness. In their first experiment, to help the observer-participants learn the names of each walker (who were strangers to the participants) they were shown a film clip of each walker while being told the name. They were then shown other clips of the same six walkers (one set of six walkers at a time) and for each had to say a name. After each time they gave a name they were told who the walker actually was. For each participant this continued until they correctly identified each of the six walkers in a set. On average, participants need to see eight sets of the six walkers before they were able to name all six correctly. From the results of this first study Stevenage et al concluded that people can learn to identify people by their gait.

In their second study, 48 participants initially saw a two-second film clip of just one walker and were given the name of that walker. Then they were shown six walkers (three female, three male) and had to say which one was the walker they had just seen. (They could see this gait line-up more than once if they wished.) Half of the participants chose the correct person, which is a level of performance considerably above what may have been the chance level (of 16%). However, since 69% picked a walker of the correct gender, perhaps such gender recognition assisted performance. That is, if the gender of the target was somehow 'known' to participants (see the studies mentioned above concerning gait gender recognition), then this would for them have narrowed down the number of possible choices from the six-person line-ups to three, creating a chance level of performance of 33%. Stevenage et al dispensed with this gender assisted notion. Importantly, they found that the level of correct identification (ie 50%) was not affected by whether the initial target recording was made in daylight conditions or dusk conditions. (No point-light displays were used in their second study and the gait line-up always involved daylight conditions.)

Stevenage et al concluded that 'humans can use gait information to identify people' (1999, 524), but in our opinion the error rates found in their second study (ie half of the identifications were incorrect) suggest that the use of gait line-ups to identify once-seen strangers are likely to be error prone. Nevertheless, they made the worthwhile suggestion that 'it might be prudent to reconsider the static nature of a conventional identity parade . . . a walking parade could . . . serve to improve . . . recognition procedures' (1999, 525).

In terms of the major focus of the present book (ie the identification/recognition of 'once-seen' crime perpetrators) few studies of gait are directly relevant. However, it does seem that people can learn how to discriminate to some extent between individuals' gait. Troje, Westhoff and Lavrov (2005) showed to observers several men walking. The walking movement was made available by attaching small reflective makers to the men's joints (etc). That is, during the experiments only the movement of the markers was visible. At the beginning of the experiment the observers could not reliably discriminate between the walkers. However, after several sessions involving feedback as to whether the observer chose the correct name of the walker, performance achieved 90% correct naming (of each of the seven walkers). It is not made clear in this 2005 publication whether or not the observers (18 students or employees of the university) already knew any of the walkers (seven students or staff at the same university) and thus already had some familiarity with their gait. Though at the beginning of the study recognition was at chance level, prior familiarity may have aided learning.

If it is possible for people to recognize/identify others by their gait (and much more research is needed on this), then an important question would involve whether people can disguise their identity by trying to alter their gait? Richardson and Johnston (2005) also used the point-light technique. In their study the recorded individuals (students) walked normally and then walked as if they were much older (ie 70 years of age). The observers were shown two video-clips of walkers and were told that in one clip a person was walking normally and in the other clip as a 70 year old. The observers had to indicate for each pair of clips whether they were of the same person or of two different people. Average performance was found to be 70% (when it would be 50% by chance alone) this deriving from 75% for 'same walker' and 64% for 'different walker'. Thus, this study suggests that attempting to disguise one's gait may not be entirely successful (also see the fourth experiment by Jacobs, Pinto and Shiffrar, 2004). However, Richardson and Johnson wisely noted that it 'is possible that accuracy would not be as high if participants were required to identify a given walker from a group of strangers' (2005, 40).

As stated above, there has not been sufficient research yet conducted involving gait recognition by humans. However, there is a growing literature on the use of computer-based systems to recognize people by their gait. This literature is not directly relevant to the present book and it therefore will not be reviewed here. (Readers interested in this topic could see Kale et al, 2004; Wang, Tan, Ning and Hu (2003); Wong and Rogers (2007); Yam, Nixon and Carter, 2004.)

Almost no studies have compared the informativeness of gait cues compared to face cues. However, this was done as part of a study of person recognition from poor quality video recordings (Burton, Wilson, Cowan and Bruce, 1999). In this study people who were well acquainted with the individuals shown in the video recordings were able to recognize them (from the four-second unedited clips as they entered or left the front door of a building). However, when the clips were edited to obscure the face or the body or the gait movement cues performance dropped (from around 90% to 83% for body obscured to 80% for gait obscured and to around 30% for face obscured). The small but significant drop in performance when gait cues were unavailable suggests that when available they had aided recognition.

Overall, the literature that is currently available on the extent to which people can recognize/identify others by their gait (especially unfamiliar others) is very limited. Thus, the likelihood of 'gait line-ups' (ie similar to person, face or voice line-ups) presently seems to be remote. We need to know much more about the psychological processes that underlie how witnesses might seek to match their memory of the gait of a culprit with the gait of the suspect/people in a gait line-up. Also, we need to know a great deal more about factors that might bias or reduce the accuracy of gait identification.

VOICE-PLUS-FACE LINE-UPS

Although the available research suggests that correct performance at voice line-ups generally will be poor, a few researchers have begun to examine whether holding a voice line-up in addition to a visual line-up would be of use for crimes in which a witness both saw and heard the perpetrator. For example, Pryke, Lindsay, Dysart and Dupuis (2004) conducted two such experiments. Witnesses were first presented with a face line-up and then (unexpectedly) with a voice line-up (of the same people as in the face line-up). Performance on the voice line-up was indeed poor (even though the foils in the voice line-up were not selected on the basis of voice similarity). Thus, at first glance, it might seem that holding a face line-up followed by a voice line-up might add nothing to the face line-up and could even detract from it (eg if a witness performed correctly on the face line-up but incorrectly on the voice line-up, in court the latter might reduce the impact of the former). However, with regard to incorrect choosing on a face line-up (eg when the perpetrator is absent), the choosing of the same person on the voice line-up would be very rare. Sensibly, Pryke et al called for more research to be conducted on this topic before any recommendations are made to practitioners.

Melara, DeWitt-Rickards and O'Brien (1989) compared performance on visual, voice and visual-plus-voice video parades. Somewhat surprisingly they found there to be more correct choices from the TP parades for voice than for visual (perhaps due to the unusual methodology they used), with performance on the simultaneously presented visual-plus-voice parades being between the voice (only) and the visual (only). However, on the TA parades performance on the voice (only) parades was very poor (ie 85% false choosing) and that for visual-plus-voice parades was poorer than for visual parades (in experiment 2A but not in experiment 2B).

CONCLUSION

Some of the chapters in this book reveal that recognizing a once-seen person via their appearance (eg their face) is a challenging task that many people are poor at. Other chapters consider possible methods of assisting witnesses to be better at recognizing people by their appearance. The present chapter has reviewed research evidence concerning trying to identify strangers via their voice or gait. Overall, such research makes it clear that voice and gait recognition usually results in rather poor performance (though the recognition of friends' gait or familiar voices can be much above chance level).

To date, few studies have attempted to examine whether holding not only a visual/appearance line-up but also a voice or gait line-up might sometimes assist in determining whether the suspect is the perpetrator. This could be beneficial if the suspect is innocent, but that is not usually the reason for holding a line-up.

FURTHER READING

LOULA, F., PRASAD, S., HARBER, K. and SHIFFRAR, M. (2005). Recognizing people from their movement. *Journal of Experimental Psychology: Human Perception and Performance, 31,* 210–220.

PHILIPPON, A., CHERRYMAN, J., BULL, R. and VRIJ, A. (2007). Earwitness identification performance: The effect of language, target, deliberate strategies, and indirect measures. *Applied Cognitive Psychology, 21,* 539–550.

STEVENAGE, S., NIXON, M. and VINCE, K. (1999). Visual analysis of gait as a cue to identity. *Applied Cognitive Psychology, 13,* 513–526.

YARMEY, A.D. (2007). The psychology of speaker identification and earwitness memory. In R. Lindsay, D. Ross, J.D. Read and M. Toglia (eds) *Handbook of Eyewitness Psychology: Volume 2, Memory for People.* Mahway, NJ: Erlbaum, 101–136.

REFERENCES

ALLPORT, G. and VERNON, P. (1933). *Studies in Expressive Movements.* London: MacMillan.

BARCLAY, C., CUTTING, J. and KOZLOWSKI, L. (1978). Temporal and spatial factors in gait perception that influence gender recognition. *Perception and Psychophysics, 23,* 145–152.

BORG, G., EDGNEN, B., and MARKLAND, G. (1973). The reliability and stability of the indicators in a simple walk test. *Reports from the Institute of Applied Psychology, No 35.* Stockholm: University of Stockholm.

BULL, R. (1981). Voice identification by man and machine: A review of research. In. S. Lloyd-Bostock (ed.) *Psychology in Legal Contexts.* London: Macmillan, 28–42.

—— (1982). Witnesses' ability to identify voices. In A. Trankell (ed.) *Reconstructing the Past.* Deventer: Norstedts, 271–278.

—— and CLIFFORD, B. (1976). Identification: The Devlin Report. *New Scientist,* 6 May.

—— and —— (1984) Earwitness voice recognition accuracy. In G. Wells and E. Loftus (eds) *Eyewitness Testimony: Psychological Perspectives.* New York: Cambridge University Press, 92–123.

—— and —— (1999). Earwitness testimony. *Medicine, Science and the Law, 39,* 120–127.

——, RATHBORN, H. and CLIFFORD, B. (1983). The voice recognition accuracy of blind listeners. *Perception, 12,* 223–226.

BURTON, A.M., WILSON, S., COWAN, M. and BRUCE, V. (1999). Face recognition in poor quality video: Evidence from security surveillance. *Psychological Science, 10,* 243–248.

CLIFFORD, B.R. and BULL, R. (1978). *The Psychology of Person Identification.* London: Routledge and Kegan Paul.

——, RATHBORN, H. and BULL, R. (1981). The effects of delay interval on voice identification. *Law and Human Behavior, 5,* 201–208.

—— and TOPLIS, (1996). A comparison of adults' and children's witnessing abilities. In N. Clark and G. Stephenson (eds) *Investigative and Forensic Decision-making: Issues in Criminological And Legal Psychology.* Leicester: British Psychological Society, 76–83.

CUTTING, J. and KOZLOWSKI, L. (1977). Recognizing friends by their walk: Gait perception without familiarity cues. *Bulletin of the Psychonomic Society, 9,* 353–356.

DEFFENBACHER, K., CROSS, J., HANDKINS, R., CHANCE, J., GOLDSTEIN, A., HAMMERSLEY, R. and READ, J.D. (1989). Relevance of voice identification research to criteria for evaluating reliability of an identification. *Journal of Psychology, 123,* 109–119.

DEVLIN, LORD P. (1976). *Report to the Secretary of State for the Home Department of the Departmental Committee on Evidence of Identification in Criminal Cases.* London: Her Majesty's Stationery Office.

ELAAD, E., SEGER, S. and TOBIN, Y. (1998). Long-term working memory in voice identification. *Psychology, Crime and Law, 4,* 73–88.

GOLDSTEIN, A. and CHANCE, J. (1985). *Voice recognition. The effects of faces, temporal distribution of practice and social distance.* Paper presented at the Biennial Convention of the American Psychology Law Society, Chicago, May.

HAMMERSLEY, R. and READ, J.D. (1996). Voice identifications by humans and computers. In. S. Sporer, R. Malpass and G. Koehnken (eds) *Psychological Issues in Eyewitness Identification*. Manwah, NJ: Erlbraum, 117–152.

HOLLEIN, H., BENNETT, G. and GELFER, M.P. (1983). Criminal identification comparison: Aural versus visual identifications resulting from a simulated crime. *Journal of Forensic Sciences, 28,* 208–221.

JACOBS, A., PINTO, J. and SHIFFRAR, M. (2004). Experience, context, and the visual perception of human movement. *Journal of Experimental Psychology: Human Perception and Performance, 30,* 822–835.

KALE, A., SUNDARESAN, A., RAJAGOPALAN, A., CUNTOOR, N. ROY-CHOWDHURY, A., KRUGER, V. and CHELLAPPA, R. (2004). Identification of humans using gait. *IEEE Transaction on Image Processing, 13,* 1163–1173.

KERSHOLT, J., JANSEN, N., VAN AMELSVOORT, A. and BROEDERS, A. (2006). Earwitnesses: Effects of accent, retention and telephone. *Applied Cognitive Psychology, 20,* 187–197.

——, ——, —— and —— (2004). Earwitnesses: Effects of speech duration, retention interval and acoustic environment. *Applied Cognitive Psychology, 18,* 327–336.

KREEZER, G. and GLANVILLE A. (1937). A method for the quantitative analysis of human gait. *Journal of Genetic Psychology, 50,* 109–136.

LOULA, F., PRASAD, S., HARBER, K. and SHIFFRAR, M. (2005). Recognizing people from their movement. *Journal of Experimental Psychology: Human Perception and Performance, 31,* 210–220.

McGEHEE, F. (1937). The reliability of the identification of the human voice. *Journal of General Psychology, 17,* 249–271.

—— (1944). An experimental investigation of voice recognition. *Journal of General Psychology, 31,* 53–65.

MELARA, R., DeWITT-RICKARDS, T. and O'BRIEN, T. (1989). Enhancing line-up identification accuracy: Two codes are better than one. *Journal of Applied Psychology, 74,* 706–713.

NIXON, M., CARTER, J., GRANT, M., GORDON, L. and HAYFRON-ACQUAH, J. (2003). Automatic recognition by gait: Progress and prospects. *Sensor Review, 23,* 323–331.

NOLAN, F. (2003). A recent voice parade. *Forensic Linguistics, 10,* 277–291.

OLSSON, N., JUSLIN, P. and WINMAN, A. (1998). Realism of confidence in earwitness versus eyewitness identification. *Journal of Experimental Psychology: Applied, 4,* 101–118.

ORCHARD, T. and YARMEY, A.D. (1995). The effects of whispers, voice-sample duration, and voice distinctiveness on criminal speaker identification. *Applied Cognitive Psychology, 9,* 249–260.

ORMEROD, D. (2001). Sounds familiar?—Voice identification evidence. *Criminal Law Review,* 595–622.

PHILIPPON, A., CHERRYMAN, J., BULL, R. and VRIJ, A. (2007a). Lay people's and police officers' attitudes towards the usefulness of perpetrator voice identification. *Applied Cognitive Psychology, 21,* 103–115.

——, ——, —— and —— (2007b). Earwitness identification performance: The effect of language, target, deliberate strategies, and indirect measures. *Applied Cognitive Psychology, 21,* 539–550.

PICKEL, K., FRENCH, T. and BETTS, J. (2003). A cross-modal weapon focus effect: The influence of weapon presence on memory for auditory information. *Memory, 11,* 277–292.

POLLICK, F., KAY, J., HEIM, K. and STRINGER, R. (2005). Gender recognition from point-lightwalkers. *Journal of Experimental Psychology: Human Perception and Performance, 31,* 1247–1265.

PRYKE, S., LINDSAY, R., DYSART, J. and DUPUIS, P. (2004). Multiple independent identification decisions. *Journal of Applied Psychology, 89,* 73–84.

RATHBORN, H., CLIFFORD, B. and BULL, R. (1981). Voice recognition over the telephone. *Journal of Police Science and Administration, 9,* 280–284.

RICHARDSON, M. and JOHNSTON, L. (2005). Person recognition from dynamic events: The kinematic specification of individual identity in walking style. *Journal of Nonverbal Behavior, 29,* 25–44.

SEITZ, K. (2003). The effects of changes in posture and clothing on the development of unfamiliar person recognition. *Applied Cognitive Psychology, 17,* 819–832.

STEVENAGE, S., NIXON, M. and VINCE, K. (1999). Visual analysis of gait as a cue to identity. *Applied Cognitive Psychology, 13,* 513–526.

TROJE, N., WESHOFF, C. and LAVROV, M. (2005). Person identification from biological motion: Effects of structural and kinematic cues. *Perception and Psychophysics, 67,* 667–675.

WANG, L., TAN T., NING, H. and HU, W. (2003). Silhouette analysis-based gait recognition for human identification. *IEEE Transaction on Pattern Analysis and Machine Intelligence, 25,* 1505–1518.

WILDING, J. and COOK, S. (2000). Sex differences and individual consistency in voice identification *Perceptual and Motor Skills, 91,* 535–538.

WINOGRAD, E., KERR, N. and SPENCE, M. (1984). Voice recognition: Effect of orienting task, and a test of blind versus sighted listeners. *American Journal of Psychology, 97,* 57–70.

WOLFF, W. (1933). The experimental study of forms of expression. *Character and Personality, 2,* 168–176.

WONG, W. and ROGERS, E. (2007). Recognition of temporal patterns: From engineering to-psychology and back. *Canadian Journal of Experimental Psychology, 61,* 159–167.

YAM, C., NIXON, M. and CARTER, J. (2004). Automated person recognition by walking running via model based approaches. *Pattern Recognition, 37,* 1057–1072.

YARMEY, A.D. (1995). Earwitness and evidence obtained by other senses. In R. Bull and D. Carson (eds) *Handbook of Psychology in Legal Contexts.* Chichester: Wiley, 262–273.

—— (2003). Earwitness identification over the telephone and in field settings. *Forensic Linguistics, 10,* 65–77.

—— (2007). The psychology of speaker identification and earwitness memory. In R. Lindsay, D. Ross, J.D. Read and M. Toglia (eds) *Handbook of Eyewitness Psychology: Volume 2, Memory For People.* Mahway, NJ: Erlbaum, 101–136.

—— and MATTHYS, E. (1992). Voice identification of an abductor. *Applied Cognitive Psychology, 6,* 367–377.

——, YARMEY, A.L., YARMEY, M. and PARLIAMENT, L. (2001). Commonsense beliefs and the identification of familiar voices. *Applied Cognitive Psychology, 15,* 283–299.

6

THE EFFECTS
OF EXPECTATIONS
AND STEREOTYPES
ON IDENTIFICATION

INTRODUCTION

At the end of the previous chapter we stated that much more needs to be known/ researched concerning factors that might bias (gait) identification. The present chapter focuses on some of the factors that have been found to bias identification. Though none of the studies to be reviewed here have involved identification by gait, their findings could also apply to gait.

BIAS USING FINGERPRINTS

We'll begin this chapter with some studies of possible bias in identification using fingerprints. In earlier chapters in this book we have described some of the processes involved when a crime witness later is shown one or more faces and has to decide if that of the perpetrator is present. Essentially, this is a 'matching' task in which the witness has to try to match his/her memory of the perpetrator with the face(s) now being seen, while bearing in mind that people's appearance does change. A crucial question focuses on how similar the memory and the current face have to be before the witness will make a match/an identification. In Britain in 1976 the report to the government by Lord Devlin's committee (on evidence of identification in criminal cases) made it clear that when eyewitnesses make such matches/identifications they can often be mistaken. This report (plus other factors) led to the requirement (in England and Wales) that judges give the 'Turnbull warning' to juries in cases involving eyewitness identification evidence (see Chapter 4). Given that eyewitnesses can sometimes make incorrect matches, perhaps some other methods of identifying criminals do not run the risk of the 'matching' problem?

Fingerprints are widely believed to be a reliable way of identifying people. However, pioneering recent research by Itiel Dror has recently revealed that the expectations which even experts have can sometimes affect their identification decisions. His first study did not involve experts but students (Dror, Peron, Hind and Charlton, 2005).

He noted that fingerprint matching is a decision-making process and that in the crime setting many fingerprints are far from perfect. The examiner has to decide whether the sample from the 'crime scene' and that from the 'suspect' are similar enough to arrive at the decision that they are from the same person. How similar they have to be can be influenced by a number of factors, possibly including what the examiner expects or needs to decide. In his first study the students were shown 96 pairs of fingerprints. Half of these pairs were chosen such that the decision of 'match versus non-match' should have been easy to arrive at (ie the prints in each pair were very clear and 24 of the pairs provided a perfect match and the other 24 an obvious non-match). The other half of the pairs were chosen because the fingerprints were incomplete and less detailed, thus providing imperfect pairs that were 'ambiguous'. For each of the 96 pairs the participants were required to say if the two fingerprints were the same or different. For the first set of 24 pairs (ie 12 'same' and 12 'different' in random order) the participants were given no further instructions. However, for the next set of 24 pairs the experimenters tried to induce a low emotional state in the participants by, prior to each pair, exposing the participants to 'background stories and photographs' (2005, 803) involving relatively common crimes such as bicycle theft, burglary that did not include physical harm to the victim. For the third set of 24 pairs these were said to involve crimes in which the victim was seriously hurt (such as personal attacks and murder) which sought to induce a higher emotional state. For the final set of 24 pairs, higher emotion background stories plus photographs were again used but in addition prior to each pair of fingerprints being displayed on the screen the words 'same' and 'guilty' were extremely briefly (ie subliminally) displayed on the screen (for 88 milliseconds) as 'primes'.

For the easy, non-ambiguous pairs Dror et al noted that 'participants correctly distinguished between match and non-match fingerprints' (2005, 805) and that performance did not significantly differ across the four sets. However, for the ambiguous pairs participants chose the response 'same' 47%, 49%, 58%, and 66%, respectively across the four sets. Thus, regarding the experimenters' manipulation of high emotion and 'primes', while this had no effect for non-ambiguous pairs, it had an effect for the ambiguous pairs. In fact, while participants' frequency of responding 'same' for the no-emotion and the low-emotion ambiguous sets was close to what it should be (ie 50%), it was significantly higher for the high-emotion set (at 58%) and for the high-emotion plus 'prime' set (at 66%). Thus, Dror et al concluded that bias induced in the participants influenced their decision-making for ambiguous pairs. (However, they noted that their participants were students and not real-life fingerprint examiners.)

Dror's next two studies did involve expert fingerprint examiners. In one (Dror, Charlton and Peron, 2006) five fingerprint experts from around the world (average 17 years' experience of examining fingerprints) consented to take part. For each of the five the experimenters were given permission to access fingerprint matches that they had made in the past in real-life cases. For each expert a match they had made in the year 2000 in the normal course of their work was chosen. Two other experts (ie not the five involved in this experiment) verified that each of the five matches (ie one for each of the five experts) was indeed a match. When filling in the consent form to take part in this experiment the five experts agreed that in the coming 12 months during the course of their normal work they would, unknown to them, be presented with a pair of fingerprints, to assess for whether they matched or not, that were actually part of this experiment. In fact, each of the five was asked by a colleague to examine a pair of fingerprints (this was a common occurrence) that the colleague said 'was the one that was erroneously matched by the FBI as the Madrid bomber' (2006, 76). After examining the pair of fingerprints three of the five experts decided that there was not a match, one said that he could not arrive at a decision, and one said that there was a match. However, in fact, the pair of fingerprints each expert was actually presented with was a pair they themselves had actually (correctly) matched in 2000! Dror et al concluded: 'This study shows that fingerprint identification decisions of experts are vulnerable to irrelevant and misleading contextual influences' (2006, 76). What the experts expected to see/decide caused some of them to make an incorrect identification response. Thus, it is not only 'lay' witnesses who can make mistaken identification decisions.

In his third study Dror again involved experts (Dror and Charlton, 2006). This time six experts (with a total of more than 35 years' relevant experience) gave permission for the experimenters to covertly access files of their past cases from some years prior. In this experiment each expert was presented with eight pairs of fingerprints from their own files (four of which unknown to them they had previously decided were a match and four of which they had decided were not a match). The correct nature of these decisions was verified for the purposes of this experiment by two other experts (each of whom had more than 20 years' experience), who also determined for each pair whether it was a 'difficult' evaluation or a 'not difficult' evaluation.

When each of the six experts was presented with the eight pairs, for four pairs they were given information that could bias them towards not deciding that a pair matched (eg 'the suspect was in police custody at the time of the crime'—2006, 608) and for the other pairs they were given information that could bias towards a match (eg 'the suspect whose print this is confessed to the crime from where the other print was taken'). For the other four pairs they were not given any biasing information. Of the six experts, two made identical decisions to their previous decisions for all eight pairs, three made seven identical decisions (out of eight), and one made five identical decisions. Of the six 'change of mind' decisions, five were of pairs independently assessed as being difficult evaluations, and four occurred when the expert had been given biasing information in the direction opposite to their own prior decision.

From the results of this study Dror and Charlton concluded that 'fingerprint experts were vulnerable to biasing information' (2006, 614) particularly in difficult cases. Even though in this experiment two of the experts made the same eight correct decisions as before, and three only changed one of their eight decisions, the results do suggest that some experts when making identification decisions can, like ordinary witnesses, make mistakes especially for difficult decisions in the presence of biasing information. Dror and Charlton also pointed out: 'This entire area of research is new in the forensic sciences and has rarely been considered before' (2006, 614) and that 'Fingerprint and other forensic experts are not immune to such psychological and cognitive factors' (2006, 612).

THE EFFECT OF EXPECTATIONS ON IDENTIFICATION

Let us now look at some other research on the biasing effects of expectations on eyewitness identifications.

In one of the earliest, comprehensive reviews of the then available research on the psychology of person identification (eg the later recognition of a once-seen crime perpetrator) Clifford and Bull (1978) noted: 'Since art began, the role of stereotypes in predisposing observers to expect individuals to behave in certain ways has been well known' (1978, 56). When choosing actors to play roles, casting directors often choose people who 'look right' for the part, so that their role becomes more believable. For example, a film director may well choose to play the role of Aimee Jones (an honest, efficient, and helpful administrator) an actress with a happy, nice, smiley face. Human beings not only expect certain looking individuals to behave in predictable ways, they also assume that particular behaviours are likely to be committed by certain looking people. Many decades ago Monaham (1941) noted that:

even social workers accustomed to dealing with all types often find it difficult to think of a normal, pretty girl as being guilty of a crime. Most people, for some inexplicable reason, think of crime in terms of abnormality of appearance and I must say that beautiful women are not often convicted. (1941, 121)

HONESTY

In one of our earliest studies (Bull, 1979) three groups of people were shown facial photographs of 11 individuals and were asked to evaluate each individual on ten rating scales (eg for attractiveness, intelligence, dishonesty). Eight of these photographs were the same across the three groups. The three other faces, however, varied across the groups. For one of these faces, one group saw him with a beard and moustache, another group saw him with just the moustache (he shaved off his beard for the purpose of this study), and the remaining group saw him neither with the beard or the moustache (ie clean shaven). For the other two faces (one male, one female) one group saw the face with two slight scars (professional make-up was used), another group saw one scar, and the remaining group saw no scars. (None of the groups saw the same amount of scarring on both faces.)

For the eight faces that were identical across the three groups, no inter-group differences were found for the ratings (as was, indeed, expected). Also, the ratings did not differ across the groups for the face that differed regarding facial hair. However, ratings did differ across the groups as a function of facial scarring. For the male face, the amount of scarring significantly affected ratings of dishonesty, unattractiveness, warmth, insincerity, and fewer friends. For the female face scarring affected ratings of dishonesty, unattractiveness, and no sense of humour. Thus, for both faces relatively minor variations in scarring affected assessments of dishonesty and unattractiveness.

A couple of years later we found (Bull and Stevens, 1981) that when a person was collecting money for a children's charity, the presence on her face (using a professional make-up artist) of a minor disfigurement resulted in fewer people donating money (and in those who did donate giving less) than when the same person had no such disfigurement. Again, it would seem that people may well have associated aspects of faces with dishonesty.

Thus, aspects of a person's facial appearance can influence judgements of that person. But can aspects of a person (eg their job, personality) affect judgements and memory for their face? Over 30 years ago Rothbart and Birrell (1977) found that students' evaluations of a stranger's face were influenced by the type of personality the experimenters ascribed to the face (ie favourable or unfavourable).

Whether honest-looking faces are easier or more difficult to recognize than less honest faces was studied by Mueller, Thompson and Vogel (1988). From their knowledge of the available literature they suggested that if dishonest faces are more distinctive and unusual than honest faces then they may be easier to recognize. However, this would depend upon which types of faces (ie dishonest or honest) were used as the 'foils' in the line-up or photo spread. In their first study participants saw 16 faces (one at a time for five seconds each). Then 25 minutes later they were presented with 32 four-person photo spreads (for 15 seconds each) half of which contained a previously seen face. From the photo spreads that did contain a previously seen face there was an effect of facial honesty in that accuracy was less (ie fewer correct choices and more incorrect choices) for arrays that contained an honest face plus dishonest foils. When the photo spreads did not contain a previously seen face many participants nevertheless chose a face, especially when a photo spread contained honest faces, which suggests greater confusion regarding honest-looking faces. In their second study the participants (who saw 32 faces—16 honest and 16 dishonest) 'were read a 100 word description of a crime in which an elderly woman was assaulted, robbed, taken to hospital, and the assailant was not captured' (1988, 120). (How this 'fits' with seeing 32 'target' faces was not explained.) As was found in their first study, recognition was less accurate for the honest faces (which were also rated higher on 'typicality' than the dishonest faces). Mueller et al concluded that honesty affects face memory because among honest faces there are more similar features than among dishonest faces. A major implication of their research is, of course, that a perpetrator who happens to have a dishonest-looking face is more likely subsequently to be recognized. However, their findings regarding target-absent photo spreads suggest that when a person has a dishonest face, but is not the perpetrator, they are less likely to be falsely identified. In their second study they tried to induce a criminal stereotyping effect, but this lacked realism and they acknowledged that in more realistic settings the stereotype that crime perpetrators have dishonest faces may have an effect. Another implication of their (first) study that is not quite so 'obvious' is that if a suspect has an honest face but is innocent, people are more likely to choose that face than a dishonest face from a (target-absent) photo spread (containing similar faces to the target).

ATTRACTIVENESS

Around 30 years ago in a seminal study by Shepherd, Ellis, McMurran and Davies, (1978) the participants constructed, using the 'photo-fit' system, a representation/ likeness of a man's face which they had just seen in a photograph. Some of the partici- pants were told that the photograph was of a lifeboat-man and the others that it was of a murderer. (However, all saw the same photograph.) The resultant 'Photofits' were shown to a new group of participants (who knew nothing of murder/lifeboat-man) who were asked to assess the Photofit faces on a number of evaluative scales. It was found that the lifeboat-man Photofits were evaluated as significantly more attrac- tive than the murderer Photofits. Thus, the actual construction of the Photofits was affected by beliefs about the person originally seen in the photograph.

COMMON KNOWLEDGE

A study by Hollin (1980) also neatly demonstrates the biasing effects of people's beliefs on their 'memory' of people. In this study a person came into/interrupted a lecture and walked around to look for the briefcase he thought he'd left there. After a while, the lecturer told the person to leave. Later the students who had been in the audience were each asked to describe the person's appearance. Regarding hair colour, 93% cor- rectly reported it as being blonde whereas only 7% correctly reported eye colour as green. In fact, of those who reported blonde hair, almost half incorrectly reported blue eyes. It seems that they had used their 'common' knowledge/beliefs that most blonde people have blue eyes incorrectly in this instance. Similarly, although members of another lecture audience all correctly reported that the person who came into their lecture had dark hair, over 50% of them incorrectly reported brown eye colour (when, in fact, it was grey), and 56% incorrectly reported dark complexion (when, in fact, it was a light complexion).

EFFECTS OF ETHNICITY

In 2004 Eberhardt, Goff, Purdie and Davies published one of the most important studies of the effects of stereotypes on memory for faces. (This study was the fourth of the five presented in their research journal paper.) Over 50 police officers from a police department in the US participated in this study. The computer-based study involved the officers having to indicate as fast as possible where a dot had briefly appeared on the computer screen. Prior to the dot appearing two faces simultane- ously briefly appeared on the screen (for around 650 milliseconds), and when these faces went off the screen the dot appeared where one of the faces had been. Unknown to the officers, for half of them just before the faces appeared a word appeared on the screen for a few milliseconds, and this 'prime' was one of ten words associated with crime (eg 'investigate', 'arrest', 'shoot'). (Later in the study it was confirmed that no participants had been aware of the primes.) These researchers were interested in whether the police officers, being from an organization in which the majority of people were 'white', would locate the dot faster if it had been preceded (in its location) by a 'black' face than a 'white' face if a crime had been on the screen (ie prior to the faces appearing). This was indeed the case, the presence of the crime prime reducing by 30% the time it took to locate the dot when in its location it had been preceded by a 'black' face.

Even more relevant to the present chapter was what happened when the officers were then presented with an unexpected facial recognition task involving five faces being presented simultaneously on the screen. These five faces (including the previous briefly seen face) purposely varied in the extent to which they were typical/stereotypical of either 'black' or 'white' facial appearance. On average the officers chose the correct face on 34% of occasions. Those officers who chose an incorrect face 'black' face, and who had been primed with the crime words, chose 'faces that were more stereotypically Black than the target' (2004, 887). No such effect took place for 'white' faces. From such findings Eberhardt et al concluded that 'Blacks who appear more stereotypically Black may be the most vulnerable to false identifications in real criminal lineups. This type of false identification may be likely even when the actual perpetrator is present in the lineup' (2004, 888).

In another of the studies reported in their 2004 paper Eberhardt et al examined whether police officers would assess 'more stereotypically Black faces as more criminal' (2004, 888). In this study 166 police officers (mostly 'White Americans') saw a series of 'colour photographs of 40 Black or 40 White male faces' (2004, 888). One third of the officers rated each face for how 'stereotypically Black or White' each seemed. Another third indicated for each face whether the person looked criminal or not. The remaining third rated the faces for attractiveness. (Overall, the two samples of faces did not differ on average attractiveness.) The 'black' faces that were rated high in stereotypicality were more frequently labelled as looking criminal than were 'black' faces rated low in stereotypicality. No such effect was found for 'white' faces. From these findings the researchers concluded that the police officers' perceptions that 'the more Black, the more criminal' (2004, 889) and the results of their police officer facial identification study (described above) could be explained by: 'Thinking of crime may have led officers to falsely identify the more stereotypically Black face because more stereotypically Black faces are more strongly associated with the concept of crime than less stereotypically Black faces' (2004, 889). (For a review of research on recognizing faces of various ethnicities, see Chapter 4).

CRIME OBJECTS

In the first of the five studies by Eberhardt el al 'white male' students tried to identify an item on the computer screen. For each item its presentation began in a severely degraded form (ie it was very difficult to see what the item was) and its presentation gradually improved in clarity 'frame by frame'. The students' task was to identify each item as soon as possible (ie while still degraded to some extent). Prior to each item being presented some of the 'participants were exposed to a Black face prime or a White face prime displayed for 30 ms'. (2004, 879). (No participants later reported being aware of primes.) Some of the items progressively presented on the screen were crime related and some were not. For the later type of item there was no effect of the type of prime. However, for the crime-related items 'Black face primes dramatically reduced the number of frames needed to accurately detect crime-relevant objects' (2004, 880).

POSITIVE BIAS

In another of their 2004 studies Eberhardt et al examined the effect of 'a positive concept associated with Black Americans' (2004, 883). 'White male' students were required to locate as quickly as possible a dot on the computer screen. Using a procedure similar to their fourth study (which was described above), some of the participants were exposed to a word prime and some were not. All participants were briefly exposed to faces where the dots would then appear. In this study the word primes were all associated with basketball and it was found that those participants exposed to these primes more quickly detected the location of the dots proceeded by 'black' faces. (There was no similar effect for 'white' faces.) From these findings Eberhardt et al concluded that this study 'demonstrates that stereotypic associations other than crime can lead to visual tuning effects' (2004, 885).

DANGEROUS BIASES

In the overall discussion of their studies' findings these researchers noted:

police officers may face elevated levels of danger in the presence of White armed suspects in comparison to Black armed suspects. For example, if police officers have a delayed response to White suspects . . . these officers may be more likely to get hurt, shot, or killed. (2004, 890)

They also noted that 'innocent Blacks may easily become the target of intense visual surveillance'. (2004, 890).

Similar points were made in 2001 by Payne who noted:

In February 1999 four White New York Police officers shot and killed . . . an unarmed Black immigrant in a hail of 41 bullets . . . at the moment that police officers ordered him to stop he moved, producing an object that later turned out to be a wallet. (2001, 181)

In Payne's first experiment (2001, 183) 'photographs of White and Black male faces were used as primes' (ie shown briefly) after which either a gun or a tool briefly appeared on the computer screen. Participants were required to indicate gun or tool as quickly as possible. The response times for guns were faster when they were preceded by a black face than a white face, but were faster for tools when primed by a white face. Payne suggested that such bias is largely automatic (ie not under conscious control), especially in situations which consume considerable cognitive resources. Thus, controlling such a process within oneself would be difficult. (Also see similar research by Payne, Lambert and Jacoby, 2002.)

A 2002 study by Correll Pank, Judd and Wittenbrink examined the effects of ethnicity on shoot/don't-shoot decisions. In a computer game setting they found that students shot at an armed target quicker when he was African American than when he was white, and that participants failed to shoot an armed target more often when he was white than when he was African American. Furthermore, if the target was not armed he was shot more often when he was African American. (Most of the participants were white.) Somewhat similarly, Greenwald, Oakes and Hoffman (2003) found in a computer simulation that the ethnicity of the target influenced whether or not the objects held by targets were 'seen' and responded to as guns or as harmless objects. Such studies as this and several of those reviewed above are likely to have relevance to the 2005 shooting by the London Metropolitan Police of the Brazilian Jean Charles de Menezes whom they misidentified as a terrorist.

REDUCING STEREOTYPES

Training people to try not to be affected by such stereotypes was examined by Kawa-Kanu Dovidio, Moll, Hermsen and Russin (2000) who found that 'participants who received extensive training in negating stereotypes were able to reduce this stereotype activation' (2000, 884). Basically the training involved responding 'No' (on many occasions) to stereotypes when they arose in association with photographs of people.

A more recent study extends our understanding of stereotypes. Sherman, Stroessner, Conrey and Azam (2005) found that participants who were higher in prejudice ignored a man's counter-stereotypical behaviour when evaluating him if he was from a group about whom they were prejudiced. Participants lower in prejudice took his behaviour into account. Furthermore, participants higher in prejudice attributed causation for the man's behaviour to himself when these behaviours were consistent with their stereotype but to factors external to him when these behaviours were inconsistent with their stereotype. Sherman et al concluded that 'higher prejudice was associated with both biased encoding and judgment processes' (2003, 618).

BIAS FOR EVENTS

Some of the studies so far mentioned in this chapter have demonstrated how people's expectations/beliefs can influence what they report about a once-seen person's facial appearance. We will now turn to studies that demonstrate similar phenomena for the reporting of what people did. Over 25 years ago Sagar and Schofield (1980) provided school pupils/students with oral descriptions plus drawings of four interpersonal acts involving two pupils/students (ie requesting food from another student, using another student's pencil without permission, bumping into another student in the hallway, poking another student in the classroom). Each interpersonal act involved one of 'four possible black/white racial permutations of actors and targets' (1980, 593). These researchers found that the participants rated 'the behaviours of the black actors more mean/threatening than identical behaviour by white actors' (1980, 594) (and that the 'race' of the participants had no effect on this). Duncan (1976) found that people described/remembered an 'ambiguous shove' as being 'more violent when it was performed by a black than when the same act was perpetrated by a white' (1976, 590).

A similar effect was found by Bodenhausen and Wyer (1985) who asked students in the US to take part in a study of disciplinary decision making. The students read (mock) employee personnel files which included a description of an employment related infraction committed by that person. Some students read a file with the name 'Albert Ellman' at the beginning, and others the file of 'Ahmad Gazah'. The infraction involved either 'uncooperativeness' or 'laziness'. (A prior study had established that uncooperativeness was stereotypically associated with 'American' employees and laziness with 'Arab' employees.) The students were asked to assume the role of a personnel manager when later answering questions about the file. It was found that the students recommended more severe disciplinary action when the infraction matched the apparent ethnicity of the name in the file. Furthermore, with regard to the other information in the file, less of it was recalled when the person's infraction was stereotypical. Bodenhausen and Wyer attributed this information recall effect to the notion that when a stereotype based explanation was available, the participants needed less information from the file. They also noted: 'Transgressions that are consistent with a cultural stereotype of the transgressor appear to be attributed to stable dispositional factors rather than to transitory or unstable ones' (1985, 279).

Boon and Davies (1996) conducted a similar but more complex study that built upon (but was more methodologically rigorous than) Hastorf and Contril's pioneering 1954 study of how beliefs influence the perceived extent of wrong-doing. Boon and Davies noted that eyewitnesses do not passively record information impartially like a video recorder. Rather, they actually select (and process) from the available information. They pointed out that 'schema theory' can account for active selection and processing (and therefore selective remembering). Schema theory involves the following four aspects of the event/person information: (i) selection; (ii) abstraction; (iii) inference; and (iv) integration. Most of the time these four aspects allow us to deal rapidly and effectively with what takes place, especially in complex, fast-moving events. However, they sometimes produce biased processing/remembering, as Boon and Davies found. In their study, students from England and from Scotland were shown 25 excerpts from a previous football match between England and Scotland. Each excerpt involved an incident involving players from both teams. After seeing each excerpt the students had to indicate which of seven actions available to the match referee was appropriate (ie send off English player, yellow card for English player, free kick to Scotland, no action, free kick to England, yellow card for Scottish player, send off Scottish player). After making their 25 decisions the participants were each asked to what extent they usually were a supporter of English/Scottish football teams. Around a quarter of the participants indicated that they had no such national team allegiance, but over a third indicated allegiance to Scotland and a similar number an allegiance to England. Each participants' assessment of what the referee should have done for each of the 25 excerpts was summed across the 25 assessments to provide a 'perceptual rating score'. Statistical analyses of these scores found that the scores of those participants with team allegiances were affected by which team they supported (whereas the 'neutral' participants' perceptual rating scores were non-partisan). Boon and Davies' study indicates that evaluations of who was responsible for wrong-doing can easily be influenced by people's partisanship.

Five years later Boon and Davies (2001) produced another important study. They noted that our comprehension of complex events (including which person did what) is dependent not only on information that was actually in the events but also on information that was not present but contributed by the observer. The knowledge/experience of the observer helps to make sense of events and to react quickly to them. However, on occasion this contribution by the observer (often referred to by psychologists as 'top-down processing') can bias interpretation and recall. They noted that Dooling and Christiaansen (1977) had developed a 'hierarchical coding model of schema theory' that holds that information attended to 'is tagged according to its perceived importance for the schema that is in operation at the time of encoding . . . details of relatively low significance . . . will be tagged accordingly and will be forgotten most quickly' (Boon and Davies, 2001, 518). In Boon and Davies' study participants saw a film of a man's visit to a country house. Half of them were told that he was an insurance man on legitimate business, and half that he was a criminal conducting a reconnaissance for a later robbery from the house. The five-and-a-half minute long film consisted of ten sequences. Two versions of a short 150-word biography of the man were produced which differed somewhat. For example, the insurance man was described as having completed military service but the criminal as having served time in a detention centre for young offenders.

Having watched the film the participants one week later participated in a recognition test involving eight pairs of film clips which they had to rate for likelihood of having been in the film. Four of these pairs of film clips involved both (i) a more suspicious and (ii) a less suspicious version of the man's original actions. The other four pairs of film clips involved (i) a correct and (ii) an incorrect version of aspects of the original film that the researchers deemed to be non-critical (eg which door of his car the man opened to put his coat into the car). The recognition test data revealed a significant effect of 'criminal versus insurance man' in that participants' told he was a criminal favoured the more suspicious sequences. (There was, as expected, no effect of 'criminal versus insurance man' for the non-critical items.) From this study Boon and Davies concluded that 'memory can be distorted by extra stimulus information' (2001, 525).

BIAS FOR HEIGHT

Indeed, an earlier and simpler study (see Bull, Bustin, Evans and Gahagan, 1983) found that people's memory of the height of a person whom they had just seen was influenced by the status (the experimenter) assigned to the person. That is, participants were told that the person was a professor or a senior lecturer, or a lecturer or a laboratory demonstrator or a student (ie there were five groups of participants). The height 'memories' systematically varied across status, with the average for 'professor' being three inches taller than for 'student'. In another study, even though the person was still in view (at distances of 20 or 50 or 80 feet) whether participants were told he was a professor or a student influenced how tall they said he was, especially at 80 feet (ie 73 inches versus 69 inches).

LINE-UP CHOICE

Faces that fit people's expectations of what criminals look like have been found easier to recognize than faces low in criminality. In MacLin and MacLin's (2004) second experiment students first saw a series of 24 faces (for one second each). Twelve of the faces had a 'high criminality' appearance (this was established in the first study) and 12 were 'low criminality'. (In the first study faces rated high in criminality were also rated as less attractive, less typical, and more memorable.) Fifteen minutes later the students were presented with a series of 48 faces (each for three seconds) and were required to say for each face whether it was one of the 24 they had seen previously. Significantly more of the high criminality faces were correctly recognized (74%) than of the low criminality faces (57%). These researchers also reported another study in which participants were asked to select from a line-up the person who matched either (a) a physical description provided by the experimenters or (b) the physical description plus that the described person was wanted for armed robbery. The results of this study demonstrated that those given only the physical description all correctly chose from the line-up. However, some in the 'physical description plus armed robbery' condition incorrectly chose the face that more closely matched (by prior study) the stereotype of an armed robber. In light of their findings MacLin and MacLin noted: 'When a person whose face would be rated high in criminality is both the suspect and the actual perpetrator, criminality works for the legal system, aiding in recognition and identification' (2004, 153). However, they also noted that sometimes a suspect's face may appear high in criminality, but this person is not the perpetrator. They concluded that: 'A more complete understanding of the effects of criminality on the psychological processes inherent in the criminal justice system is needed' (2004, 153).

CAN SOME STEREOTYPES BE ACCURATE?

So far, this chapter has focused on psychological research which demonstrates how stereotypes can have an unduly biasing effect. However, a few remarkable studies have been published (some long ago) that suggest that people's beliefs about what criminals look like may be accurate.

It is relatively easy to run a study which demonstrates that people share beliefs about which facial appearances are associated with different types of criminal (eg drug-dealing, company fraud, robbery with violence). For example, Bull and Green (1980) showed people ten photographs of different looking men (in fact, of friends and acquaintances) and asked people to say which of 11 crimes each man had committed. For eight of the crimes people (independently) consistently chose a face (which differed across the crimes). However, none of the faces were actually of criminals. A remarkable 1939 study used the faces of actual criminals. From prison files, Thornton chose (without seeing the faces) 20 case files regarding four different crimes. Participants in the study saw (only) the 20 faces and were asked to indicate which of the four crimes each man had committed. The results demonstrated that participants were correct more often than would be accountable by chance. Thus, something in the faces matched with people's stereotypes. In 1962 a somewhat similar and equally remarkable study was published by Kozeny. In this German study photographs of 730 criminals were put into one of 16 piles depending on what the person had been convicted of. From each of these 16 piles a composite was photographically produced. Participants were asked to indicate which composite went with which crime type and a fair proportion did this with some accuracy. Thus, it is possible that, to an extent, people's expectations of which faces match which crimes may sometimes have some accuracy to them.

CONCLUSION

This chapter has demonstrated that human perception and memory are regularly influenced by the expectations and stereotypes held about people. These stereotypes and expectations are likely not only to bias ordinary witness memory for who did what and what perpetrators looked like, but also relevant professionals, such as experienced fingerprint experts. It seems that even the perception of the possession of a weapon can be affected. Aspects of facial appearance such as honesty and attractiveness can also influence which faces are identified. Clearly, the complex functioning of the human brain, so often of benefit, can sometimes lead to errors.

FURTHER READING

EBERHARDT, J., GOFF, P., PURDIE, V. and DAVIES, P. (2004). Seeing Black: Race, crime, and visual processing. *Journal of Personality and Social Psychology, 87*, 876–893.

DROR, I., PERON, A., HIND, S-L. and CHARLTON, D. (2005). When emotions get the better of us: The effect of contextual top-down processing on matching fingerprints. *Applied Cognitive Psychology, 19*, 799–809.

MACLIN, O. and MACLIN, M.K. (2004). The effect of criminality on face attractiveness, typicality memorability and recognition. *North American Journal of Psychology, 6*, 145–154.

REFERENCES

BODENHAUSEN, G. and WYER, R. (1985). Effects of stereotypes on decision making and information processing strategies. *Journal of Personality and Social Psychology, 48*, 267–282.

BOON, J. and DAVIES, G. (1996). Extra-stimulus influences on eyewitness perception and recall: Hastorf and Cantril revisited. *Legal and Criminological Psychology, 1*, 155–164.

—— and —— (2001). The influence of biographical information on event memory. *Journal of General Psychology, 120,* 517–530.

BULL, R. (1979). The psychological significance of facial deformity. In M. Cook and G. Wilson (eds) *Love and attraction.* Oxford: Pergamon, 21–25.

——, BUSTIN, B., EVANS, P. and GAHAGAN, D. (1983). *Psychology for Police Officers.* Chichester: Wiley.

—— and GREEN, J. (1980). The relationship between physical appearance and criminality. *Medicine, Science and the Law, 20,* 79–83.

—— and STEVENS, J. (1981). The effects of facial disfigurement on helping behaviour. *Italian Journal of Psychology, 8,* 25–33.

CORRELL, J., PANK, B., JUDD, C. and WITTENBRINK, B. (2002). The police officer's dilemma: Using ethnicity to disambiguate potentially threatening individuals. *Journal of Personality and Social Psychology, 83,* 1314–1329.

DROR, I. and CHARLTON, D. (2006). Why experts make errors. *Journal of Forensic Identification, 56,* 600–616.

——, —— and PERON, A. (2005). Contextual information renders experts vulnerable to making erroneous identifications. *Forensic Science International, 156,* 74–78.

——, ——, HIND, S-L. and CHARLTON, D. (2005). When emotions get the better of us: The effect of contextual top-down processing on matching fingerprints. *Applied Cognitive Psychology, 19,* 799–809.

DUNCAN, B. (1976). Differential social perception and attribution of intergroup violence. *Journal of Personality and Social Psychology, 34,* 590–598.

EBERHARDT, J., GOFF, P., PURDIE, V. and DAVIES, P. (2004). Seeing Black: Race, crime, and visual processing. *Journal of Personality and Social Psychology, 87,* 876–893.

GREENWALD, A., OAKES, M. and HOFFMAN, H. (2003). Targets of discrimination: Effects of race on responses to weapon holders. *Journal of Experimental Social Psychology, 39,* 399–405.

HASTORF, A. and CONTRIL, H. (1954). They saw a game. A case study. *Journal of Abnormal and Social Psychology, 97,* 129–134.

HOLLIN, C. (1980). *An investigation of certain social, situational, and individual factors in eyewitness testimony.* Unpublished PhD thesis, North East London Polytechnic.

KOZENY, E. (1962). Experimental investigation of physiognomy utilising a photographic statistical method. *Archiv fur die Gesamte Psychologie, 114,* 55–71.

MACLIN, O. and MACLIN, M.K. (2004). The effect of criminality on face attractiveness, typicality memorability and recognition. *North American Journal of Psychology, 6,* 145–154.

MONAHAN, F. (1941). *Women in Crime.* New York: Ives Washburn.

MUELLER, J., THOMPSON, W.B. and VOGEL, J. (1988). Perceived honesty and face memory. *Personality and Social Psychology Bulletin, 14,* 114–124.

PAYNE, B. K. (2001). Prejudice and perception: The role of automatic and controlled processes in misperceiving a weapon. *Journal of Personality and Social Psychology, 81,* 181–192.

——, LAMBERT, A. and JACOBY, L. (2002). Best laid plans: Effects of goals on accessibility bias and cognitive control in race-based misperceptions of weapons. *Journal of Experimental Social Psychology, 38,* 384–396.

ROTHBART, M. and BIRRELL, P. (1977). Attitude and the perception of faces. *Journal of Research in Personality, 11,* 209–215.

SAGAR, H.A. and SCHOFIELD, J.W. (1980). Racial and behavioural cues in black and white children's perceptions of ambiguously aggressive acts. *Journal of Personality and Social Psychology, 39,* 590–598.

SHEPHERD, J., ELLIS, H., McMURRAN, M. and DAVIES, G. (1978). The effect of character attribution on photofit construction of a face. *European Journal of Social Psychology, 8,* 263–268.

SHERMAN, J., STROESSNER, S., CONREY, F. and AZAM, O. (2005). Prejudice and stereotype maintenance processes: Attention, attribution and individuation. *Journal of Personality and Social Psychology, 89,* 607–622.

THORNTON, G. (1939). The ability to judge crimes from photographs of criminals. *Journal of Abnormal and Social Psychology, 34,* 378–383.

7

RECOMMENDATIONS FOR CONDUCTING IDENTIFICATION PARADES

INTRODUCTION

Throughout the course of this book many different factors that affect the accuracy of eyewitness identification evidence have been discussed. In Chapter 4 we reviewed factors relating to the witness (eg age), the perpetrator (eg distinctiveness), and the crime event itself (eg duration). Wells (1978) termed these factors *estimator variables*. The Criminal Justice System is unable to control these factors and their effect on subsequent identification accuracy can only be estimated after the crime has occurred. Conversely, *system variables* are factors that are under the control of the Criminal Justice System. Examples of system variables include construction of a line-up, presentation of a line-up, and instructions given to witnesses relating to a line-up. Vast amounts of research have been conducted which examine the impact of system variables on identification accuracy and some of this research relates to, and in some cases has guided, current legislation and guidelines concerned with the conduct of identification procedures here in the UK (Police and Criminal Evidence Act (PACE) Code D), in the US (Wells et al, 1998; Technical Working Group, 1999), and in Canada (Turtle, Lindsay and Wells, 2003). This chapter will give an overview of the empirical research upon which some of the recommendations for conducting identification procedures have been made.

MULTIPLE WITNESSES VIEWING AN IDENTIFICATION PARADE

Sometimes crimes are witnessed by more than one person. If this occurs it is easy to understand that multiple witnesses (referred to as co-witnesses in relevant research) will naturally discuss with one another what happened, bearing in mind that the event they witnessed is likely to be out of the ordinary. Indeed, Paterson and Kemp (2006) found that in 86% of criminal cases where multiple witnesses were present the witnesses discussed what occurred. Gabbert, Memon and Allen (2003) found that 71% of witnesses reported erroneous information which was presented to a co-witness with whom they had a discussion about the event but which the 'original' witnesses had not directly seen in the event. Beaudry, Lindsay and Dupuis (2006) suggest that separation of witnesses, including emergency personnel (police, paramedics, and fire), should occur as soon as possible after the crime has been committed, prior to even obtaining a description of the perpetrator. In terms of identification, PACE Code D stipulates that the officer responsible for conducting an identification procedure should ensure that multiple witnesses are not able to communicate with each other prior to them viewing a parade, nor overhear a witness who has already viewed the parade, and that only one witness at a time should view the parade.

Research investigating to what extent multiple witnesses' influence each other in relation to line-ups has also focused on the role of co-witness feedback on judgements of confidence that the identification made is accurate. This is important because jurors are more likely to believe confident witnesses (Wells, Lindsay and Ferguson, 1979). Luus and Wells (1994) found that witnesses who had received feedback that their fellow witness (co-witness) identified the same person as they had reported increased confidence, while witnesses told that a co-witness had identified somebody different or had not made an identification reported decreased confidence. In a more recent study Skagerberg (2007) found that pairs of witnesses who directly gave their partners (opposed to an experimenter or someone perceived to be in authority) confirming feedback that they had picked the same person from the line-up were more certain that they were correct in their identification decision than pairs whose partners gave disconfirming feedback. Moreover, pairs who agreed on their line-up choice were more likely to say (i) they had a better look at the perpetrator and (ii) would be more likely to testify in court compared to pairs who disagreed over their line-up choice.

CONSTRUCTING A LINE-UP

Constructing a line-up is by no means a simple task. There are several issues to be considered. Underlying all of these issues is the notion that the line-up needs to be a fair test of identification for the witness as well as being fair to suspects. For example, the line-up needs to be constructed in a manner so that the suspect does not stand out so that the witness is not inadvertently led to the suspect for any other reason except a valid recognition of the suspect as the perpetrator of the crime they witnessed. Bearing this in mind, it is important to consider the number of suspects per parade, size of parade, and bias in a parade when constructing line-ups.

ONE OR MORE SUSPECTS IN A PARADE

The US *Eyewitness Evidence: A Guide for Law Enforcement* (Technical Working Group, 1999) stipulates that only one suspect should be included in each identification parade. PACE Code D stipulates that only one suspect shall appear in any set (line-up), unless there are two suspects of roughly similar appearance, in which case they may be shown in a larger line-up containing extra foils. This in reality happens very rarely (personal communication, Crossley, 2007). Wells and Turtle (1986) cite findings from a survey of line-up practices from 22 police departments in the Midwestern US which suggested that a number of police departments did use an all suspect model where every member of the line-up was a suspect for that particular crime. As a result of this Wells and Turtle highlighted the importance of being able to identify when a witness has made a known error (ie has identified a known-to-be innocent foil). This can only occur when a line-up contains one suspect and the rest of the members are known-to-be innocent foils (compared to a line-up that contains only suspects). They also pointed out that the inclusion of more than one suspect increases the probability that a suspect is identified by chance alone. For these reasons, if there are multiple suspects for one crime it is better to create separate line-ups for them.

LINE-UP SIZE

The larger the line-up the less likely it is that the suspect will be identified by chance alone (Wells and Turtle, 1986). PACE Code D stipulates there should be at least eight other people in addition to the suspect. *Eyewitness Evidence: A Guide for Law Enforcement* stipulates there should be a minimum of five fillers in addition to the suspect. Research has considered line-up size but none has demonstrated an optimal number. Nosworthy and Lindsay (1990) investigated 'nominal size' (the mere number of line-up members) and found that as long as a line-up contained three good-quality foils increasing the number of foils (between 3 and 20) had no effect on line-up accuracy.

LINE-UP BIAS

When considering constructing line-ups we need to go beyond nominal size and think about the quality of the foils. A large line-up with 11 foils would produce a nominal size of 12, but if the quality of all the foils is poor and the suspect stands out, functionally this is a line-up of one (Wells, 1993). A classic example to illustrate this comes from a case in the US where a witness described the perpetrator as being a black male. The police constructed a line-up containing one black suspect and five white foils (Ellison and Buckhout, 1981). Essentially this line-up had a functional size of one (ie it was a show-up rather than a line-up). The purpose of a line-up is to give the witness a fair opportunity to see if they can recognize the perpetrator of the crime they witnessed from an array of similar looking individuals. In so doing it is important to have good foils in the line-up. Therefore, the suspect should not stand out in anyway and all the foils should be viable alternatives to the suspect.

METHODS FOR SELECTING LINE-UP FOILS

PACE Code D stipulates that people (line-up foils) should be selected who, so far as possible, resemble the suspect in age, height, general appearance, and position in life. In light of this, in the UK foils are selected using a 'match to similarity of the suspect method'. Furthermore, 83% of respondents to a questionnaire sent to US police jurisdictions asking about line-up construction and delivery stated they adopted a match to similarity of the suspect approach when constructing line-ups (Wogalter,

Malpass and McQuiston, 2004). However, some research suggests that selecting foils based on their similarity to the suspect may present some difficulties. Luus and Wells (1991) suggest two related issues. First, how far do you go in matching the similarity of various facial features? This method gives no guidance on how similar foils need to be in order for the line-up to be fair. Second, if a line-up administrator had a very large database of potential foils, one could potentially end up with a line-up full of clones of the suspect. This would make the witnesses' task too difficult.

An alternative method for selecting foils is to use a 'match to witnesses' description of the perpetrator method'. In fact, the *Eyewitness Evidence: A Guide for Law Enforcement* stipulates that fillers should be selected who generally fit the witnesses' description of the perpetrator. The underlying notion with this method is that line-up foils will be selected on the basis that they match key features given by witnesses in their description but that they will differ on certain features not mentioned in the witnesses' description. This means the suspect should not stand out relative to the foils and equally all foils should be viable alternatives. However, the witness could recognize particular features of the perpetrator that they were unable to recall in their verbal description (Wells, Rydell and Seelau, 1993).

Using a match to witnesses' description of the perpetrator however, does have some practical limitations. First, witnesses rarely provide adequate descriptions and may even sometimes leave out key pieces of information such as race and sex. (This problem may also be exacerbated if the witness has been subject to a poor interview, eg they were asked leading questions relating to the description of the perpetrator (see Chapter 3).) It is unlikely that witnesses do not remember the race and sex of a perpetrator but more likely they simply presume a 'default value' (Lindsay, Martin and Weber, 1994). Therefore, when witnesses are interviewed care needs to be taken to ensure that such default values are not left out of their descriptions. Second, if there are multiple witnesses of a crime there is every possibility that there will be differences in their descriptions. Assuming the differences are not great Malpass, Tredoux and McQuiston-Surrett (2007) suggest creating a composite description that includes all the descriptors given by all witnesses. However, if there are meaningful differences between witnesses' descriptions the need for creating separate line-ups for different witnesses could arise. Third, a situation may occur where a feature in the description may be discrepant from the suspect. For example, the description may state the perpetrator had facial hair but when the suspect arrives he is clean shaven. In this situation, to ensure the suspect does not stand out, all foils should also be clean shaven (Beaudry et al, 2006; Valentine, 2006).

THE EFFECT OF LINE-UP CONSTRUCTION METHODS ON LINE-UP PERFORMANCE

Some research has investigated the effect of line-ups constructed using the 'match to similarity of the suspect' method versus line-ups constructed using a 'match to witnesses description of the perpetrator' method on witnesses' line-up performance. Wells et al (1993) found in a laboratory study that line-ups constructed using 'match to witnesses' description of the perpetrator' led to higher correct identifications and lower false identifications compared to line-ups constructed using a 'match to similarity of the suspect' method. In a further laboratory study Lindsay et al (1994) also found higher correct identifications (though not significantly) with a line-up composed using a 'match to composite description of the perpetrator' compared to a 'similarity to suspect' constructed line-up. Tunnicliff and Clark (2000) report two studies where police officers (study 1) and undergraduate students (study 2) constructed line-ups using not only 'similarity to suspect' methods but also 'similarity to witnesses' description of the perpetrator'. However, no significant differences were found in correct or false identifications between the two methods across the two studies. In the most recent investigation, Darling, Valentine and Memon (2008) selected line-up foils adopting either a 'similarity to suspect' method or a 'similarity to witnesses' description of the perpetrator' method from the VIPER database (see Chapter 9 for a description of VIPER) used by approximately half of the police forces in England and Wales to construct video parades. There were no significant differences in witnesses' performance on either target present (TP) or target absent (TA) video line-ups according to line-up construction method. The findings reported by Darling et al were obtained from an ecologically valid study, and when coupled with the findings of Tunnicliff and Clark (2000), they suggest that currently there is little reason to change the way in which line-ups are constructed in the UK using a 'similarity to the suspect' method.

MEASURING LINE-UP FAIRNESS

Once a line-up has been constructed researchers have devised various methods of assessing the fairness of the line-up. Methods have focused on measuring line-up bias (eg whether the line-up is biased towards the suspect) and line-up size (eg whether there are a sufficient number of foils that are viable alternatives to the suspect to reduce the possibility of an innocent suspect being identified by chance). Such research began with Doob and Kirshenbaum (1973) which was based on their assessment of a real line-up in a Canadian case. They showed 'mock witnesses' who had not seen the actual crime the description of the culprit given by the witness. Having read the description these mock witnesses were asked to view the 12-person line-up and guess who they thought the police suspect was. Had the line-up been fair, one would have expected the rate of guessing whom the suspect was to be 1/12. In this case 11 out of 21 mock witnesses guessed who the suspect was (just based on reading a description of the perpetrator), indicating that the line-up was biased towards the suspect. This method is known as the proportions technique and is a measure of line-up bias. Other measures of line-up fairness have all used mock witnesses to evaluate fairness of line-ups.

Examples of Measures of Line-up Fairness

Functional Size is a measure of line-up bias. It is calculated by dividing the total number of mock witnesses by the number who select the suspect (Wells, Leippe and Ostrom, 1979). For example, if there are 20 mock witnesses, and based only on reading the description of the perpetrator, 15 of them select the suspect from a six-person line-up then the functional size is 1.3. This would mean the line-up is very biased towards the suspect. Conversely, if there are 20 mock witnesses and only four of them select the suspect, the functional size would be five, which suggests that the line-up is not biased towards the suspect. However, one of the problems with functional size is that it fails to take into account the distribution of foil choices (ie whether one or more foils are being chosen at an above chance rate or are never chosen).

Effective Size is a measure of line-up size which measures the number of viable foils. Those foils chosen by mock witnesses at a rate which differs to that expected by chance (eg are never chosen) are deemed not to be effective alternative choices (Malpass, 1981). The maximum effective size is the maximum number of line-up members. The minimum effective size is one (assuming that a mock witness chooses one member of the line-up). Effective size is calculated by subtracting from the nominal size of the line-up for each foil chosen by mock witnesses at a rate which differs to that expected by chance.

For more details on these and other measures of line-up fairness see Malpass et al (2007).

All the above methods of measuring line-up fairness use mock witnesses. It is therefore important to consider the extent to which such evaluations of fairness are likely to translate to actual eyewitness performance. Malpass et al (2007) suggest that because mock witnesses (who have only seen a description of the perpetrator) differ from actual witnesses (who have a visual memory of the perpetrator), a line-up that is evaluated as fair on the basis of verbal description may not be fair for real witnesses who may rely more on visual memory. However, surprisingly little published research has examined this question. Lindsay, Smith and Pryke (1999) found some evidence that measures of line-up bias were linked with witness performance on a line-up. For example, a simultaneous line-up deemed to be unfair to the suspect on the basis of a measure of line-up bias did lead to more false identifications of a designated innocent suspect on a TA line-up. For TP simultaneous line-ups, fairer line-ups lead to fewer correct identifications of the perpetrator compared to unfair line-ups. Thus, on the basis of this study measures of line-up fairness do appear to relate to witness performance. However, further research is required before firm conclusions should be drawn regarding the utility of mock witness measures of line-up fairness for actual witnesses.

PRESENTING A LINE-UP

Once a line-up has been constructed, decisions still need to be made as to how to present it. Research has focused on two issues in relation to line-up presentation. First, through what media should line-ups be presented, either live, on videotape, or photographs? Second, whether all line-up members should be presented together (simultaneously) or whether each line-up member should be presented one at a time (sequentially). These two issues will be examined in turn.

LINE-UP MEDIA

The US *Eyewitness Evidence: A Guide for Law Enforcement* gives guidance for presenting both live line-ups and photographic line-ups. In the UK identification parades, until recently, were live but now the vast majority of them are presented using video/DVD. Some research has examined the effectiveness of live line-ups versus photo line-ups versus videotaped line-ups on witness performance using a mock witness paradigm. Cutler and Fisher (1990) found there was no significant effect of line-up media (live, photo, video) for participants who had viewed a staged event and then after a delay of 16 days attempted to identify the perpetrator from either a TP or TA line-up. However, when the line-up was TA participants who had seen either a live or videotaped line-up were significantly less likely to make false identifications compared to participants who had viewed a photographic line-up. In a more thorough investigation Cutler, Berman, Penrod and Fisher (1994) reviewed findings from seven studies which had specifically tested the effect of line-up media on witness performance. They concluded that there seems to be little difference between live and videotaped line-ups. They found it more difficult to draw any firm conclusion as to whether photograph line-ups might lead to poorer performance (due to their lack of richness of information). When Cutler et al (1994) considered the findings relating to line-up media from Shapiro and Penrod's (1986) meta-analysis, which examined studies that adopted widely varying methods (alongside the seven studies they reviewed), they suggested that line-up media is unlikely to have a robust effect on witness performance.

Therefore, at present, the findings from mock witness studies suggest that (i) live and videotaped line-ups may not be significantly better than photographic line-ups (though this finding could result from the fact that different studies employed slightly different methodologies to examine the effects of line-up media), and (ii) there is little difference between video line-ups and live line-ups. If there is little difference between live and videotaped line-ups, it is worth considering the practical issues associated with each. Slater (1994) identified several issues which can arise with live line-ups including, the costs, problems with a suspect arriving for a parade where foils have been organized only to find the suspect has changed his/her appearance, and the stress involved for a witness viewing a live parade. With videotaped line-ups, once the necessary initial financial investment has been made, they are cheaper to run in the long term, a suspect's image can be captured as soon as they are arrested to reduce the chance that their appearance has changed substantially, and stress for the witness is likely to be reduced. Furthermore, there are additional advantages of videotaped line-ups including: (i) foils can be selected from a very large database, meaning they are likely to be better quality than foils selected for live line-ups; (ii) there is no risk that line-up members will 'act up' thus invalidating the procedure; and (iii) parades can be shown at a time that is convenient to the witness(es) (Pike, Brace and Kynan, 2002).

PACE Code D gives instructions for live and video line-ups, but as mentioned above, nearly all identification procedures in the UK are now shown on videotape/DVD. Valentine and Heaton (1999) considered the fairness of video line-ups compared with live line-ups. They used mock witnesses to evaluate the fairness of real police identification parades that had either been shown on videotape or that were live (and a photograph had been taken of the live parade). Mock witnesses were given a witnesses description of the culprit and asked on the basis of that description alone to identify who they thought the suspect was (as per the Doob and Kirshenbaum (1973) procedure for evaluating line-up fairness described above). One would expect for a line-up containing nine members that the suspect should be identified by mock witnesses (just using a description of the culprit) with a one in nine chance (ie at a rate of 11%). However, 25% of mock witnesses identified the suspect from the photos of live parades, compared to only 15% from the videotape parades. The probability that the suspect was chosen from the videotape parades was not significantly different from that assuming equal distribution of choices among all parade members but the proportion of witnesses identifying the suspect from live parades was significantly higher than would be expected by chance alone. In a further study to evaluate the fairness of video line-ups for white suspects and African-Caribbean suspects Valentine, Harris, Colman Piera and Darling (2003) showed white and African-Caribbean mock witnesses descriptions of white European suspects, African-Caribbean suspects, and white European/African-Caribbean dual ethnicity suspects. There was no significant effect of identification parade race (or mock witness race) on mock witness identifications of the suspect. Thus, it seems that video parades are fair to white suspects as well as to suspects from other ethnic groups, possibly because with video parades the police usually have a much fuller database of faces from which they can select appropriate foils.

The media in which a parade is shown has clear implications for how members of a line-up are presented, for example in either a sequential or simultaneous fashion.

SIMULTANEOUS VERSUS SEQUENTIAL LINE-UP PRESENTATION

Simultaneous versus sequential line-up presentation has been one of the most debated topics in eyewitness identification research in recent years. In the first study to investigate sequential line-ups Lindsay and Wells (1985) showed half of their participants a simultaneous line-up (ie all faces were viewed at the same time) and half of their participants a sequential line-up. The sequential presentation involved participants viewing the line-up photos one at a time and deciding for each whether or not that photo was the criminal. They were told that they could take as long as they wanted looking at each photo but they would only see the photo once. The six line-up photos were held in a pack of 12 photos to help to persuade witnesses that there may be more than six photos in the line-up to reduce the possibility that they would feel pressured to make a 'yes' response as they neared the end of the line-up. After photo six the line-up was stopped. Lindsay and Wells found that sequential presentation led to a significant reduction in false identifications compared to simultaneous presentation, without any significant impact on correct identifications. They suggested that this could be due to participants adopting different decision strategies for simultaneous rather than sequential line-ups. When witnesses view a simultaneous line-up they can select the member of the line-up (relative to the other line-up members) who most resembles their memory for the perpetrator (a relative judgement). A relative judgement strategy is adequate when the target is present in a line-up, however, it can lead to false identifications when the target is absent. With a sequential line-up witnesses are forced to decide 'yes' or 'no' as to whether this is the perpetrator or not for each line-up member (an absolute judgement strategy). Lindsay and Wells believe that the change in judgement strategy from relative to absolute with a sequential line-up led to the reduction in false identifications. Indeed Kneller, Memon and Stevenage (2001) examined the use of relative and absolute judgement strategies across sequential and simultaneous line-ups. The results revealed that witnesses reported both relative and absolute judgement strategies when viewing simultaneous line-ups but only absolute judgement strategies when viewing sequential line-ups. Witnesses reporting use of absolute judgement strategies were more likely to be accurate.

Since their pioneering 1985 experiment, many studies have also found a beneficial effect of sequential line-up presentation in reducing false identifications compared with simultaneous line-up presentation (for example, see the meta-analysis conducted by Steblay, Dysart, Fulero and Lindsay, 2001). However, this 2001 meta-analysis (which involved 23 studies) also noted that sequential presentation of target present line-ups led to a reduction in correct identifications (compared to simultaneous presentation). Furthermore, in the years since this meta-analysis was published, other studies (which have adopted more real world conditions) have also found that sequential presentation can lead to a significant reduction in correct identifications from TP line-ups made by young and elderly witnesses (eg Memon and Gabbert, 2003; Wilcock, Bull and Vrij, 2005). While it is desirable to develop a procedure that reliably reduces the rate of false identifications, this should not be at the cost of decreasing the rate of correct identifications of the crime perpetrator. *Eyewitness Evidence: A Guide for Law Enforcement* does give instructions for presenting live and photo line-ups in either a sequential or simultaneous presentation. This may be somewhat premature bearing in mind the different findings obtained in research.

One possible reason for different results across studies of sequential versus simultaneous presentation is related to the methods used to present the sequential line-ups. McQuiston-Surrett, Malpass and Tredoux (2006) conducted a review of these different methods and suggested that one key methodological difference relates to the 'stopping rule'. One of the original notions of sequential presentation was that if witnesses made an identification during the line-up it was immediately ended (ie before all the photos had been shown). However, many studies have abandoned this rule and instead let witnesses view the whole line-up (regardless of whether they make a choice or not during its presentation). McQuiston-Surrett et al (2006) found that sequential presentations which are immediately halted do not result in their normal beneficial effect (ie reduced false identifications), suggesting that witnesses should be allowed to see all members of a sequential line-up. However, at present the *Eyewitness Evidence: A Guide for Law Enforcement* gives sequential instructions for either showing all line-up members or halting the line-up as soon as an identification is made.

In addition to understanding how differences in methodologies may contribute to differing results, it is important to consider theoretical explanations underlying the effects of sequential presentation compared to simultaneous presentation. As described above, many researchers have suggested that with sequential presentation people are forced to adopt an absolute judgement strategy where they compare each individual line-up member directly with their own memory for the perpetrator. Conversely, when viewing a simultaneous line-up witnesses can examine all members of the line-up and compare them with one another before selecting who looks the most similar (relative to the other line-up members) to their memory for the perpetrator. However, an alternative explanation could be that rather than adopting an absolute judgement strategy when viewing a sequential presentation, people instead adopt stricter decision criterion (Ebbesen and Flowe, 2002; Meissner, Tredoux, Parker and MacLin, 2005). That is, participants may take greater care and only identify a member of a sequential line-up if they are really certain that that individual is the perpetrator (ie that there is a very high match between this line-up member and their memory of the perpetrator). This would explain why there is a reduction in both correct identifications and false identifications with sequential line-ups. However, even if stricter decision criteria are adopted when viewing a sequential line-up, such criteria may vary as a witness progresses through a sequential line-up presentation. At the beginning, the decision criteria may be very stringent because witnesses probably don't want to identify an early face when in fact there may be a better option later on. However, later on in the sequential presentation they may adopt more lenient decision criteria when they realize they maybe running out of line-up members to view. This has clear implications for positioning of the suspect in a sequential line-up (Ebbesen and Flowe, 2002). Positioning of the suspect may also be moderated by the similarity of line-up foils. For example, if the foils are very similar to the culprit and the culprit is towards the end of line-up a witness may falsely identify a very similar looking foil presented earlier in the line-up and then miss the culprit presented later on (Flowe and Ebbesen, 2007). At this point in time further research is required in order to more fully understand the theoretical explanations as to why sequential presentation reduces both correct identifications and false identifications. Furthermore, it is also important to consider additional factors that could modify the sequential effect, such as whether a witness viewed the perpetrator under good or poor viewing conditions and is thus likely to have a good or poor memory for the perpetrator.

As discussed above, identification procedures in the UK are presented on videotape meaning that line-up members are naturally presented sequentially. However, the relevant PACE Code D instructions for showing a video parade differ to a considerable extent from the type of sequential presentation used in psychological research (and from the instructions given in *Eyewitness Evidence: A Guide for Law Enforcement*). In the UK witnesses are advised that they will see the whole set of images twice through before they should make any decision and that they can go back and see any images (or all of them) they want to again or have them 'frozen' as many times as they need to. Thus, there are three clear differences between such instructions and psychological researchers' sequential line-ups. First, witnesses see all images twice before making a decision. Second, witnesses can see any or all of the images as many times as they want to. Third, witnesses know how many people are contained in the line-up. Valentine, Darling and Memon (2007) compared the current PACE Code D instructions for video line-ups to the instructions usually used in research on sequential line-ups (most of which is conducted in North America). Participants witnessed a live (surprise) simulated theft. A few days later half the witnesses viewed either a TP or TA VIPER line-up parade twice through from start to finish with an opportunity to revisit any member of the parade (as per the current PACE Code D guidelines). The remaining half of the participants viewed either a TP or TA VIPER line-up parade but if they identified anyone during it the parade was halted (ie they were not able to go back to look at a line-up member once they had rejected it, and they did not know how many people the parade contained as per most strict researchers' sequential instructions). Participants who received the researchers' sequential instructions were significantly less likely to make a correct identification than participants given instructions as per PACE Code D. In a similar study, Wilcock, Milne and Hughes (in preparation) found that witnesses given instructions as per PACE Code D made significantly more choices (both hits and foil identifications) from a TP video line-up parade compared to witnesses given researchers' sequential line-up instructions.

On the basis of the available research regarding sequential line-up presentation, we would suggest that it is premature to draw the conclusion that sequential presentation (as recommended by many researchers) is beneficial compared to simultaneous presentation. Further research is needed which explicitly investigates (i) the effect of different methods associated with sequential presentation, and (ii) the theoretical explanations thought to underlie the sequential effect.

ADMINISTRATION OF A LINE-UP

Wells (1993) describes how police line-ups can be likened to psychological experiments. For example, when the police conduct an identification procedure they have a hypothesis that their suspect is the culprit. Witnesses could be seen as participants in a study when they view the parade and, depending upon their performance, acceptance or rejection of the police hypothesis is considered. If we consider the line-ups and experiments analogy further, in well controlled psychological experiments it is good practice that participants are naive to the condition they are in (*blind*) and also that the investigator is naive to the conditions participants are in to avoid giving off any cues (*double blind*). Similarly, a person conducting an identification parade with knowledge of who the suspect is can give off cues either intentionally or unintentionally. Wells et al (1998) have therefore suggested that line-ups should be conducted 'double blind' (ie the line-up administrator should not have knowledge of which position the suspect is in and the witness should be told that the perpetrator may or may not be present).

Evidence that line-up administrators who know the position of the suspect can inadvertently give off cues to witnesses and affect their decision comes from Phillips, McAuliff, Kovera and Cutler (1999). They found that when participants acting as line-up administrators knew the identity of the suspect participant witnesses were significantly more likely to identify the suspect from a sequential line-up presentation than when the participant administrators were blind to the position of the suspect. This finding is all the more worrying because participant administrators did give instructions informing the witnesses that the perpetrator may or may not be present (and the line-up should be rejected if the perpetrator was not present). Furthermore, the administrators were explicitly told to be as fair as possible and not tell mock witnesses the position of the suspect.

In an effort to overcome the effect of administrator bias Haw and Fisher (2004) showed participants a video event and then varied the contact between line-up administrators and witnesses who viewed photographic line-ups. The line-up administrators were led to believe that the line-ups they were to show to the witnesses contained the culprit and they were told which position the culprit was in. The administrators were allocated to one of two conditions: either a high contact condition where they sat at a table with the witness showing them the line-up photos and recording the witness' decision or a low contact condition where the administrator handed witnesses the line-up instructions, line-up photos, a recording form, and then sat out of the witnesses' direct view. Results revealed that witnesses in the high contact condition chose the culprit replacement on the TA line-up at an above chance rate. This rate was reduced in the low contact condition where the administrators sat behind the witness.

On the basis of the available psychological research, the safest thing to do would be for line-up administrators to be blind to the identity of the suspect in the line-up. PACE Code D currently gives no instructions that the identification officer conducting the parade should be blind, however, this is about to be considered in a review of PACE Code D (personal communication, Valentine, 2007). Whilst there may be logistical problems in running video identification parades double blind, researchers have considered ways in which this could happen. For example, Valentine (2006) suggested that several 'identical' video parades (but with the suspect in different positions on each) be made available for the witness to choose from. The witness would view the chosen parade on one screen but the identification officer would view the same parade on another screen (which is back-to-back to the screen which the witness views). The screen viewed by the identification officer would be obscured except for the position number for each member of the parade, thus the identification officer would not know when the suspect is being viewed by the witness. Only once the witness' decision has been recorded and the witness has left the room should the parade be seen by the identification officer and suspect's legal representative.

An additional reason for conducting line-ups 'double blind' could be that administrator knowledge of the identity of the suspect may influence witnesses' confidence that they made the correct decision on a line-up. As discussed in Chapter 4, eyewitness confidence is very important because it affects jurors' beliefs about the accuracy of eyewitness identification evidence and in turn juror verdicts (Cutler, Penrod and Stuve, 1988). Research has indeed shown that line-up administrator knowledge of a suspects' position can increase witnesses' confidence. Garrioch and Brimacombe (2001) found that mock witnesses were significantly more confident when the line-up administrator believed such witnesses had correctly identified the suspect than were mock witnesses whose participant administrators had no information about the suspect's identity. The administrators did not, however, give blatant feedback, such as 'Good, you identified the actual suspect' (see Chapter 4 for discussion of the post-identification feedback effect). Instead, Garrioch and Brimacombe (2001) found that post-identification feedback was via administrators' voice intonation and non-verbal behaviours. For example, when administrators asked mock witnesses whom they believed had correctly identified the suspect how confident they were using a 1 to 10 confidence scale, line-up administrators stressed the words '10 is extremely confident' and made eye contact simultaneously. This study provides yet more evidence that line-ups should be administered 'double blind'.

INSTRUCTIONS TO WITNESSES

Non-biased Line-up Instructions

Malpass and Devine (1981) demonstrated the importance of non-biased line-up instructions which inform witnesses that the perpetrator may or may not be present in the line-up. They found that failure to warn witnesses that the culprit may or may not be in the line-up (biased instructions) resulted in 78% of witnesses making identifications from a TA line-up, whilst maintaining a high level of hits in the TP line-up. With the warning that the perpetrator may not be in the TA line-up (non-biased instructions) the false identification rate fell to 33%. Steblay (1997) conducted a meta-analysis of 18 studies and confirmed that after witnesses receive biased line-up instructions a higher level of choosing ensues. When the line-up is target present this presents less of a problem (see Clark, 2005). However, if the suspect in the line-up is innocent, non-biased line-up instructions are crucial. Nowadays the importance of giving witnesses non-biased line-up instructions is recognized in several countries. For example, informing witnesses that the perpetrator may or may not be present in the line-up has been required of police forces in England and Wales since 1986 (Zander, 1990). PACE Code D stipulates that prior to the parade being shown witnesses should be told that the person they saw may or may not be in the parade and that they should say if they cannot make an identification. Similarly *Eyewitness Evidence: A Guide for Law Enforcement* instructs witnesses that the person who committed the crime may or may not be present.

Ascertaining Witness Confidence

As mentioned above, the confidence that a witness shows in court can be crucial because jurors are persuaded by confident witnesses (Cutler et al, 1988). It is therefore important that witness statements of confidence about the accuracy of their identification for use in court are taken immediately after they make the identification before there is any opportunity for their confidence to be altered due to learning new information. Evidence was been presented in Chapter 4 on the very robust post-identification feedback effect where Wells and Bradfield (1998) found that if a line-up administrator told mock witnesses who had made false identifications (after viewing a TA line-up) 'Good, you identified the actual suspect', they were significantly more confident that their identification was accurate compared to those who had received no feedback. *Eyewitness Evidence: A Guide for Law Enforcement* instructs witnesses that they will be asked to state in their own words how certain they are about their identification. PACE Code D does not currently allow for this, however, this is about to be considered in a review of PACE Code D (personal communication, Valentine, 2007).

ALTERNATIVE LINE-UP PROCEDURES

Thus far in this chapter we have discussed research which relates to legislation such as PACE Code D or recommendations made such as *Eyewitness Evidence: A Guide for Law Enforcement*. However, there is some additional research which has examined novel methods of presenting line-ups aimed at increasing the accuracy of eyewitness identifications.

MODIFIED SEQUENTIAL LINE-UP

Levi (1998) has suggested that the sequential line-up (as described above) could be modified in two ways to reduce the risk of false identifications being made. First, by enlarging the line-up to around 20 people (because the larger the line-up the less likely it is an innocent suspect will be chosen by chance). Second, by allowing witnesses to make more than one identification—referred to as multiple choices (Levi, 2006). The reasoning behind allowing witnesses to make multiple choices comes from the suggestion that if a line-up is large then a witness may find it more difficult to correctly identify the perpetrator (eg they may have already identified a foil before they see the perpetrator). Clearly, if they are allowed another choice from the line-up then they have the opportunity to also identify the perpetrator. A court viewing the identification evidence would realize that such a witness cannot be entirely relied on because they have made one false identification but there is still some evidence from their identification of the suspect that the suspect is guilty. Levi (1998) tested mock witnesses' performance on TP or TA modified 20-person sequential line-ups viewed on videotape. The suspect appeared in the fourth, ninth, fourteenth, and eighteenth positions in the line-up an equal number of times (ie for different witnesses). For the TP line-up 43% of mock witnesses correctly identified just the perpetrator, 8% identified the perpetrator plus one foil, and 18% chose the perpetrator plus more than one foil. For the TA line-up no mock witnesses chose just the designated innocent suspect and just 5% chose the innocent suspect plus one or more foils, 33% chose one or more of the foils, and 61% of mock witnesses correctly rejected the line-up. Levi then considered the effect of each of the modifications to the sequential line-up. First, line-up size, where line-ups which contained the suspect in position four and nine (ten-person line-ups) were compared to line-ups which contained the suspect in position 14 and 18 (20-person line-ups). For TP line-ups there were fewer correct identifications from 20-person line-ups compared to ten person line-ups, though this effect was not statistically significant. However, there was a significant effect of line-up size for the target absent line-ups where 20-person line-ups led to more foil identifications and fewer correct rejections. Second, witnesses were allowed to have more than one choice from the line-up. When only witnesses' first choice data was considered there was an increase from 43% to 49% for correct identifications of the suspect, and an increase from 17% to 38% for identifications of a member of the TA line-up. Levi argued that the increase in identifications from a TA line-up would result in more false identifications of a suspect.

In a further paper Levi (2006) compared the multiple choice modified sequential line-up with a simultaneous and sequential line-up. For the TP line-up, when considering perpetrator identifications, the simultaneous line-ups led to more correct identifications (62.5%) than the sequential line-up (35%) which in turn elicited more correct identifications than the modified sequential line-up (20%). However, when considering perpetrator identifications plus foil identifications, for the modified sequential line-up, identification rose to 42.5% which was not significantly different from the correct identification rate from the simultaneous and sequential line-ups. For the TA line-up, the simultaneous line-up led to more mistaken identifications (48.7%) than the sequential or modified sequential line-up (both 30%). Further research would need to be conducted before drawing any firm conclusions as to the effectiveness of the modified sequential line-up. There would also need to be due consideration given as to the practicalities for the police to conduct such large line-ups and the likely effect of multiple choices from line-ups on the decision-making of those involved in the criminal justice system.

ELIMINATION LINE-UP

A different method of showing a line-up has been put forward by Pozzulo and Lindsay (1999). Their 'elimination line-up' was developed to help reduce false identifications made by children viewing TA line-ups (see Chapter 8 for discussion of child eyewitness identification performance). The 'elimination line-up' involves showing witnesses all the members of the line-up together as with a simultaneous line-up presentation but then asking witnesses to eliminate, one at a time, all but one member of the line-up. The process of elimination involves a relative judgement because witnesses are comparing all members of the line-up relative to each other. However, with the one remaining member of the line-up witnesses are asked to make an absolute judgement as to whether this is the perpetrator or not. Pozzulo and Lindsay (1999) found evidence that for children the elimination line-up reduced false identifications whilst having no impact on correct identifications. In a more recent study Pozzulo and Balfour (2006) found that the elimination line-up resulted in more correct rejections of a target absent line-up (when the line-up members matched child and adult mock witnesses' descriptions of the perpetrator). Beresford and Blades (2006) also investigated the elimination line-up with children and their data for line-ups shown photographically suggest that elimination line-ups may be helpful. Further research is required to confirm the beneficial effect of elimination line-ups, particularly with adults.

PRACTICE LINE-UPS

Other research investigating methods of increasing the accuracy of witnesses viewing identification line-ups has focused on instructions/practice given to witnesses prior to them viewing the actual line-up. Goodman, Bottoms, Schwartz-Kenney and Rudy (1991) found that three practice line-ups (a TP animal line-up, a TP line-up for the experimenter, and a TA line-up for the child's mother) reduced the numbers of false identifications made by older children. These findings have also been supported by those of Parker and Ryan (1993) who found that practice with a TA and a TP array reduced children's errors on a simultaneous line-up. The beneficial effect of practice has also recently been found to reduce the number of false identifications made by elderly witnesses whilst having no detrimental effect on the rate of correct identifications of the perpetrator (Wilcock and Bull, manuscript in preparation). However, firm conclusions about the beneficial effect of practice should not be drawn yet because there is some evidence to suggest that practice line-ups may not always be beneficial (eg Parker and Myers, 2001), and research examining the effectiveness of practice line-ups with young adults has not yet been conducted. (For further information on practice line-ups see Chapter 8.)

PRE-IDENTIFICATION LINE-UP QUESTIONS

In a study aimed to reduce the rate of false identifications made by young adults Dysart and Lindsay (2001) asked mock witnesses, prior to a line-up, three questions:

1. How clear a memory do you have for the face of the criminal?
2. How confident are you that you will be able to select the criminal if you see a photograph of him in a line-up?
3. How confident are you that you will realize that the guilty person is *not* in the line-up if you are shown a line-up with only innocent people in it?.

These pre-identification questions successfully reduced the rate of false identifications by young adults viewing a simultaneous TA line-up. Dysart and Lindsay concluded that question 3 may have encouraged participants to adopt stricter decision criteria by encouraging them to use an absolute decision strategy (compared to a relative decision strategy) that led to a reduction in false identifications. This is supported by the fact that they did not observe a similar reduction in false identifications when the TA line-up was presented sequentially (when participants would have been likely to have already adopted an absolute decision strategy). However, Memon and Gabbert (2003) investigated whether the same pre-identification questions would be beneficial for elderly witnesses and found no beneficial effect. Again, further research needs to be conducted before firm conclusions can be drawn about the beneficial effect of pre-identification questions.

CONCLUSION

In this chapter we have reviewed research which has relevance to (and in some cases has guided) legislation for showing witnesses identification line-ups. It is clear that some of these empirical findings have great value and have contributed to line-up procedures which are fairer to witnesses viewing a line-up and also to innocent suspects. It is also clear from the discussions in this chapter that in some countries, for example, the UK and the US, there is a good level of cooperation between academics and members of the Criminal Justice System, and this is to be celebrated. Whilst there are many robust effects in the research on system variables, researchers must always take great care not to draw premature conclusions and make recommendations to the Criminal Justice System before developing adequate theoretical understanding.

FURTHER READING

Dupuis, P.R. and Lindsay, R.C.L. (2007). Radical alternatives to traditional lineups. In R.C.L. Lindsay, D.F. Ross, J.D. Read and M.P. Toglia (eds) *Handbook of Eyewitness Psychology Volume 11*. Mahwah, NJ: Lawrence Erlbaum Associates, 179–200.

Malpass, R.S., Tredoux, C.G. and McQuiston-Surrett, D. (2007) Lineup construction and lineup fairness. In R.C.L. Lindsay, D.F. Ross, J.D. Read and M.P. Toglia (eds) *Handbook of Eyewitness Psychology Volume 11*. Mahwah, NJ: Lawrence Erlbaum Associates, 155–178.

Wells, G.L., Small, M., Penrod, S., Malpass, R.S., Fulero, S.M. and Brimacombe, C.A.E. (1998). Eyewitness identification procedures: Recommendations for lineups and photospreads. *Law and Human Behavior, 22*, 603–647.

REFERENCES

Beaudry, J., Lindsay, R.C.L. and Dupuis, P. (2006). Procedural recommendations to increase the reliability of eyewitness identification. In M.R. Kebbell and G. Davies (eds) *Practical Psychology for Forensic Investigations and Prosecutions*. Chichester: John Wiley and Sons, 25–46.

Beresford, J. and Blades, M. (2006). Children's identifications of faces from lineups: The effects of lineup presentation and instructions on accuracy. *Journal of Applied Psychology, 91*, 1102–1113.

Clarke, S.E. (2005). A re-examination of the effects of biased lineup instructions in eyewitness identification. *Law and Human Behaviour, 29*, 575–604.

Cutler, B.L., Berman, G.L., Penrod, S. and Fisher, R.P. (1994). Conceptual, practical, and empirical issues associated with eyewitness identification test media. In D.F. Ross, J.D. Read and M.P. Toglia (eds) *Adult Eyewitness Testimony Current Trends and Developments*. New York: Cambridge University Press, 163–181.

—— and Fisher, R.P. (1990). Live lineups, videotaped lineups, and photoarrays. *Forensic Reports, 3*, 439–448.

——, Penrod, S.D. and Stuve, T.E. (1988). Juror decision making in eyewitness identification cases. *Law and Human Behavior, 12*, 41–55.

Darling, S., Valentine, T. and Memon, A. (2008). Selection of lineup foils in operational contexts. *Applied Cognitive Psychology, 22*, 159–169.

Doob, A.N. and Kirshenbaum, H.M. (1973). Bias in police lineups: Partial remembering. *Journal of Police Science and Administration, 1*, 287–293.

Dysart, J.E. and Lindsay, R.C.L. (2001). A preidentification questioning effect: Serendipitously increasing correct rejections. *Law and Human Behavior, 25*, 155–165.

Ebbesen, E.B. and Flowe, H.D. (2002). *Simultaneous versus sequential lineups: What do we really know?* at <http://psy.ucsd.edu/~eebbesen/SimSeq.htm> (accessed 22 March 2006).

ELLISON, K.W. and BUCKHOUT, R. (1981). *Psychology and Criminal Justice.* New York: Harper and Row Publisher.

FLOWE, H.D. and EBBESEN, E.B. (2007). The effect of lineup member similarity on recognition accuracy in simultaneous and sequential lineups. *Law and Human Behavior, 31,* 33–52.

GABBERT, F., MEMON, A. and ALLAN, K. (2003). Memory conformity: Can eyewitnesses influence each other's memories for an event. *Applied Cognitive Psychology, 17,* 533–543.

GARRIOCH, L. and BRIMACOMBE, C.A.E. (2001). Lineup administrators' expectations: Their impact on eyewitness confidence. *Law and Human Behavior, 25,* 299–315.

GOODMAN, G., BOTTOMS, B., SCHWARTZ-KENNEY, B. and RUDY, L. (1991). Children's testimony for a stressful event: Improving children's reports. *Journal of Narrative and Life History, 1,* 69–99.

HAW, R.M. and FISHER, R.P. (2004). Effects of administrator-witness contact on eyewitness identification accuracy. *Journal of Applied Psychology, 6,* 1106–1112.

KNELLER, W., MEMON, A. and STEVENAGE, S. (2001). Simultaneous and sequential lineups: Decision processes of accurate and inaccurate eyewitnesses. *Applied Cognitive Psychology, 15,* 659–671.

LEVI, A.M. (1998). Protecting innocent defendants, nailing the guilty: A modified sequential lineup. *Applied Cognitive Psychology, 12,* 265–275.

—— (2006). An analysis of multiple choice in MSL lineups, and a comparison with simultaneous and sequential ones. *Psychology, Crime and Law, 12,* 273–285.

LINDSAY, R.C.L., MARTIN, R. and WEBBER, L. (1994). Default values in eyewitness descriptions. A problem for the match to description lineup foil selection strategy. *Law and Human Behavior, 18,* 527–542.

——, SMITH, S.M. and PRYKE, S. (1999). Measures of lineup fairness: Do they postdict identification accuracy? *Applied Cognitive Psychology, 13,* 93–107.

—— and WELLS, G.L. (1985). Improving eyewitness identifications from lineups: Simultaneous versus sequential lineup presentation. *Journal of Applied Psychology, 70,* 556–564.

LUUS, C.A.E. and WELLS, G.L. (1991). Eyewitness identification and the selection of distractors for lineups. *Law and Human Behavior, 15,* 43–57.

—— and —— (1994). The malleability of eyewitness confidence: Co-witness and perseverance effects. *Journal of Applied Psychology, 79,* 714–723.

MALPASS, R.S. (1981). Effective size and defendant bias in eyewitness identification lineups. *Law and Human Behavior, 5,* 299–309.

—— and DEVINE, P.G. (1981). Eyewitness identification: Lineup instructions and the absence of the offender. *Journal of Applied Psychology, 66,* 482–489.

——, TREDOUX, C.G. and McQUISTON-SURRETT, D. (2007). Lineup construction and lineup fairness. In R.C.L. Lindsay, D.F. Ross, J.D. Read and M.P. Toglia (eds) *Handbook of Eyewitness Psychology Volume 11.* Mahwah, NJ: Lawrence Erlbaum Associates, 155–178.

McQUISTON-SURRETT, D., MALPASS, R.S. and TREDOUX, C.G. (2006). Sequential versus simultaneous lineups: A review of methods data and theory. *Psychology, Public, Policy and Law, 12,* 137–169.

MEISSNER, C.A., TREDOUX, C.G., PARKER, J.F. and MacLIN, O.H. (2005). Eyewitness decisions in simultaneous and sequential lineups: A dual-process signal detection theory analysis. *Memory and Cognition, 33,* 783–792.

MEMON, A. and GABBERT, F. (2003). Improving the identification accuracy of senior witnesses: Do pre-lineup questions and sequential testing help? *Journal of Applied Psychology, 88,* 341–347.

NOSWORTHY, G. J. and LINDSAY, R.C.L. (1990). Does nominal lineup size matter? *Journal of Applied Psychology, 75,* 358–361.

PARKER, J. and MYERS, A. (2001). Attempts to improve children's identifications from sequential-presentation lineups. *Journal of Applied Social Psychology, 31,* 796–815.

—— and RYAN, V. (1993). An attempt to reduce guessing behavior in children's and adults' eyewitness identifications. *Law and Human Behavior, 17,* 11–26.

PATERSON, H.M. and KEMP, R.I. (2006). Co-witness talk: A survey of eyewitness discussion. *Psychology, Crime and Law, 12,* 181–191.

PHILLIPS, M.R., MCAULIFF, B.D., KOVERA, M. and CUTLER, B.L. (1999). Double-blind photoarray administration as a safeguard against investigator bias. *Journal of Applied Psychology, 6,* 940–951.

PIKE, G., BRACE, N. and KYNAN, S. (2002). *The visual identification of suspects: Procedures and practice.* London: Home Office.

Police and Criminal Evidence Act 1984. Code D Code of Practice for the Identification of Persons by Police Officers (2005 edition) available at <http://police.homeoffice.gov.uk/publications/operational-policing/previous-PACE-codes-2005/PACE_Chapter_D.pdf?view=Binary> (accessed 1 September 2006).

POZZULO, J. and BALFOUR, J. (2006). Children's and adults' eyewitness identification accuracy when a culprit changes his appearance: Comparing simultaneous and elimination lineup procedures. *Legal and Criminological Psychology, 11,* 25–34.

—— and LINDSAY, R. (1999). Elimination lineups: An improved identification procedure for child eyewitnesses. *Journal of Applied Psychology, 84,* 167–176.

SHAPIRO, P.N. and PENROD, S. (1986). Meta-analysis of facial identification studies. *Psychological Bulletin, 100,* 139–156.

SLATER, A. (1994). *Identification parades: A scientific evaluation.* London: Home Office.

SKAGERBERG, E.M. (2007). Co-witness feedback in line-ups. *Applied Cognitive Psychology, 21,* 489–497.

STEBLAY, N.M. (1997). Social influence in eyewitness recall: A meta-analytic review of lineup instruction effects. *Law and Human Behavior, 21,* 283–297.

STEBLAY, N., DYSART, J., FULERO, S. and LINDSAY, R.C.L. (2001). Eyewitness accuracy rates in sequential and simultaneous lineup presentations: A meta-analytic comparison. *Law and Human Behavior, 25,* 459–476

TECHNICAL WORKING GROUP FOR EYEWITNESS EVIDENCE (1999). *Eyewitness Evidence: A Guide For Law Enforcement.* WASHINGTON, D.C.: Office of Justice Programs, National Institute of Justice.

TUNNICLIFF, J.L. and CLARK, S.E. (2000). Selecting foils for identification lineups: Matching suspects or descriptions? *Law and Human Behavior, 24,* 231–258.

TURTLE, J., LINDSAY, R.C.L. and WELLS, G.L. (2003). Best practice recommendations for eyewitness evidence procedures: New ideas for the oldest way to solve a case. *The Canadian Journal of Police and Security Services, 1,* 5–18.

VALENTINE, T. (2006). Forensic facial identification. In A. Heaton-Armstrong, E. Shepherd, G. Gudjonsson, and D. Wolchover (eds) *Witness testimony: Psychological, Investigative, and Evidential Perspectives.* Oxford: Oxford University Press, 281–307.

——, DARLING, S. and MEMON, A. (2007). Do strict rules and moving images increase the reliability of sequential identification procedures? *Applied Cognitive Psychology, 21,* 933–949.

——, HARRIS, N., COLMAN PIERA, A. and DARLING, S. (2003). Are police video identifications fair to African-Caribbean suspects? *Applied Cognitive Psychology, 17,* 459–476.

—— and HEATON, P. (1999). An evaluation of the fairness of police line-ups and video identifications. *Applied Cognitive Psychology, 13,* 59–72.

WELLS, G.L. (1978). Applied eyewitness testimony research: System variables and estimator variables. *Journal of Personality and Social Psychology, 36*, 1546–1557.

—— (1993). What do we know about eyewitness identification? *American Psychologist, 48*, 553–571.

—— and BRADFIELD, A.L. (1998). 'Good you identified the suspect': Feedback to eyewitnesses distorts their reports of the witnessing experience. *Journal of Applied Psychology, 83*, 360–376.

——, LIEPPE, M.R. and OSTROM, T.M. (1979). Guidelines for empirically assessing the fairness of a lineup. *Law and Human Behavior, 3*, 285–293.

——, LINDSAY, R.C.L. and FERGUSON, T.J. (1979). Accuracy, confidence, and juror perception in eyewitness identification. *Journal of Applied Psychology, 64*, 440–448.

——, RYDELL, S.M. and SEELAU, E.P. (1993). The selection of distractors for eyewitness lineups. *Journal of Applied Psychology, 78*, 835 – 844.

——, SMALL, M., PENROD, S., MALPASS, R.S., FULERO, S.M. and BRIMACOMBE, C.A.E. (1998). Eyewitness identification procedures: Recommendations for lineups and photospreads. *Law and Human Behavior, 22*, 603–647.

—— and TURTLE, J.W. (1986). Eyewitness identification: The importance of lineup models. *Psychological Bulletin, 99*, 320–329.

WILCOCK, R.A. and BULL, R. (manuscript in preparation). *Novel lineup methods for improving the performance of older eyewitnesses.*

——, —— and VRIJ, A. (2005). Aiding the performance of older eyewitnesses: Enhanced non-biased lineup instructions and lineup presentation. *Psychiatry, Psychology, and Law, 12*, 129–140.

——, MILNE, R. and HUGHES, C. *A comparison of real world police lineup presentation versus laboratory recommended lineup presentation.* In preparation.

WOGALTER, M.S., MALPASS, R.S. and McQUISTON, D.E. (2004). A national survey of US police on preparation and conduct of identification lineups. *Psychology, Crime and Law, 10*, 69–82.

ZANDER, M. (1990). *The Police and Criminal Evidence Act.* London: Sweet and Maxwell.

8

ASSISTING VULNERABLE WITNESSES

INTRODUCTION

The term 'vulnerable witnesses' covers a wide range of people whose performance could be substantially improved if appropriate special assistance/measures were made available to them. In terms of their identification performance, only a limited amount of relevant research has, to date, been conducted. This research has included children, elderly adults, and people with a learning disability. This chapter reviews what is currently known on this important topic. (The authors wish to thank Kristjan Kask for his assistance with aspects of this chapter.)

CHILD WITNESSES

There can be little doubt that developments in the last 15 years or so have resulted in very substantial improvements in a number of countries regarding the gathering of verbal accounts from child witnesses/victims about what they may have experienced (Westcott, Davies and Bull, 2002). This has, in part, been due to the now widespread recognition that children are often witnesses to and victims of crime.

Relevant professional guidance and training has, quite rightly, focused on assisting children to recall as much as possible about what may have happened while not biasing their accounts (Milne and Bull, 2006). However, such improvements in investigative procedures have not focused directly on assisting children to make correct identifications. A recently developing body of research has found that while child witnesses can perform fairly well when choosing from a set of faces that does indeed include the perpetrator/target, they often do not correctly indicate that a target-absent set of faces actually does not contain the perpetrator (eg when the police suspect in the set of faces is not, in fact, the perpetrator). That is, children make 'false positive' choices from a set of faces that does not, in fact, contain the 'target'. However, little guidance is yet available that relevant professionals could use to assist children to perform better at identification tasks.

In 1999, Pozzulo and Lindsay made the important point that because children are prone to making false positive choices from line-ups, this 'may discourage police officers and prosecutors from seeking and using the identification of child witnesses (1999, 167). Prior to taking part in an identification task witnesses will typically be asked by the police to describe the perpetrator. In 1996, Schwartz-Kenney, Bottoms and Goodman made the following point:

> Little is known about young children's ability to report pertinent information about the appearance of formerly unknown people, and even less is known about how to obtain accurate descriptive reports from children. (1996, 121).

They noted that few researchers have considered the problems of improving children's person descriptions and identifications. A major issue they raised was the limited amount of descriptive information that young children (of primary school age and younger) spontaneously seem able to provide when asked questions such as 'What did the man look like?'. They suggested that this was likely to be due to their limited ability to use retrieval strategies. Indeed, Davies, Tarrant and Flin (1989) found that children's descriptions of a once-seen person were very brief (ie an average of 1.00 descriptors from six-year-olds and 2.21 from ten-year-olds). Even at age 12 years children's descriptions contain fewer items than adults' (eg 7.61 versus 9.85 in Pozzulo and Lindsay's (2003) first experiment).

In a seminal paper on the ability of children to respond correctly to target present (TP) and target absent (TA) arrays of facial photographs, Parker and Carranza (1989) made the following point:

> In the past few years there has been an upsurge in the interest of eyewitness testimony of children. With the heightened concern of child abuse, children are more evident in the courtrooms thus magnifying the need to determine their credibility. Researchers are focusing on the interaction of laws, legal practices, and current psychological knowledge in evaluating children's eyewitness testimony. (1989, 133).

PREVIOUS STUDIES OF CHILD EYEWITNESSES

Parker and Carranza (1989) noted that while a considerable number of studies had previously been conducted on children's face-processing abilities (eg studies in which each child sees many target faces and then is required to state for an even larger sample of faces which of these they were shown previously), few studies had examined children's ability to select from a small set of photographs the one face they had been shown previously. The latter type of study being closer to the eyewitness situation. Parker and Carranza also made the point that 'a more ecologically valid line-up procedure . . . . can reflect the witness's natural tendency to choose or guess' (1989, 134) (ie when looking for only one target face among the set of faces). They hypothesized that children may feel more pressured than adults to choose a photo. They found a trend toward reduced accuracy of child witnesses in target absent line-ups compared to adult witnesses. While for TP line-ups the difference in the level of correct identifications between adult and child witnesses was small (31% versus 40%), for TA line-ups the level of correct performance (ie indicating that the target face was not in the array) differed more between adult and child witnesses

(46% versus 25%). Parker and Carranza concluded that child witnesses are more likely to guess than are adults, and also:

Children may be more likely to assume that the target must be in the line-ups especially with an adult authority figure presenting the photo-spread . . . Social factors as well as cognitive factors most likely play a role in this behaviour, and further studies are needed to determine how these factors contribute to the child witness's propensity to guess. (1989, 142–3)

Indeed, several other studies (eg Davies, Stevenson-Robb and Flin, 1988; Parker and Ryan, 1993) have also shown that when the target face is not in the set or array shown, young children, more so than older children or adults, still choose a face (but see Davies et al, 1989; Yarmey, 1988). With TP arrays children have sometimes been found to perform no poorer than adults (eg Parker, Haverfield and Baker-Thomas, 1986).

More recently, Beal, Schmidt and Dekle (1995) and Gross and Hayne (1996) similarly found that children's correct performance was generally much poorer when tested with TA photo spreads than with TP arrays. Gross and Hayne asked: 'Given that children were generally accurate when tested with target present line-ups, why were they so inaccurate when tested in the target absent condition?' (1996, 369). In reply they suggested that one explanation could relate to the notion that to be correct on a TP line-up merely requires 'recognition' of the target face but to be correct on a TA line-up requires 'recall' (ie retrieval from memory) of sufficient information about the face to be sure that it is not present. An additional explanation they offered relates to the established finding (see, eg, Milne and Bull, 1999; Westcott, et al, 2002) that:

when children are questioned, they generally attempt to provide answers . . . In the case of line-up identifications, the mere presentation of a line-up by an adult may create an implicit demand for the child to pick someone even if the target is not present . . . It is possible, therefore, that children's poor performances on target absent trials are not always a reflection of a memory deficit, but rather may reflect the child's increased attempt to comply with what he or she perceives to be the social demands of the task. (1996, 369–70)

In concluding, Gross and Hayne argued that future research designed to improve children's performance regarding the TA condition is sorely needed.

From their 1998 meta-analysis (a form of overview) of all published prior studies on the eyewitness identification accuracy of children Pozzulo and Lindsay (2001) concluded: 'When presented with a target absent line-up, children were consistently less likely than adults to correctly reject a line-up' (2001, 181). They pointed out: 'Low rates of correct rejection are a serious problem reducing the credibility of children's identification evidence' (2001, 181). They suggested that these low rates were likely to be the result of both social factors (eg the child thinks he or she must make a choice) and of memory/cognitive factors (eg being able to retrieve the target face from memory). (For more on this see the next section.)

In the years since Lindsay and Pozzulo's (1998) overview a number of other relevant studies have been published. Kask, Bull and Gillett (in submission) recently performed an up-to-date meta-analysis of the 28 studies now available involving children. In this we found for correct identifications the performance of children aged three to four years was poorer than that of children aged five and over, however the performance of children (all ages combined) was not different from that of adults. Regarding correct performance in TA settings, there was for children a small improvement with age but this effect was not strong enough to be significant. For TA settings children's average correct performance was 47% and for adults was 74%, however this difference did not prove to be statistically significant (possibly due to the variability in the data across the number of relevant but different studies). Our overview also revealed that increasing the number of faces/persons in the test setting reduced children's accurate choosing of the target, but for TA tests their false choosing rate was high irrespective of the number of persons (ie four or six or eight).

Combining all the studies that had varied the delay intervals between (i) initially seeing the target and (ii) the later test produced no consistent effect of increased delay (for TP tests; there are too few delay studies regarding TA tests). (For more on delay see Cain, Baker-Ward and Eaton, 2005.)

For TP tests, overall, children performed rather better for simultaneous (57%) than for sequential (47%) presentations. Also, for TA tests the rate of correct performance was better for simultaneous (47%) than for sequential (31%) presentations. The mode of exposure at test (ie live or photographs or video) had no significant effect on children's performance either for TP or for TA tests.

Given that this most recent meta-analysis has again confirmed that children' correct performance on TA tests is poor (it averaged only 47%), ways of improving such child performance are needed. Also needed is more research on the effect of child witnesses' correct and incorrect performance on courts/jurors (Pozzulo, Lemieux, Wells and McGuaig, 2006).

POSSIBLE WAYS TO IMPROVE CHILD EYEWITNESS PERFORMANCE

Given that it is very likely that children's poorer performance in the TA condition is due to the combination of 'cognitive' and 'social' factors (for more on such factors see Ceci and Bruck, 1993), we conducted three studies that were designed to assist children in these regards (Bull, George, Knight and Paterson, 2001).

Cognitive factors would include children's abilities (i) initially to attend to the target face when they first see it, then (ii) to put what they attend to into memory (ie to encode), (iii) to store that information in memory, and (iv) to retrieve that information from memory. In connection with the ways that an investigator (eg a police officer) may assist a child to 'identify' a face seen before (of a person previously unknown to the child) say, by showing the child a set of faces, it is only at the retrieval stage that such help could be given. It is now well established that young children have relatively poor meta-memory skills. That is, they have not yet learned how best to retrieve what they have in memory (Milne and Bull, 1999). Also, young children's facial descriptions may not be as good as older children's or adults' (Flin, Markham and Davies, 1989). Therefore, our research project sought to establish that if younger children spontaneously provide fewer descriptors than do older children (which we indeed found—see results of study one, below), would the prompting of children to provide further (appropriate) descriptors (especially 'holistic' and 'configurational' ones, known to aid face processing—see Chapter 2) result in subsequent improved performance (especially in the TA condition)? This was the aim of our second study (described below). Although Pozzulo and Warren (2003) found that for children (around 12 years of age) there was no relationship between number of descriptors spontaneously provided and identification accuracy (for TA and TP arrays), they did note that procedures which might elicit greater amounts of correct descriptive information could be worth developing.

Social factors would include the pressure children feel under to choose a face. In the TA condition, helping the child to realize that (i) TA facial arrays do exist, and (ii) that the person conducting the 'test' would welcome a 'not there' or 'don't know' response (when this is correct), may result in more correct responses in the TA condition. This was the aim of our third study (which also was designed, in part, to replicate our second study regarding prompting). Goodman, Bottoms, Schwartz-Kenney and Rudy (1991) found that using 'practice' photo arrays including a TA array (regarding the child's mother) reduced children's false identifications in a subsequent task (however, only for the older children). Similarly, Parker and Ryan (1993) found that practice with a TA and a TP array reduced errors when a test presented the faces together in a single array (but not when the test faces were presented sequentially one at a time). (However, Davies et al, 1988; Lindsay, Pozzulo, Craig, Lee and Corber, 1997; and Pozzulo and Lindsay, 1997, found no beneficial effect of practice.) Parker and Myers (2001) also found no effect of practice for TA arrays.

With regard to making it clearer to children that an 'I don't know' response is acceptable, Schwartz-Kenney, Bottoms and Goodman (1996) found in the first of their two studies that not making the acceptability of this response explicit to children resulted in few 'don't know' responses (even when this was the correct response). In their second study which made it more explicit, there was an increase in 'don't know' responses. However, they noted that this effect was not as strong as it could have been, and they recommended that children undertake practice involving TA line-ups. Indeed, in another identification study (Memon and Rose, 2002), although 'children were given the option to say "don't know", not a single child took this up' (2002, 10). However, Mulder and Vrij (1996) found that 'don't know' instructions improved children's verbal responses to questions.

Ethnicity

In order to reflect the fact that England is a multi-ethnic society, children from various ethnicities (African Caribbean, Indian Asian, and white) were invited to participate in our research (Bull et al, 2001) and the faces we showed them were Indian Asian, white, and African Caribbean (all photographed in England). We also showed them Japanese faces (photographed in Japan). Few previous studies had been conducted on whether children recognize better faces of their own ethnicity. (See Chapter 4 for a review of such studies with adults.) In North America Feinman and Entwistle (1976) had found ethnicity to affect children's recognition of photographs (of other children), but Goldstein and Chance (1980) and Chance, Turner and Goldstein (1982) found no such effect (using photographs of adults). These rather contradictory findings led Pezdek, Blandon-Gitlin and Moore (2003) to state that 'it is difficult to know what advice expert witnesses should offer jurors regarding whether the cross-race effect operates for children' (2003, 760). However, they noted that while in the 1976 study children of two ethnicities had participated, in the 1980 and 1982 studies only children of one ethnicity participated and photographs of their own ethnicity and of Japanese people had been shown to them. In their own study Pezdek et al (2003) found that for children and adults (in Los Angeles) 'for each age group, own-race identification was more accurate than cross-race identification' (2003, 761). However, for the 'third graders' (mean age 8.63 years) while the 'black' children recognized the 'black' faces better than the 'white' faces, the 'white' children recognized both faces equally well. Nevertheless, Pezdek et al (2003) concluded that 'expert witnesses on eyewitness identification should be confident testifying that for children as well as adults, own-race faces are recognised more accurately than cross-race faces' (2003, 763). A more recent study by Corenblum and Meissner (2006) produced results that seem to support this 2003 conclusion (but again the children who participated were all of only one ethnicity—'Euro-Canadian'), as did a study conducted in France by Sangrigoli and de Schonen (2004) with three-to-five-year-old white children whose experience of Asian faces was small (though it is not clear from the report of their study whether ethnicity had a statistical 'main effect').

Our three related studies involved: (i) noting the descriptors that children of different ages spontaneously used to describe various faces; (ii) prompting half the children (using a list generated from study one) to provide more descriptors than provided by themselves spontaneously to see if this improved later face identification performance; and (iii) replication/repeat of study two but with the additional factor of 'standard' or 'enhanced' instructions regarding TA photo spreads.

Study one

In study one 140 children were individually asked to describe in their own words each of 12 different faces shown to them which varied in (i) ethnicity (African Caribbean, white, Indian Asian, Japanese) and (ii) age (child, younger adult, older adult). The boys and girls were aged six to eleven years, their ethnicity was Indian Asian, white, African Caribbean, and for the white children they were from London or from the Isle Of Wight (where the vast majority of the population are white and thus their more limited familiarity with other ethnicities might affect their performance—see Brigham and Malpass, 1985; Feinman and Entwistle, 1976).

It was found that the children very rarely provided descriptors that could be classified as 'incorrect'. The psychological literature on face processing suggests that such processing (and therefore identification) will be less successful/less 'mature' if it only involves the processing of separate facial features rather than 'configurational' or 'holistic' processing (see Chapter 2). In our study the older children did provide more holistic descriptors. Regarding possible effects of ethnicity, similar numbers of descriptors were provided across all four ethnicities of face by all three ethnicities of child. Similarly, when we analysed the data for each descriptor separately (eg of hair, of eyes) there were very few effects of ethnicity. Thus, study one was successful in gathering for each face a list of descriptors that children provided.

Study two

The main purpose of study two was to see if prompting some of the children to provide more descriptors of each face (derived from study one) would aid their subsequent photo spread performance. In this study 154 children African Caribbean, white, and Asian Indian girls and boys (aged six to seven or ten to eleven years) were shown each of two male faces (one at a time—a younger adult and an older adult) for ten seconds and asked what type of job each might have (to try to ensure that they concentrated on the face). Directly after seeing each face (one of their own ethnicity and one of another ethnicity) they then described it from memory (prompted to provide more descriptors or not prompted). Two hours later they were shown two photo spreads (one at a time) and asked to say for each face seen earlier (job now mentioned back to them) whether or not it was in the relevant photo spread and if it was to point to it. Each photo spread was of faces of the same ethnicity and age as the 'target' face. Some photo spreads contained the target and some did not.

In this second study the children's performance was significantly better on TP photo spreads than on TA ones (92% versus 60%), this being in line with the results of previous research. However, there was no effect on identification performance of prompting half of the children to provide more (correct) descriptors (77% versus 75%).

Also, there was no effect of 'own' versus 'other' ethnicity for TP performance (96% versus 88%). For TA correct performance, there was no effect of 'own' versus 'other' ethnicity for the older adult face (various faces/targets were used) but a significant effect for the younger adult face (again, various faces were used) (70% versus 49%). With regard to 'familiarity' (ie white in London or Isle of Wight), while there were no effects for the TP, or for TA older adult photo spread, for the TA young adult photo spread, lower familiarity children performed significantly better for 'own' than for 'other' ethnicity (56% versus 0%). Thus, the effects of ethnicity and familiarity were limited.

Study three

The main purposes of the third study were (i) again to see whether prompting might assist children (this study had already been decided upon before the results of study two were known so as to try to replicate whatever the findings of study two turned out to be) and (ii) to see if 'enhanced' instructions might reduce false choosing from TA photo spreads. In this study another 154 children (white, Indian Asian, African Caribbean) were shown for ten seconds each of two young adult male faces and asked to state what job each might have, one face was of 'own' ethnicity and one of 'other' ethnicity. A week later they were asked to describe each face (job mentioned to them) from memory either spontaneously or with prompting. Two hours later they were shown two photo spreads, one of which was target-absent and one target-present. Half the children were given 'enhanced' instructions (explained below) concerning the possibility of TA photo spreads.

The 'standard' TA instructions mentioned that the target face 'may or may not be there' (ie the instructions police in England and Wales are required to give).

Those children who received the 'enhanced' instructions received the 'standard' instructions and additionally for them beneath each six faces photo spread was a 'Not there' card and a 'Don't know' card that they were told they could point to. These children were encouraged at test to look at the whole of each face and they also experienced a practice TA photo spread for which they were asked if their school head teacher were present. These children's performance on this practice photo spread was very impressive, as we had indeed hoped. Not one of them chose a face, indicating that they had understood that the face they were looking for may not be present. However, and rather surprisingly, the enhanced instructions did not improve performance on the main task.

Again there were very limited effects of ethnicity and familiarity, which does not support the conclusion of Pezdek et al (2003). We suggest that the country (and cities/towns) in which such studies are conducted will probably turn out to be an important factor due partly to their varying social and ethnic histories and their current situations regarding immigration, employment prospects, prejudice and so on.

Although the enhanced instructions had no effect on photo spread performance regarding the once-seen face, there were some interesting findings regarding the notion that better descriptions might help. For example, in the spontaneous description condition the children who provided more descriptors more often correctly rejected the TA array; prompting did lead to more holistic and configurational descriptors being provided; asking children the reasons for their line-up decision revealed that for TA arrays those who did mention either holistic or configurational descriptors performed better than those who only mentioned featural descriptors (Schwarzer, 2002).

The findings of this research project involving the three studies described above suggests that trying to improve children's facial recognition performance, especially for TA photo spreads, will be a very challenging task.

OTHER IDEAS

Another way of possibly improving children's descriptions is to enable them to use the interviewer as a comparison or 'standard' to guide their descriptions (eg the interviewer might say 'Was he taller or shorter than me?'). Unfortunately, we have recently found the use of 'a standard' not to be generally effective for children (Kask, Bull, Heinla and Davies, 2007) or adults (Kask, Bull and Davies, 2006).

Miller, Fremouw, Aljazireh and Parker (1996) conducted a study to examine whether (a) use of the cognitive interview (Milne and Bull, 1999) or (b) the provision of a number of prompt cards (eg for actions or for the event setting or for people in the event) would produce enhanced memory of witnessed events. While both of these techniques improved verbal recall, neither of them improved performance on the photo spreads. For the adults, the lack of improvement could be due to the fact that without these techniques performance on the photo spread (which always contained the target) was very good. For the children (aged seven to ten years), performance without either technique averaged 67% thus leaving some room for improvement. However, neither technique led to a significant improvement, and photo spread performance was actually significantly poorer for the prompt card technique. Thus, yet again, it was not possible to improve children's face/person identification performance.

Pozzulo and Lindsay (1999) noted: 'To date, attempts to find training tasks or instructions that reduce children's false-positive line-up decisions have faired poorly' (1999, 168). However, they did find that their 'elimination procedure resulted in children making fewer false-positives' (1999, 174). This procedure essentially involves requiring witnesses to eliminate all but one of the faces in the presented array before they are asked if the remaining face is the target. However, Beresford and Blades (2006) found that their version of the 'elimination procedure' was no better at improving children's performance on a TA line-up than were instructions that highlighted the negative consequences of choosing the wrong person.

Sometimes a crime perpetrator's appearance can change considerably in the time between the crime and the later line-up (eg from long to short hair). Pozzulo and Balfour's more recent (2006) study did again find the 'elimination procedure' to result in children making fewer choices from TA arrays when the target's/suspect's appearance had not changed. But when the suspect's hair length had changed (and the people in the array matched this change in hair length), the 'elimination procedure' did not improve performance. Thus, yet again, it seems that improving children's performance is an unresolved challenge.

INTERVIEWER MANNER

Although ever-growing numbers of research studies and of professional guidance documents are becoming available on the topic of gathering information from child witnesses, the vast majority of these relate to topics such as memory and question types rather than to how the interviewer should behave (eg either in a business-like/formal manner or in an informal/supportive manner). An overview of the limited number of available studies on this topic (Memon, Vrij and Bull, 2003) noted that interviewer manner may well play a (complex) role, especially regarding the effects of unskilled questioning (Bull and Corran, 2002). However, almost no studies have examined whether interviewer manner might influence the person/face identification performance of vulnerable witnesses. Paterson, Bull and Vrij (2002) found not only that a supportive manner/style influenced children's correct verbal recall, but that it had an almost significant effect on their photo spread performance.

CONCLUSION REGARDING CHILDREN

Near to the end of their 1996 paper, Schwarz-Kenney et al stated:

we are confident that future investigations will culminate in the development of a line-up interview technique that will effectively facilitate children's person identification . . . It is up to empirical researchers to help ensure the attainment of this goal so that children's actual abilities are not underestimated . . . So that questions of guilt and innocence are answered. (1996, 131)

We hope that this review of the literature will prove to be a worthwhile addition to the, as yet, rather sparse literature on assisting child witnesses' identification performance. Even though research to date has usually not resulted in the development of effective techniques, the outcomes are likely to be useful in point-ing future research in alternative directions.

OLDER ADULTS

IMPORTANCE OF ELDERLY WITNESSES

Many developed countries have an ageing population. In the UK, between 1971 and 2005 the proportion of the population of adults aged 65 and over increased from 13% to 16% (National Statistics, 2006). Within this age group even larger increases have been seen in adults aged 85 and over, where between 1971 and 2004 the proportion of the UK population aged 85 and over had more than doubled from 0.9% to 1.9% (National Statistics, 2005). By 2031 the proportion of the population aged 65 and over is projected to rise to 23%. Not only is the population in many countries ageing but older adults are also remaining fit, active, and healthy for longer which in turn means they may be more likely to witness crime and be involved in the Criminal Justice System (Rothman, Dunlop and Entzel, 2000). Additionally, older adults may also be victims of crime. Thornton et al (2003) found that in 2001/02 there were 19,400 reported cases of distraction burglary where the victim was aged 60 years and over. In light of these factors researchers have recently become interested in examining the performance of older adult witnesses.

There are some issues for researchers examining the effects of ageing on eyewitness performance. First, when should one classify a witness as an 'older witness'? Bear in mind that Valentine, Pickering and Darling (2003) found in an archival study that suspects were significantly more likely to be identified by witnesses younger than 30 years! However, most of the research discussed below classifies older witnesses as either 60 and over or 65 and over. This is in accordance with the age at which women in the UK are currently able to receive their state pension at 60 years (though this will rise to 65 by 2020) and men at 65 years. Second, should researchers differentiate between young-old (75–84 years) and old-old (85 years and over) adults? There is some evidence to suggest that young-old and old-old adults may perform differently on line-ups (Memon, Gabbert and Hope, 2004) and thus if we examine the perform-ance of older witnesses as one large group (eg defined as anyone above 74 years) we may overlook some important individual differences.

Prior to examining the performance of older witnesses on line-ups and how we may be able to aid their performance we will briefly review the possible effects of ageing on the memory processes of encoding, storage, and retrieval.

IMPLICATIONS OF AGEING FOR WITNESS PERFORMANCE

As discussed in Chapter 2, in order to successfully identify a perpetrator witnesses must first have perceived, paid attention to, and encoded the crime event. There is then a retention period during which time the information is stored in memory prior to it being retrieved and/or the perpetrator being recognized. Ageing can affect any or all of these stages.

Older adults are immediately at a disadvantage compared to younger adults at the initial stage of perceiving the crime event due to losses in the sensory systems. Changes in the structures of the eye associated with ageing result in less efficient processing of visual stimuli. Hearing is also likely to be affected by ageing, with half of individuals aged between 75 and 79 years having measurable hearing loss (Schneider and Pichora-Fuller, 2000). Witnesses must also selectively pay attention to the crime/criminal whilst ignoring other surrounding irrelevant information. Evidence suggests that older adults are more likely to demonstrate attentional deficits (McDowd and Shaw, 2000), meaning that they may not encode information as efficiently as younger adults. Rabinowitz, Craik and Ackerman (1982) found that older adults were less likely to encode specific contextual details (about to-be-remembered words). Instead they encoded more general and less distinctive information which is likely to lead to poorer retrieval.

The period between encoding an event and subsequently trying to remember it is known as the retention period. Few studies have investigated the effect of length of retention period on older witness performance. Memon, Bartlett, Rose and Gray (2003) studied the identification performance of older and younger witnesses after a 20 minute delay and a one week delay. After a week older adults were less accurate than when the delay was just 20 minutes. Other researchers, rather than looking specifically at the effect of length of delay, have been more interested in what occurs during the delay. During the period in which information is being retained, additional information relating to a crime may be learnt from newspapers or other witnesses. This new information could be integrated with or overlay the existing memory, and then when the information is recalled it may include the additional information (which may or may not be accurate). Cohen and Faulkner (1989) showed young and older participants an event on video and then they read a written version of the event containing some misinformation (ie incorrect information). Older participants were more often misled by the misinformation compared to the younger adults. However, it should be noted that other research has found no evidence that older adults are more prone to suggestibility (Coxon and Valentine, 1997). For more details of suggestibility in older eyewitness testimony and interviewing older witnesses see the review by Mueller-Johnson and Ceci (2007).

One factor that may explain why older witnesses may be more susceptible to misinformation is that older adults are more likely to make source-monitoring errors (Hastroudi, Johnson and Chrosniak, 1989). Source monitoring refers to identifying where information was learnt, for example: (a) did a person experience an event and therefore the information comes directly from that experience; or (b) did they hear about an event from another person, dream or imagine it? In the eyewitness context, after a witness has seen a crime they may learn new information about the crime (which could be either accurate or inaccurate) through other witnesses, by reading the newspaper, or through information mistakenly being introduced during an interview. If the witness is an older adult they may make mistakes in their source monitoring and recount the crime including the new information that was learnt subsequently to the crime.

EFFECT OF AGE ON IDENTIFICATION PERFORMANCE

Some of the early research investigating the accuracy of young and old 'mock' eye-witnesses who had viewed a simulated crime (depicted in a series of slides) found there was no effect of age on correct identification of the perpetrator (Yarmey and Kent, 1980; Yarmey, Tressillian Jones and Rashid, 1984). However, Yarmey et al (1984) also found that older witnesses made substantially more false identifications from both TP and TA line-ups. More recently, Searcy, Bartlett and Memon (1999) showed younger (18 to 30 years) and older (60 to 80 years) mock witnesses a video recorded re-enactment of a real crime involving two perpetrators. Older witnesses were significantly more likely to make false identifications than younger witnesses on both line-ups, regardless of whether the line-up was target present or target absent. This finding has been replicated in a number of subsequent studies (Memon and Bartlett, 2002; Searcy, Bartlett and Memon, 2000; Rose, Bull and Vrij, 2005; Wilcock, Bull and Vrij, 2005, 2007). These findings have been replicated using a delay of a week (Memon et al, 2003). A further study by Memon, Hope and Bull (2003) found that length of exposure to the perpetrator's face (either 12 seconds or 45 seconds) had a significant effect on older witnesses' identification performance with longer duration of exposure leading to more accurate line-up performance in terms of correctly identifying the perpetrator, correctly rejecting a TA line-up, and making fewer false identifications.

All of the above studies have considered the older participant group as one large group, however, Memon et al (2004) investigated the identification abilities of young-old witnesses aged between 60 and 68 years and old-old mock witnesses aged between 69 and 81 years. They found significant differences between these two groups of older witnesses, in that 75% of the old-old witnesses made false identifications from a TA line-up compared to just 13% of the young-old witnesses. This would suggest that witnesses who could be classified as old-old may be particularly prone to making false identifications.

One study has investigated the effect of showing mug shots prior to the line-up on older witnesses' identification performance. Memon, Hope, Bartlett and Bull (2002) asked participants to view a crime event on videotape and then look at a mug shot album to see if they could identify the perpetrator. They found that older mock witnesses were more likely to make a choice from the mug shot album than younger mock witnesses. In a subsequent line-up one of the already seen mug shots was included (the 'critical foil'). If a witness had made a choice from the mug shot album they were more likely to falsely identify the critical foil as the perpetrator (regardless of whether they had chosen the critical foil from the mug shot book or another mug shot). Memon et al suggested that participants who chose from the mug shot book and then chose the critical foil in the line-up were likely to be responding due to a feeling of familiarity for the face rather than being able to recall the specific details of the face. This would explain why older witnesses were more likely than younger witnesses to choose from the mug shot book (because they may not have encoded fully the details of the perpetrators face and were therefore only able to respond using perceived familiarity for a face). For a more in-depth discussion of the effect of viewing mug shots on identification performance see Chapter 4.

Some research has examined the relationship between eyewitness confidence and older witnesses' line-up accuracy. Scogin, Calhooon and D'Errico (1994) examined young (18 to 35 years), young-old (59 to 74 years) and old-old (75 to 94 years) adults' performance on a photographic line-up task having viewed a crime shown on video-tape. They found no significant correlation between line-up accuracy and self-ratings of confidence in any age group, meaning that even if an older witness is extremely confident that they have correctly identified the perpetrator this does not necessarily mean they are correct in their identification. Other researchers have also found no correlation to exist between confidence and line-up accuracy in older adults (Adams-Price, 1992; Memon et al, 2002, 2003; Wilcock et al, 2007). (See Chapter 4 for a fuller discussion of the relationship between confidence and accuracy.) Researchers have also investigated whether older adults are as confident in their line-up decisions as younger adults. Some research suggests they are less confident than younger adults (Memon et al, 2002; 2003; Wilcock et al, 2003), whilst other research has found no difference between the two groups (Adams-Price, 1992; Searcy et al, 1999). Neuschatz et al (2005) investigated whether the post-identification feedback effect found in young adults translates to older adults. They found that older adults were as suscep-tible as younger adults to the effects of feedback from a line-up administrator. When the administrator said to participants that they had correctly identified the suspect, this had the effect of inflating their confidence that they had correctly identified the perpetrator compared to those who had received no feedback. (See Chapter 4 for a fuller discussion of the relationship between feedback on identification performance and subsequent confidence.)

AIDING OLDER WITNESSES' PERFORMANCE

It would be more helpful to develop methods for aiding the performance of older wit-nesses. Some research has demonstrated with young adults that context reinstatement (CR) instructions (eg to mentally recreate the context in which the target face was ini-tially seen) can lead to greater identification accuracy (eg Cutler, Penrod and Martens, 1987; Gwyer and Clifford 1997; Malpass and Devine, 1981a; O'Rourke, Penrod, Cutler and Stuve, 1989). Thus far, just three studies have investigated whether the beneficial effect of CR instructions might translate to older witnesses. Searcy, Bartlett, Memon and Swanson (2001) and Memon et al (2004) found that the cognitive interview (CI) compared with a structured interview had no effect on the number of false identifi-cations made by older adults. Similarly, Memon at al (2002) found CR instructions failed to reduce the rate of false identifications made by older adults after exposure to mug shots. Wilcock et al (2007), instead of using standard CR instructions, examined the effect of photographic CR on line-up accuracy. That is, older participants viewed a series of photographs taken at the scene of the mock crime event and of objects in the crime event. They then used these photographic cues to aid mental reinstate-ment of context. There were three main reasons for using photographic context rein-statement. First, verbal recall of contextual details often shows age-related deficits (Schacter, Norman and Koutstaal, 1998). Using photographs means that participants have the context reinstatement in front of them, and they are not explicitly asked to try to mentally recreate context (as in previous investigations of effectiveness of context reinstatement by older witnesses). Second, using photographs of the crime scene may well often be feasible in the forensic setting. Third, older people are probably very familiar with looking at photographs, whereas they may not be familiar with mnemonic methods such as context reinstatement. Photographic context reinstatement led to significantly fewer false identifications in older 'mock' witnesses on one of two line-ups. Further research investigating whether some form of context reinstatement could aid the performance of older adults on line-ups is warranted.

Other research investigating how best to aid older witnesses has examined the role of older witnesses' memory for non-biased line-up instructions. Malpass and Devine (1981b) were the first to demonstrate the importance of non-biased line-up instructions (ie informing witnesses that the perpetrator *may or may not* be present in the line-up). They found that failure to warn witnesses that the culprit may or may not be in the line-up (biased instructions) resulted in 78% of witnesses making false identifications from a TA line-up, whilst maintaining a high level of hits in the TP line-up. With the warning that the perpetrator may not be in the TA line-up (non-biased instructions) the false identification rate fell to 33%. More recently, Steblay (1997) conducted a meta-analysis of 18 studies which confirms that after witnesses receive biased line-up instructions a higher level of choosing ensues. Nowadays the importance of giving witnesses non-biased line-up instructions is recognized in several countries. Thus, informing the witness that the perpetrator may or may not be present in the line-up has been required of police forces in England and Wales since 1986 (Zander, 1990) and, more recently, has been recommended by the Attorney General in the US (Wells, Malpass, Lindsay, Fisher, Turtle and Fulero, 2000).

However, older witnesses may not actually remember being given non-biased line-up instructions prior to them making a line-up decision. Rose, Bull and Vrij (2003) found a significant effect of age group on reported memory for line-up instructions in that 91% of young adults said they remembered the instructions compared to only 75% of the older adults. However, these results were based on a simple 'yes/no' question. In a follow-up study, Rose et al (2005) asked younger and older participants an open question about their memory of the line-up instructions and again found a significant effect of age on recall of the line-up instructions (with 68% of younger participants being able to recall them correctly compared to only 46% of older participants). Further, and more importantly, there was a significant effect of memory for line-up instructions on line-up accuracy, with participants who failed to remember the line-up instructions making significantly more false identifications.

In light of these findings more recent research has investigated ways in which to increase older witnesses' memory for the non-biased line-up instructions. Wilcock et al (2005) attempted to enhance the non-biased line-up instructions by giving a fictitious example of a case of false identification and briefly reviewing a DNA exoneration case before giving participants the standard non-biased line-up instructions. Though the enhanced line-up instructions led to significantly better memory concerning the possibility the perpetrator may or may not be present in the line-up, they had no significant effect on line-up performance. Memon and Gabbert (2003a) found that some 'pre-identification questions' (which had previously been found to reduce false identifications in young adults—Dysart and Lindsay, 2001) had no effect on older adults. One further study has investigated a different method of illustrating the standard non-biased line-up instructions by giving older mock witnesses a practice TA line-up prior to the line-up for the perpetrator shown in a videotaped mock crime event. Wilcock and Bull (manuscript in preparation) showed half of the mock witnesses a practice line-up composed of famous female faces and asked them to identify the Queen's face (which was absent). They then received standard non-biased line-up instructions. The practice line-up led to significantly fewer false identifications from a TA line-up, whilst maintaining the same rate of correct identifications from a TP line-up (compared to mock witnesses who just received the standard non-biased line-up instructions). Thus, such practice, though not benefiting young children (see earlier in this chapter) may benefit older adults.

The final area of research examining possible methods for enhancing older witnesses' performance has focused on line-up presentation methods. The majority or research examining the performance of older witnesses has used simultaneous line-ups (where all faces are shown together). Despite this, substantial amounts of research have demonstrated that showing members of a line-up one at a time in a sequential fashion substantially reduces the number of false identifications made by witnesses viewing TA line-ups (Steblay, Dysart, Fulero and Lindsay, 2001) (See Chapter 7 for a full discussion of sequential versus simultaneous line-ups.) Four studies of simultaneous versus sequential line-up presentation have found that, as with young adults, sequential line-up presentation reduces the rate of false identifications made by older adults viewing TA line-ups (Memon and Gabbert, 2003a; Rose et al, 2005; Wilcock et al, 2005). However, all four studies also found a reduction in correct identifications of the perpetrator from TP line-ups (Memon and Gabbert, 2003a, 2003b; Rose et al, 2005; Wilcock et al, 2005).

CONCLUSION REGARDING ELDERLY EYEWITNESSES

We know that older witnesses in general are likely to be less accurate than younger witnesses. We are currently less sure of how we can aid older witnesses' performance on line-ups. In addition to investigating interventions designed to improve the performance of older witnesses, we need to focus on the role of individual differences in line-up performance, in that it may not always be the case that the older a witness the more likely they are to perform poorly. We should also consider the role of line-up administrators and how they can best interact with this group of witnesses (see Wright and Holliday, 2005).

WITNESSES WITH INTELLECTUAL DISABILITIES

In many countries the view may still be held that people with 'intellectual disabilities' (ie what used to be called 'mental handicap' or 'mental retardation') rarely witness criminal activity or other types of wrongdoing. However, it is becoming ever clearer, at least in some countries, that such people do have these experiences, either as victims or as 'bystanders' (Ericson and Isaacs, 2003). This is not only for those who may be in residential care but also for those who live independently in the community (which is being encouraged in a number of countries). Those who live in the community may be more likely to witness things done by people whom they do not already know well than those living in residential care where most people they see are well or fairly well known to them. However, in both types of setting the person identification/recognition abilities of people with intellectual disabilities is likely to be important. Unfortunately, almost no relevant research studies have been conducted.

In Canada, Ericson and Isaacs (2003) showed to adults with intellectual disabilities a film clip of a non-violent purse theft (which they also showed to adults without disabilities). Then the participants were shown a photo spread of five different men and were told:

I would like you to look carefully at the pictures and tell me if you see the man who played the thief (first man who ran out of the store). He may be in the pictures you see or he may not be in the pictures. If you don't remember/aren't sure of what he looks like don't guess, just say 'I don't know'. If you are sure that you see the thief, tell me which person that you think it is. You can have as much time as you want to look at the pictures. (2003, 166)

The photo spread that all participants then saw did not, in fact, contain the thief, but five men whose photographs Ericson and Isaacs had carefully selected to look like the thief (ie as in a 'good' or 'fair' photo spread). The adults without intellectual disabilities chose a person from this photo spread (ie made a false identification) 24% of the time, whereas those with intellectual disabilities did so 55% of the time. Such a differential rate of error between the two groups could have been due to the people with intellectual disabilities either (i) having a poorer memory of the thief or (ii) feeling more obliged to make a choice (or, of course, to both). In order to compare these alternative explanations (one based largely on 'cognitive' processes and the other on more 'social' processes) Ericson and Isaacs then showed to all the participants a second photo spread that, this time, did contain the thief. For this photo spread the rates of correctly identifying the thief were 20% and 23% respectively (ie those with intellectual disabilities performed slightly better), suggesting that memory for the actual thief did not differ between the two groups. On this TP photo spread the rates of choosing a wrong face were 5% and 30% respectively, suggesting that those with intellectual disabilities felt more obliged to make a choice.

The much higher rates of incorrect choosing (both for TP and TA photo spreads) by those with intellectual disabilities occurred even though for each man in the photo spreads there were five different photographs of him, these being: 'A full frontal view, a close up frontal shot of the face and upper body, one view of each three quarter profile, and a (left) side view' (2003, 166). Perhaps having so many photographs of each man encouraged those with intellectual disabilities to choose, even though they had been told (see above) that the thief may or may not be in the photographs. Also, being paid for their participation may have affected some individuals' choosing rates.

All of the participants who did not make a choice from either photo spread were asked to indicate the reason for this. The possible explanations were:

(i)   the participant did not think that the target was present;
(ii) the participant could not remember what the target looked like; or
(iii) the participant was not sure which of the men in the photo spread was the target (ie could not distinguish between the men or did not feel sure enough to make a choice).

Among these non-choosers, around three-quarters of those with intellectual abilities indicated that the explanation was that they were not sure which of the men was the target and only 6% (ie one) indicated that the explanation was that the target was not present. However, of those without intellectual disabilities just over half indicated that the explanation was that the target was not present and only a third that the explanation was that they were not sure which was the target.

Ericson and Isaacs pointed out that the participants with intellectual disabilities made as many correct identifications (ie for TP photo spreads) as did the participants without intellectual disabilities. However, the former made many more false choices (both from TP and TA photo spreads). Also the former rarely in terms of non-choosing indicated that this was because the target was not present. Thus these researchers concluded that 'participants with intellectual disabilities were under the impression that the suspect must be present' (2003, 168), even though they had been told that the target/suspect/perpetrator 'may or may not be present'. Thus they recommended that individuals with intellectual disabilities may need practice with identification tasks and additional detailed instructions in order to understand better that the target/perpetrator may not be present (in the photo spread). Sensible as this recommendation is, this is what our 2001 study (for the Home Office) with children examined in an attempt to reduce their false choosing from TA photo spreads. As described earlier in this chapter, although in that child study the practice (at the head teacher TA photo spread) was 100% successful, this practice did not generalise to the test situation. Thus, those who seek to build on Ericson and Isaacs sensible recommendation will need to devote considerable thought to the question of what effective practice should involve.

CONCLUSION

The research reviewed above makes it clear that while the identification performance of vulnerable witnesses may not differ much from that of ordinary witnesses when the perpetrator is indeed among the persons seen, when the perpetrator's face is not present they are considerably prone to choosing a face (and more so than ordinary adults). While some pioneering attempts have been made to try to improve their performance, most of these have, to date, been unsuccessful.

FURTHER READING

MUELLER-JOHNSON, K. and CECI, S. (2007). The elderly eyewitness: A review and prospectus. In M.P. TOGLIA, J.D. READ, D.F. ROSS and R.C.L. LINDSAY (eds) *Handbook of Eyewitness Psychology: Memory for Events Volume 1.* Mahwah, NJ: Lawrence Erlbuam Associates, 577–603.

POZZULO, J. and BALFOUR, J. (2006). Children's and adults' eyewitness identification accuracy when a culprit changes his appearance: Comparing simultaneous and elimination lineup procedures. *Legal and Criminological Psychology, 11,* 25–34.

REFERENCES

ADAMS PRICE, C. (1992). Eyewitness memory and aging: Predictors of accuracy in recall and person recognition. *Psychology and Aging, 7,* 602–608.

BEAL, C., SCHMIDT, K. and DEKLE, D. (1995). Eyewitness identification of children: Effects of absolute judgements, nonverbal response options, and event encoding. *Law and Human Behavior, 19,* 197–216.

BERESFORD, J. and BLADES, M. (2006). Children's identifications of faces from lineups: The effects of lineup presentation and instructions on accuracy. *Journal of applied Psychology, 91,* 1102–1113.

BRIGHAM, J. and MALPASS, R. (1985). The role of experience and contact in the recognition of faces of own- and other-race. *Journal of Social Issues, 41,* 139–155.

BULL, R. and CORRAN, E. (2002). Interviewing child witnesses: Past and future. *International Journal of Police Science and Management, 4,* 315–322.

——, GEORGE, P., KNIGHT, S. and PATERSON, B. (2001). *Trying to improve children's facial identifications.* Final report to the Home Office. London: Home Office.

CAIN, W., BAKER-WARD, L. and EATON, K. (2005). A face in the crowd: The influences of familiarity and delay on preschoolers' recognition. *Psychology, Crime, and Law, 11,* 315–327.

COHEN, G. and FAULKNER, D. (1989). Age differences in source forgetting: Effects on reality monitoring and on eyewitness testimony. *Psychology and Aging, 4,* 10–17.

CORENBLUM, B. and MEISSNER, C. (2006). Recognition of faces of ingroup and outgroup children and adults. *Journal of Experimental Child Psychology, 93,* 187–206.

COXON, P. and VALENTINE, T. (1997). The effects of age of eyewitness on the accuracy and suggestibility of their testimony. *Applied Cognitive Psychology, 11,* 415–430.

CROSS, J.F., CROSS, J. and DALY, J. (1971). Sex, race, age and beauty as factors of recognition of faces. *Perception and Psychophysics, 10,* 393–396.

CUTLER, B.L., PENROD, S.D. and MARTENS, T.K. (1987). Improving the reliability of eyewitness identifications: Putting context into context. *Journal of Applied Psychology, 72,* 629–637.

DAVIES, G., STEVENSON-ROBB, Y. and FLIN, R. (1988). Tales out of school: Children's memory for an unexpected event. In M. Gruneberg, R. Sykes and P. Morris (eds) *Practical Aspects of Memory: Vol. 1. Memory in Everyday Life.* Chichester: Wiley, 122–127.

——, TARRANT, A. and FLIN, R. (1989). Close encounters of the witness kind: Children's memory for a simulated health inspection. *British Journal of Psychology, 80,* 415–429.

DYSART, J.E. and LINDSAY, R.C.L. (2001). A pre-identification questioning effect: Serendipitously increasing correct rejections. *Law and Human Behavior, 25,* 155–165.

ERICSON, K. and ISAACS, B. (2003). Eyewitness identification accuracy: A comparison of adults with and those without intellectual disabilities. *Mental Retardation, 41,* 161–173.

FEINMAN, S. and ENTWISLE, D. (1976). Children's ability to recognise other children's faces. *Child Development, 47,* 506–510.

GOODMAN, G., BOTTOMS, B., SCHWARTZ-KENNEY, B. and RUDY, L. (1991). Children's testimony for a stressful event: Improving children's reports. *Journal of Narrative and Life History, 1,* 69–99.

GROSS, J. and HAYNE, H. (1996). Eyewitness identification by 5- to 6-year-old children. *Law and Human Behavior, 20,* 359–373.

GWYER, P. and CLIFFORD, B.R. (1997). The effects of the cognitive interview on recall, identification, confidence and the confidence/accuracy relationship. *Applied Cognitive Psychology, 11,* 121–145.

HASHTROUDI, S., JOHNSON, M.K. and CHROSNIAK, L.D. (1989). Aging and source monitoring. *Psychology and Aging, 4,* 106–112.

KASK, K., BULL, R. and DAVIES, G. (2006). Trying to improve young adults' person descriptions. *Psychiatry, Psychology, and Law, 13,* 174–181.

——, —— and GILLETT, R. (In submission, 2008). *A meta-analysis of child identification studies.*

——, ——, HEINLA, I. and DAVIES, G. (2007). The effect of a standard to assist children's person descriptions. *Journal of Police and Criminological Psychology, 22,* 77–83.

LINDSAY, R., POZZULO, J., CRAIG, W., LEE, K. and CORBER, S. (1997). Simultaneous lineups, sequential lineups, and showups: Eyewitness identification of adults and children. *Law and Human Behavior, 21,* 391–404.

MALPASS, R.S. and DEVINE, P.G. (1981a). Guided memory in eyewitness identification. *Journal of Applied Psychology, 66,* 343–350.

—— and —— (1981b). Eyewitness identification: Lineup instructions and the absence of the offender. *Journal of Applied Psychology, 66,* 482–489.

McDOWD, J.M. and SHAW, R.J. (2000). Attention and aging: A functional perspective. In F.I.M. Craik and T.A. Salthouse (eds) *The Handbook of Aging and Cognition.* Mahwah, NJ: Lawrence Erlbaum Associates, 221–292.

MEMON, A. and BARTLETT, J.C. (2002). The effect of verbalisation on face recognition in young and old adults. *Applied Cognitive Psychology, 16,* 635–650.

——, ——, ROSE, R. A. and GRAY, C. (2003). The aging eyewitness: Effects of age of face, delay and source memory ability. *The Journal of Gerontology: Psychological Sciences, 58,* 338–345.

—— and GABBERT, F. (2003a). Improving the identification accuracy of senior witnesses: Do pre-lineup questions and sequential testing help? *Journal of Applied Psychology, 88,* 341–347.

—— and —— (2003b). Unravelling the effect of sequential lineup presentation in culprit present lineups. *Applied Cognitive Psychology, 17,* 1–12.

—— and ROSE, R. (2002). Identification abilities of children: Does a verbal description hurt face recognition? *Psychology, Crime and Law, 8,* 229–242.

——, —— and HOPE, L. (2004). The ageing eyewitness. In J. Adler (ed.) *Forensic Psychology: Debates, Concepts, and Practice.* Uffcolme, Devon: Willan, 96–112.

——, HOPE, L., BARTLETT, J.C. and BULL, R. (2002). Eyewitness recognition errors: The effects of mugshot viewing and choosing in younger and older adults. *Memory and Cognition, 30,* 1219–1227.

——, —— and BULL, R. (2003). Exposure duration: Effects on eyewitness accuracy and confidence. *British Journal of Psychology, 94,* 339–354.

——, VRIJ, A. and BULL, R. (2003). *Psychology and Law: Truthfulness, accuracy and credibility* (2nd edn). Chichester: Wiley.

MILLER, C., FREMOUW, W., ALJAZIREH, L. and PARKER, B.K. (1996). Two methods of recall enhancement for child and adult eyewitness testimony. *American Journal of Forensic Psychology, 14,* 67–84.

MILNE, R. and BULL, R. (1999). *Investigative Interviewing: Psychology and Practice.* Chichester: Wiley.

—— and —— (2006). Interviewing victims of crime, including children and people with intellectual disabilities. In M. Kebbell and G. Davies (eds) *Practical Psychology For Forensic Investigations.* Chichester: Wiley, 7–24.

MUELLER-JOHNSON, K. and CECI, S.J. (2007). The elderly eyewitness: A review and prospectus. In M.P. Toglia, J.D. Read, D.F. Ross and R.C.L. Lindsay (eds) *Handbook of Eyewitness Psychology: Memory For Events. Volume* 1. Mahwah, NJ: Lawrence Erlbaum Associates, 577–603.

MULDER, M. and VRIJ, A. (1996). Explaining conversation rules to children: An intervention study to facilitate children's accurate responses. *Child Abuse and Neglect, 20,* 623–631.

NEUSCHATZ, J.S., PRESTON, E.L., BURKETT, A.D., TOGLIA, M.P., LAMPINEN, J.M., NEUSCHATZ, J.S., FAIRLESS, A.H., LAWSON, D.S., POWERS, R.A. and GOODSELL, C.A. (2005). The effects of post-identification feedback and age on retrospective eyewitness memory. *Applied Cognitive Psychology, 19,* 435–454.

O'ROURKE, T.E., PENROD, S.D., CUTLER, B.L. and STUVE, T.E. (1989). The external validity of eyewitness research: Generalizing across subject populations. *Law and Human Behavior, 13,* 385–395.

PARKER, J. and CARRANZA, L. (1989). Eyewitness testimony of children in target-present and target-absent lineups. *Law and Human Behavior, 13,* 133–149.

—— and MYERS, A. (2001). Attempts to improve children's identifications from sequential-presentation lineups. *Journal of Applied Social Psychology, 31,* 796–815.

—— and RYAN, V. (1993). An attempt to reduce guessing behavior in children's and adults' eyewitness identifications. *Law and Human Behavior, 17,* 11–26.

——, HAVERFIELD, E. and BAKER-THOMAS, S. (1986). Eyewitness testimony of children. *Journal of Applied Social Psychology, 16,* 287–302.

PATERSON, B., BULL, R. and VRIJ, A. (2002). *The effects of interviewer style on children's recall.* Paper presented at the 25th International Congress of Applied Psychology, Singapore.

PEZDEK, K., BLANDON-GITLIN, I. and MOORE, C. (2003). Children's face recognition memory: More evidence for the cross-race effect. *Journal of Applied Psychology, 88,* 760–763.

POZZULO, J. and BALFOUR, J. (2006). Children's and adults' eyewitness identification accuracy when a culprit changes his appearance: Comparing simultaneous and elimination lineup procedures. *Legal and Criminological Psychology, 11,* 25–34.

——, LEMIEUX, J., WELLS, E. and MCCUAIG, H. (2006). The influence of eyewitness identification decisions and age of witness on jurors' verdicts and perceptions of reliability. *Psychology, Crime, and Law, 12,* 641–652.

—— and LINDSAY, R. (1997). Increasing correct identifications by children. *Expert Evidence, 5,* 126–132.

—— and —— (1999). Elimination lineups: An improved identification procedure for child eyewitnesses. *Journal of Applied Psychology, 84,* 167–176.

—— and —— (2001). Eyewitness identification accuracy of children. In R. Bull (ed.) *Children and the Law.* Oxford: Blackwell.

—— and WARREN, K. (2003). Descriptions and identifications of strangers by youth and adult eyewitnesses. *Journal of Applied Psychology, 88,* 315–323.

RABONOWITZ, J.C., CRAIK, F.I.M. and ACKERMAN, B.P. (1982). A processing resource account of age differences in free recall. *Canadian Journal of Psychology, 36,* 325–344.

ROSE, R. A., BULL, R. and VRIJ, A. (2003). Enhancing older witnesses' identification performance: Context reinstatement is not the answer. *The Canadian Journal of Police and Security Services, 1,* 173–184.

——, —— and —— (2005). Non-biased lineup instructions do matter—A problem for older witnesses. *Psychology, Crime, and Law, 11,* 147–159.

ROTHMAN, M.B., DUNLOP, B.D. and ENTZEL, P. (2000). *Elders, Crime, and the Criminal Justice System. Myth, Perceptions, and Reality in the 21st Century.* New York: Springer Series on Life Styles and Issues in Aging.

SANGRIOLI, S. and DE SCHONEN, S. (2004). Effect of visual experience on face processing: A developmental study of inversion and non-native effects. *Developmental Science, 7,* 74–87.

SCHACTER, D.L., NORMAN, K.A. and KOUTSTAAL, W. (1998). The cognitive neuroscience of constructive memory. *Annual Review of Psychology, 49,* 289–318.

SCHNEIDER, B.A. and PICHORA-FULLER, M.K. (2000). Implications of perceptual deterioration for cognitive aging research. In F.I.M. Craik and T.A. Salthouse (eds) *The Handbook of Aging and Cognition.* Mahwah, NJ: Lawrence Erlbaum Associates, 155–219.

SCHWARTZ-KENNEY, B., BOTTOMS, B. and GOODMAN, G. (1996). Improving children's person identification. *Child Maltreatment, 1,* 121–133.

SCHWARZER, G. (2002). Processing of facial and non-facial visual stimuli in 2–5 year old children. *Infant and Child development, 11,* 253–269.

SCOGIN, F., CLAHOON, S.K. and D'ERRICO, M. (1994). Eyewitness confidence and accuracy among three age cohorts. *Journal of Applied Gerontology, 13,* 172–184.

SEARCY, J.H., BARTLETT, J.C. and MEMON, A. (1999). Age differences in accuracy and choosing in eyewitness identification and face recognition. *Memory and Cognition, 27,* 538–552.

——, —— and —— (2000). Relationship of availability, lineup conditions and individual differences to false identification by younger and older eyewitnesses. *Legal and Criminological Psychology, 5,* 219–236.

——, ——, —— and SWANSON, K. (2001). Aging and line-up performance at long retention intervals: Effects of metamemory and context reinstatement. *Journal of Applied Psychology, 86,* 207–214.

STEBLAY, N.M. (1997). Social influence in eyewitness recall: A meta-analytic review of lineup instruction effects. *Law and Human Behavior, 21,* 283–297.

——, DYSART, J., FULERO, S. and LINDSAY, R.C.L. (2001). Eyewitness accuracy rates in sequential and simultaneous lineup presentations: A meta-analytic comparison. *Law and Human Behavior, 25,* 459–476.

THORNTON, A., HATTON, C., MALONE, C., FRYER, T., WALKER, D., CUNNINGHAM, J. and DURRANI, N. (2003). *Distraction burglary amongst older adults and ethnic minority communities.* Home Office Research Study 269. Development and Statistics Directorate.

VALENTINE, T., PICKERING, A. and DARLING, S. (2003). Characteristics of eyewitness identifications that predict the outcome of real lineups. *Applied Cognitive Psychology, 17,* 969–993.

WELLS, G.L., MALPASS, R.S., LINDSAY, R.C.L., FISHER, R.P., TURTLE, J.W. and FULERO, S.M. (2000). From the lab to the police station. A successful application of eyewitness research. *American Psychologist, 55,* 581–598.

WESTCOTT, H., DAVIES, G. and BULL, R. (2002). *Children's Testimony: A Handbook of Psychological Research and Forensic Practice.* Chichester: Wiley.

WILCOCK, R.A. and BULL, R. (manuscript in preparation). *Novel lineup methods for improving the performance of older eyewitnesses.*

——, —— and VRIJ, A. (2005). Aiding the performance of older eyewitnesses: Enhanced non-biased lineup instructions and presentation. *Psychiatry, Psychology, and Law, 12,* 129–140.

——, —— and —— (2007). Are older witnesses always poorer witnesses? Identification accuracy, context reinstatement, own age bias. *Psychology, Crime, and Law, 13,* 305–316.

WRIGHT, A.M. and HOLLIDAY, R.E. (2005). Police officers' perceptions of older eyewitnesses. *Legal and Criminological Psychology, 10,* 211–224.

YARMEY, A.D. and KENT, J. (1980). Eyewitness identification by elderly and young adults. *Law and Human Behavior, 4,* 359–371.

YARMEY, A.D., TRESSILLIAN JONES, H.T. and RASHID, S. (1984). Eyewitness memory of elderly and young adults. In D.J. Muller, D.E., Blackman and A.J. Chapman (eds) *Psychology and Law.* Chichester, UK: John Wiley and Sons, 215–228.

ZANDER, M. (1990). *The Police and Criminal Evidence Act.* London: Sweet and Maxwell.

9

NEW INNOVATIONS: APPLYING PSYCHOLOGICAL SCIENCE TO THE REAL WORLD

INTRODUCTION

The preceding chapters of this book have clearly outlined that the process of recalling and/or identifying a person(s) who committed an offence is by no means a perfect one. To the contrary it is a very difficult and fragile process and can lead to miscarriages of justice. For example, in the US it has been estimated that almost 80% of the exoneration cases (on the basis of DNA evidence) of individuals wrongly convicted are at least in part due to faulty eyewitness identification evidence (McQuiston-Surrett, Topp and Malpass, 2006; see <http://www.innocenceproject.org>). Scheck, Neufeld and Dwyer (2001) further highlight that it is the inadequate procedures used by law enforcement organizations that are primarily responsible for this current state of affairs (in some countries), and that these inadequate systems even *facilitate* mistaken identifications (see Chapter 7 for system variables in identification procedures).

As a result numerous aids to memory have been developed over the years to try to help witnesses with the very difficult task of remembering 'who'. These 'memory aids' have over time become more technologically advanced; starting with a sketch artist attempting to draw a likeness with pen and paper, and leading to operators developing three dimensional computer-generated images. This chapter will therefore chart the history of the development of these tools and will examine whether they do in fact help in the plight of trying to attain a full and accurate description of a person or an accurate identification (ie do they help elicit memory for a person?).

IMPORTANCE OF FACIAL MEMORY TOOLS TO THE INVESTIGATION PROCESS

As noted in Chapter 3 the primary goal of any investigation is to answer two primary investigative questions: (i) what happened (if anything did indeed occur), and (ii) who committed the offence (Milne and Bull, 2006)? It should be crystal clear by now, having read the prior chapters in this book, that the endeavour to answer these two basic questions is not an easy one. For the witness, the investigative process typically starts with an interview, in which at some point the witness is asked to describe in detail the perpetrator(s) of the incident they have experienced (though see Chapter 3 for information on the initial call handling phase of the investigative process; Ambler and Milne, 2006). As has also been detailed in Chapter 3, witnesses have great difficulty eliciting from memory a full and accurate description of a perpetrator. As a result, in serious cases (eg sexual assault and murder) where the perpetrator(s) is unknown to the witness, witnesses are sometimes asked, a number of days or even weeks later, to construct a facial composite of the culprit from memory. In the UK the Association of Chief Police Officers Scotland (ACPOS) Facial Imaging Guidance outlines that such facial composites should be constructed within 24 to 36 hours. This timeframe however is rarely met. What is a facial composite? And how are facial composites used within an investigation?

The Association of Chief Police Officers of England, Wales, and Northern Ireland (ACPO) *National Working Practices in Facial Imaging Guidance* (2003) for practitioners clearly defines a facial composite as:

a pictorial record of the memory of a witness from their recall. The objective is to achieve a 'likeness' of the suspect and the composite image is therefore intended as an aid to the investigation of crime together with provision of corroborative evidence. (2003, 2)

These facial composites are used within an investigation in a number of ways. A facial composite can be used to help identify potential suspects. For example, such images are sometimes released to the media, loaded onto the Internet, and distributed within the local area where the crime was committed, in an attempt to prompt memory of a witness as to who the culprit actually is. The purpose here is to get a name or possible location of where this person lives and/or works etc. It has been estimated however, that only 10% of such images are actually used in this way (Davies and Valentine, 2007). Instead the majority of facial composites are used within internal police enquiries. For example, facial composites are often shown to police informants and other law enforcement agencies (Davies and Valentine, 2007). In addition, the image could also be used to actually narrow down a pool of potential suspects by using the general features produced by a witness. This in turn helps to focus the investigation.

So what do these facial composites consist of? How are they constructed? As mentioned earlier the tools for developing facial composites have evolved over time, in line with the development of technological advances. Thus the following five subsections of this chapter will detail the evolution of the different systems and will also examine the effectiveness of each.

SKETCH ARTISTS' IMPRESSIONS

The use of artists to sketch a likeness of a suspect from a witness' memory has been used by police investigators to help enquiries for over 100 years. The infamous Dr Crippen was identified, after fleeing London having viciously killed his wife, travelling on a transatlantic liner under a different name. His capture was due to the distribution by the Metropolitan Police and subsequent identification of him from an artist's impression (Davies and Valentine, 2007; Taylor, 2001). Nevertheless, the actual *process* used by sketch artists is somewhat of a mystery. Unfortunately, there is limited research, guidance, and/or standard procedures outlining such a process. It seems that each individual artist develops their own method or style and that experience and practice are important features when examining accuracy of such likenesses. However, The International Association for Identification has a Forensic Artist Certification Board and the Federal Bureau of Investigation (FBI) do run an annual training course (Domingo, 1984).

From the meagre work that has been published it seems that the majority of artists work directly with the witness, though FBI operatives work from descriptions provided by a field officer (Clifford and Davies, 1989). The problem with this latter method cannot be understated. It has been well documented within this book and elsewhere (Milne and Bull, 1999, 2006; Wright and Alison, 2004) that the police investigative interviewing process is by no means perfect. Interviewers often use leading questions (eg 'He had red hair didn't he?') and specific closed questions (eg 'What colour hair did he have?') to obtain person description from a witness. These question types are far from ideal when trying to elicit a full and accurate person description as they produce descriptions which are less complete and reliable. Instead, when interviewing a cooperative adult interviewers should start with a free recall description of the person in question and then follow up using open-ended questions for elaboration (eg 'Tell me more about his head region'). It is believed that a well-conducted interview is characterized by the interviewer using predominately open-ended questions. For example, Powell and Snow (2007; see also Powell, Fisher and Wright, 2005) noted that 80% of questions asked of cooperative adults should be open-ended. This is because open-ended questions provide the best balance of full and accurate detail from a witness (Milne and Bull, 1999).

Furthermore, if the interview process is not digitally recorded the interviewer is also relying on their own memory of this interaction. Research (eg McLean, 1995: see also Milne and Bull, 2006; and Milne and Shaw, 1999, for a more detailed description of the problems of a lack of recording the interview process) has demonstrated that a lack of recording leads to descriptions which are less complete and less reliable than those which are electronically recorded. As a result, artists basing their sketch on an account recorded in a hand-written form by an investigator may be constructing their impression on inaccurate and unreliable information, resulting in an imperfect likeness. More worryingly, if such investigators have a hypothesis as to whom they believe has committed the offence it is well established that adult memory is so fragile interviewers can in fact bias the interviewing process in such a way as to attain the information that 'fits' with their pre-conceived views (Ask and Granhag, 2005; Shepherd and Milne, 1999, 2006). As a result the facial composite may indeed show a similarity to the suspect, but a miscarriage of justice could occur if the investigators' pre-conceived views as to who the culprit is are unjustified and wrong.

It follows therefore, that independent sketch artists who actually work with the witness themselves should be more open-minded, compared to an investigator working within the enquiry. Indeed, it is recommended here that such artists should be given limited information about the case, and not told what the witness has already said in the prior police interview, to counteract such biases occurring. Indeed, it is seen as best practice (Milne, Shaw and Bull, 2007) for advanced witness interviewers in the UK to be given limited information about the incident before interviewing witnesses and victims in serious and major crime (eg murder enquires).

How artists actually produce such impressions seems to depend on each individual artist. A number of experienced artists have written books concerning their own unique methods (eg Taylor, 2001) but it seems that their techniques differ. Some use photographic material to help in the construction process, whereas others rely more on freehand drawing, and some believe that caricature should be used to emphasize distinctive features (Davies, 1986). Taylor (2001) documented her approach, which she noted usually took up to three hours to navigate. She also subdivided her process into four main stages: (i) the rapport building stage: where the artist gets to know the witness and explains the process and that the product is aimed to be a likeness and not an exact portrait; (ii) the initial drawing stage: where the artist elicits a detailed verbal description from the witness and this forms the basis of an outline and priority is given to features that are emphasized by the witness; (iii) the fine-tuning drawing stage: where the drawing is progressively refined, maybe using photographs highlighting particular features to aid the witness; and (iv) the final finishing touches stage: where a review of the individual features is made and an attempt at expression given (Davies and Valentine, 2007). The witness may then be asked to give a score out of ten as to the degree of likeness (see later in chapter for details of the extent to which we are able to assess our own ability at constructing such likenesses).

In the UK witnesses are often asked to describe the face by the sketch artist using the cognitive interview (ACPO, 2003; see Chapter 3 for more detail about this interviewing procedure; also for full description see Milne and Bull, 1999; Fisher and Geiselman, 1992), and then asked to select features/shapes and work on face proportions. These features are next drawn by hand, initially as an outline drawing and then in more detail (Frowd, Carson, Ness, McQuiston-Surrett, Richardson, Baldwin and Hancock, 2005a). This approach attempts to develop detail for groups of individual features (Davies and Little, 1990). In the UK this whole process is visually recorded (ACPO, 2003) and this is recommended here as best practice, as it seems attaining an account from the witness is pivotal to the sketch artist process. It is therefore imperative that *how* this interviewing part of the process is conducted is open to scrutiny. With a recording one can ensure the level of interviewing skill of the artist and in turn ensure that a full and accurate description is elicited from the witness, which is then used to produce the likeness.

How effective are artist impressions? Unfortunately there is limited research examining the effectiveness of such drawings. There are many anecdotal accounts highlighting the success of such artists (eg Boylan, 2000) but there is no systematic attempt to gauge their overall effectiveness under police operational conditions (see later in this chapter for an experimental examination comparing various construction tools). What is clear however is that an artist needs not only to be skilled at drawing likenesses but also be adept in investigative interviewing—a rare combination (Davies and Valentine, 2007). Indeed, there are few such artists and thus the police tend to rely on more mechanical and computer-based systems to produce facial impressions and it is to these that we now turn.

MECHANICAL COMPOSITE SYSTEMS

One of the first of these systems to be developed was Identikit created by a Californian police officer. The original system consisted of line drawings of different facial features (eg eyes) reproduced onto acetate sheets. The package contained approximately 550 features for the operator and witness to work from. (A later system Identikit II utilized photographic images). The process of putting together the facial composite requires the witness to describe each feature individually, the operator then selects the feature which best resembles the description and once all features have been deliberated upon all the individual acetates are combined to produce a composite face. This can then be refined as necessary (Davies and Valentine, 2007). Again there is limited empirical research examining the effectiveness of this procedure though individual success stories exist (eg Jackson, 1967). The original tool, however, has been criticized due to the use of line drawings (which were later replaced) as not being very realistic. Indeed research has shown that even the naming of *known* famous people is very difficult from mere line drawings (Bruce, Hanna, Dench, Healy and Burton, 1992). Thus one would expect composites created in such a way to be at a disadvantage compared to those that utilize photographic images.

Photofit, developed in the UK, was one of the first facial composite systems to utilize photographic representations of facial features (Penry, 1970), though many countries followed suit and developed very similar systems (eg France uses Portrait Robot—see Davies, 1981 for a review). Nevertheless, all such systems have the following common features. The photographic images are printed on jigsaw like pieces that slot into a template to produce the facial composite. The final version of Photofit, for example, contains approximately 850 such features (eg hairstyles) (Frowd, Carson, Ness, Richardson, Morrison, McLanaghan and Hancock, 2005b). There are, however, no standardized instructions accompanying these tools, though most operators first elicit a verbal description from the witness, who then is directed to particular features in the 'visual index' or feature library which best resembles the described feature. The individually selected features are then all combined and slotted together to produce the final composite which could be amended if necessary.

How successful are such mechanical systems? A series of studies was conducted by Professor Graham Davies and his colleagues in the 1970s to evaluate Photofit. For example, Ellis, Davies and Shepherd (1978) asked witnesses to produce a Photofit aided by an operator after briefly viewing a photograph (within a group of photos). Afterwards a panel of judges had to identify the correct individual from an array of 36 faces. It was found that accuracy was rather low, with only 12.5% of first choices being correct. Thus it can be said that likenesses produced in this way are not very helpful for prompting memory to help a witness point out an individual. However, the police also use such composites to help focus an enquiry, as opposed to actually pinpointing an individual. Indeed, Christie, Davies, Shepherd and Ellis (1981) found that when the accuracy measure used was relaxed to include 'correct type likeness' accuracy did increase to 48% (from 23% in this study for pinpointing). Worryingly this means that there is a larger 52% 'inaccurate type likeness' rate which could lead the police to disregard the true culprit in an investigation (see field research later).

Interestingly and rather surprisingly, Christie and Ellis (1981) found that verbal descriptions from a witness were a better guide to likeness than the Photofit composites themselves. As Chapter 3 highlights, attaining a verbal description of a face is a difficult and imperfect process. As Davies himself notes 'an impression of a face should be worth a thousand words' (Davies and Valentine, 2007, 64).

Experimental research examining the US Identikit system (eg Green and Geiselman, 1989) has had similar disappointing outcomes, where artist sketches were judged to be superior to Identikit composites by an independent panel of people (Laughery and Fowler, 1980). Furthermore, both impressions produced by artists and Identikit were poor with regard to accuracy, with both performing at the chance level (Davies and Valentine, 2007). It has been found, however, that the effectiveness of the systems is related to the experience of the operator, where expert operators have been found to produce better quality composites than novices (Davies, Milne and Shepherd, 1983). These authors believed that this was due to the fact that experienced operators spent longer with the witness at the start of the process, when interviewing them, and as a result obtained a description which was more complete. Thus, the effectiveness of these systems comes down to the ability of the operator to *interview* the witness appropriately to gather a full and accurate account upon which to base the construction of the facial composite. As it has been demonstrated yet again communication is at the heart of all investigation processes.

However, these evaluations were conducted in the sterile environment of a laboratory and therefore cannot be said to resemble the real world. For example, there is little personal investment for the mock witness to create likenesses that are highly accurate from memory—a cognitively demanding task. What about field research? Unfortunately, due to the difficulty of establishing the 'ground truth' in a real investigation (ie knowing definitely who has committed the offence) and the multitude of factors affecting the ability of a real eyewitness to remember a person or persons within an event, no field research examining the actual effectiveness of such a memory tool has been attempted. Kitson, Darnbrough and Shields (1978) asked for the views of investigating officers who had used composites within their enquiry as to the operational effectiveness of such images. In all, this related to 729 composites produced by Photofit over a six-month period in the UK. After two months some 140 cases had been cleared up and the investigating officer in each case was then contacted to establish what role the facial composite had had in solving the crime. In 5% of cases it was deemed that the facial composite was entirely responsible for the resolution of the case, ie the impression produced by the witness led immediately to an identification and arrest. In 50% of cases investigators found the composite 'useful' or 'very useful' where a likeness narrowed the focus of the investigation. Conversely, in 45% of cases the composites were thought to be 'not very useful' or of 'no use at all' where composites diverted enquiries and wasted police time (see also Bennett, 1986 for similar findings with the Metropolitan Police). As Davies and Valentine (2007) conclude it seems therefore that mechanical composite systems are of questionable forensic value. Why is this? Common sense would tell us that such systems should work. Does psychological theory help us to understand the limited performance of such systems?

Theoretical research examining face processing may have the answer to our question. It is thought that faces are normally encoded as a whole (ie holistically) where individual features are subsumed within a general impression of the whole face (Tanaka and Farah, 2003), rather than individual features such as the eyes and nose being encoded separately (Davies and Valentine, 2007). This holistic processing of a face is also termed configural processing and research shows that this sort of processing is beneficial for face recognition tasks. However, recall of a face, especially within the tasks set by the sketch artist or mechanical facial composite system operator requires a witness to translate the whole face into discrete individual features, one at a time. The artist or operator then asks a witness to match these to features within the kit library. This is, a near on impossible task, and concerns what is termed feature-based processing (Wells and Hryciw, 1984). Research has also shown that age and face shape are important features when judging likeness (Ellis, 1986) however, these are global dimensions involving many features in combination, again relying more on holistic processing (Bruce and Young, 1998). In addition, the mechanical systems do not allow for global changes, such as length of face to be changed easily, and such factors are important when producing useful likenesses (Gibling and Bennett, 1994). Therefore, perhaps witnesses need to manipulate a whole face in order for facial composite systems to be more effective, and thus forensically useful. Computer-based systems that allow one to do just this may be more in line with our internal memory face processing system, allowing the witness to use configural processing, which is helpful in recognizing faces.

COMPUTER-GENERATED COMPOSITE SYSTEMS

One of the first computer-generated composite systems was developed in the UK under the auspices of the Home Office and was named the Computer-Aided Design Centre (CADC; Gillenson and Chandrasekaren, 1975). The system used the features from Photofit in a digitized form and could be manipulated to produce a more life-like facial image (Davies and Valentine, 2007). Many realizing the potential of such systems were close to following suit and similar products evolved across the globe (eg Mac-a-Mug Pro a US-based Apple Mac system and E-fit a UK-based PC system). One thing in common with all these packages is that the majority of these systems still require a witness to create the desired face from a library of features.

The Mac-a-Mug Pro system (Shaherazam, 1986) uses line drawings of facial features (eg 65 types of noses) which can be manipulated within the programme (eg reduced in size). Again there is the lack of realism with line drawings used as noted before (see Identikit section earlier) and also the package was not accompanied by a standard procedure on how to use the system. Generally operators start by obtaining a brief verbal description from the witness. This description is then used as a guide for the operator to go to relevant features that are viewed on the screen (or in a visual reference catalogue) and amended if necessary. A facial composite is then produced by combining the selected features (Davies and Valentine, 2007; Koehn and Fisher, 1997).

More research has been conducted examining the effectiveness of the computer-generated composite systems, for example the Mac-a-Mug Pro system compared to the prior tools in the evolutionary history. It has been found that in an ideal world with an experienced operator compiling the facial composite from a photograph the system can produce a very good likeness (eg 49% accuracy: Cutler, Stocklein and Penrod, 1988). However, in the real world of investigation if a photograph of the assailant existed then there would be little point creating a facial composite in the first place. Wogalter and Marwitz (1991) found that facial composites produced from memory of a target seen for eight seconds produced good matching scores (40%) but this was only after a delay of 20 minutes. Again, a situation that is unlikely to be true in the real world. Unfortunately when research attempts to attain greater forensic realism the effectiveness of the system seems to depreciate. In Koehn and Fisher's study (1987) participants met a stranger and then had to individually compile a facial composite which was rated for likeness and tested for quality in an identification task. In this study 69% of the facial composites produced received the lowest two ratings on a ten point scale. In addition, accuracy in the identification task was only 4%, which rose to 77% when the facial composites were produced from photographs and not from memory. It seems therefore that there is not a problem with the system per se but with the memory process itself. Indeed it could be that the system is incompatible with the memory process, that is, it asks witnesses to use feature-based processing as opposed to configural-holistic processing.

E-fit (Aspley Ltd, 1993), another computer-generated composite system, tries to use a more configural approach and thus may prove to be more successful. This system was developed in the UK and is one of the most favoured systems in the UK for producing facial composites in actual investigations. E-fit uses photographic images and has specific guidance in its use and training courses for operators to attend (Clark, 2002; ACPO, 2003). Again there are similar systems in existence around the globe; these being PRO-fit, FACES, and Identikit 2000 (Frowd, et al, 2005a). FACES 3.0 (IQ Biometrix, 2000—see Wells, Charman and Olson, 2005 for a full description) has one large mixed gender, age, and race feature library, whereas E-fit and PRO-fit have different libraries for these global facial constructs. FACES is less sophisticated compared to E-fit with regard to the facilities within the software, however, it is commonly used in the US and is used by more than 5,000 police and intelligence agencies including the FBI and military (McQuiston-Surrett, Topp and Malpass, 2006).

The method suggested for use with E-fit involves an extensive initial interview to establish the witness' encoding conditions (ie to ensure that the witness has visually encoded sufficient information regarding the target face). Then the witness provides a detailed verbal description of the assailant's facial features using a cognitive interview (Clark, 2002). The operator then inputs the description onto the computer, normally in the absence of the witness (to avoid biasing the witness). The computer then produces the first rough image based on this description. Operators then differ with regard to what they ask the witness to do when attempting to fine tune and manipulate the face within the system. Clark (2002) found, after surveying 230 operators in the UK, that two methods emerged to be the most popular. The first method tasks witnesses to provide further descriptions early on in the process by getting witnesses to answer on screen multiple-choice questions in description boxes. The second method requires witnesses to picture the assailant in their mind's eye (akin to the mental rein-statement of context instruction, a constituent component of the cognitive interview) and to correct the ambiguities as they emerge in the image. The answers and informa-tion given within these methods then in turn drive an algorithm that selects the most appropriate features from the database. These are then displayed within the whole face and can be amended within the whole face. This process concludes with a fine-tuning stage where the operator can change individual features using free-hand and again imaging is often used (Clark, 2002). Nevertheless, it still seems that within the initial account the individual features are given through a featural processing task and it is from this that the initial composite is produced. It is only later in the process when the witness may use a more configural type of face processing.

How effective are these systems? Davies, van der Willick and Morrison (2000) found that when the E-fit was constructed from a photograph the naming rate was 49%, and much better than the likenesses produced using the PhotoFIT method. However, when facial composites were produced from memory any advantages diminished. Indeed, not one composite was named correctly and many incorrect names were given when the face was unknown to the witness. Davies and Oldman (1999) asked witnesses to construct from memory or a picture with the help of an operator one of four famous faces. E-fits produced from memory not only received lower rankings for likeness, compared to those produced from the photographs, only 6% were correctly identified and there was a 25% false naming rate (indeed there was only a 10% identifi-cation rate when the likeness was produced directly from a picture). This is a worrying situation in a real-life enquiry as false positives equate to the wrong people being in the frame and investigated. In addition, the real offender could be disregarded from a pool of potential suspects.

Similar findings have emerged when the other systems within this category have been evaluated. For example, Frowd et al (2005a) found a 3.2% naming rate for com-posites produced using FACES. However, Bruce, Ness, Hancock, Newman and Rarity (2002) found a higher 19% correct naming rate for PRO-fit when facial composites were created *immediately* after the target had been viewed. It seems that time may be a crucial factor in determining efficacy, but it often takes days if not weeks and even months before such a facial composite process is embarked upon.

Effectiveness of systems also depends on how the facial composites are used to prompt memory, within the investigation. The key question is: does the perpetrator have to be in view at the same time as the composite for it to be effective? A real-life example would be a member of the public spotting a perpetrator whilst holding a newspaper article containing their facial composite. A similar situation would be using it as a confirmation tool after a suspect has been apprehended. However, how useful are these facial likenesses over time in the memory of the public? For example, the 'potential spotter' could have just put the paper down or saw the likeness in last week's paper, would it still be helpful then? Oswald and Coleman (2007) evaluated the effects of different delays on the usefulness of facial composites produced using the FACES system. Over a series of four experiments it was found that accuracy (as measured by a target present line-up) decreased over time from a 74% accuracy rate with no delay (where line-up and facial composite were viewed at the same time), to a 58% accuracy rate when there was a 30-second delay between viewing the composite and the target in the identification task. This accuracy rate further decreased to 54% when there was a four-minute delay between viewing the composite and seeing the target. Thus it seems that facial composites are most useful when the target is present at the time of viewing the facial composite. However, there needs to be a word of warning when interpreting these findings. The facial composites were produced from photographs from actual police mug books (to add realism) but the operator had the photographs in view when they created the composite and they were not compiled from memory. As has been noted earlier such conditions are not true to life and as soon as composites are produced from memory their quality decreases. Thus, further research needs to examine this important issue with facial composites produced from memory.

The process in which the E-fit is created also seems to affect the effectiveness of the likeness produced. Clark (2002) used a more realistic design and utilized facial composites produced 22 hours after a witness viewed a brief video of a minor crime. The perpetrator in the video was in fact a police officer and the resultant composites were placed around the officer-perpetrator's station area and there was a reward for his identification. It was found that when description boxes were used to elicit the witness description identification accuracy was 43% but when imaging was used in the interviewing part of the process only an 18% accuracy rate was elicited. It therefore seems that the interview and memory process is key to the effectiveness and quality of the likeness produced. More research is needed to investigate this important area. Indeed, research has shown that the cognitive interview (CI)/enhanced cognitive interview (ECI) is effective at producing additional accurate information in a recall task, like an interview (see Kohnken, Milne, Memon and Bull, 1999, for a meta-analysis). However, the CI superiority effect has not been replicated within a recognition task (Gwyer and Clifford, 1997). As both recall and recognition are required in the production of facial composites and imaging is embedded within the CI/ECI process it is necessary to evaluate the effectiveness of such an interview method further within the facial composite construction process. Indeed, in the UK sketch artists and operators are trained in the use of the CI/ECI (ACPO, 2003).

Due to memory processes (eg selective attention) witnesses will give differing descriptions of the same perpetrator (see Milne and Bull, 1999). Investigatively this causes numerous problems. For example, what description should be used? It could be that combining all respective facial composites into one morphed likeness may result in a more effective likeness. Indeed, research does show that morphs are perceived to be more similar to a target than individual composites that produce the morph (Hasel and Wells, 2007). However, research has demonstrated that even when this is done it only seems to help memory for familiar faces, not often the case in the forensic setting where the offender is almost always unknown to the witness for such procedures to go ahead (Bruce et al, 2002).

Thus it seems that such systems have limited forensic use. How do investigators therefore use these questionable systems within investigations? The next section focusses on the limited work that actually examines the operational use of facial composite systems in the forensic context.

THE USE OF FACIAL COMPOSITE SYSTEMS
IN A REAL WORLD CONTEXT

McQuiston-Surett, Topp and Malpass (2006) surveyed 163 US law enforcement operatives regarding facial composite procedures. It was found that both manual and computer systems were in use, with Identikit (94%) being the preferred manual kit and Identikit 2000 being the preferred computer system (36%), followed closely by FACES 3.0 (32%). The preferred option in the UK, E-fit, had only been used by 3% of the US respondents. With regard to satisfaction the sketch artists and computer-based systems were seen to be superior to the manual systems, with sketch artists scoring highest for satisfaction rating. It seemed from responses that there was a varied use of the systems with haphazard selection criteria (eg cost and ease of use) and no standard training regime. This is again unlike the UK where there is a definitive training course not only in the facial composite package but in the cognitive interview as well (ACPO, 2003).

Worryingly the US operatives also had no direct guidance with what to do with multiple witnesses, whereas the majority reported treating the witnesses separately, 6% mentioned interviewing witnesses together and producing one likeness. The ACPO (2003) guidance in the UK rightly dictates that 'where there has been more than one witness, each should be dealt with individually, providing individual facial composites and with different operators where possible' (2003, 12). This is to ensure limited contamination of the fragile witness memory process.

Interestingly when examining how police operatives assessed quality of facial composites, 98% said that they used the witness' own feedback and views of satisfaction. Indeed some reported filing and not using likenesses which witnesses were unhappy with. This is worrying as it has been demonstrated that confidence is not a helpful measurement tool (eg Oswald and Coleman, 2007), this is akin to the majority of research examining the confidence-accuracy relationship within the eyewitness setting (see Chapter 4 for a discussion of confidence and accuracy). Furthermore, Hasel and Wells (2007) found that when witnesses rated their own facial composite likeness to their memory of the target, they were not very accurate. Thus investigators could be throwing away an accurate likeness and thus a potential resolution to a case.

In summary it seems that even these popular systems within the law enforcement world, have limited forensic value. Again this could be due to the fact that such systems still in part require featural based processing. A new generation of systems, termed fourth generation systems have recently been produced in an attempt to counteract this core theoretical problem.

FOURTH GENERATION SYSTEMS

Face space or face similarity space concerns a new generation of computer-based facial composite systems that try to reflect holistic-configural face processing within memory (Davies and Valentine, 2007) and is partly based on the fact that when we encode new faces we tend to compare them to similar faces with regard to texture and shape (Valentine, 2001). The construction of a facial composite within a fourth generation system first concerns the production of a random set of artificial facial images within a face space using a statistical technique called principal component analysis (PCA). The witness then selects the image(s) that is most similar to their memory of the perpetrator. In the initial set of images there are a wide range of facial appearances. The witness then selects those images which most resemble the culprit and they are used to 'breed' a new set of images into 'mutations' around the 'parent' face(s) generated by computed genetic algorithms. This process is repeated until the witness decides they are either happy with the faces which are very similar to each other and the perpetrator, or they are not happy with the faces because they are not sufficiently similar to the perpetrator (Davies and Valentine, 2007). (See problems with witness ability to assess quality mentioned earlier.)

There are three possible ways of reaching the target likeness within these systems (ie three evolutionary algorithms; Gibson, Pallares Bejarano and Solomon, 2003). The first is 'Scale Rating' where the witness rates each face in each generation on a scale (eg 1 to 10) for similarity to the target and then the 'best' two faces are used to breed the next generation. The second is called 'Select Multiple Mutate' where the witness picks the best likeness and this is then reproduced with random mutation in all but one of the faces for the next generation. The third is termed 'Follow the Leader' and it is where a witness is shown a new face alongside the current best likeness face and the witness chooses which of that pair most resembles the culprit. Each 'new' face is produced by breeding the current best likeness with a new face and this decision process then determines the direction the evolution takes. As can be seen these systems allow for the gradual holistic change of faces and thus capitalizes upon our naturalistic holistic face processing systems (Frowd et al, 2005a and 2005b).

One such fourth generation system is Evo-fit and it is being developed by Frowd, Hancock, and colleagues at the University of Stirling (Scotland). To construct an Evo-fit facial composite witnesses first select a hairstyle and facial shapes, then facial textures. This selection process helps to produce the initial face space within which to work (the PCA). The witness then views approximately 70 faces with random characteristics within this basic face space. From this selection witnesses are asked to choose the best six (approximately) and then Evo-fit breeds these faces together to produce another similar sized population. This process occurs until an acceptable likeness occurs. The facial composite is created by 'evolution' hence the name Evo-fit.

As all these fourth generation systems are still under construction and trials are being run there are few published evaluations. Frowd and his colleagues have however published a series of evaluations of Evo-fit. For example, Frowd, Hancock and Carson (2004) found that judges could name 25% of Evo-fit facial composites of celebrities produced from memory compared with 17% produced by E-fit. Frowd et al (2005a and 2005b) then later evaluated a number of facial composite systems (Evo-fit, E-fit, PRO-fit, FACES, and sketch artists) in a more forensically realistic experimental design. The witness viewed an unfamiliar target and then after three hours (2005a) or two days (2005b; most of the results below will concern the two-day delay study as this more accurately reflects the real world and face recall and recognition performance does decrease over time) each witness was cognitively interviewed and worked with an operator to produce a facial composite using one of the aforementioned methods.

First, it was found that construction time across the different systems varies, with the sketch artist taking the longest time on average—over two hours, and the shortest time being equated to the FACES system (mean time 34 minutes). The resultant composites then underwent three assessment procedures: (i) naming; (ii) sorting—where the rater was given ten targets and the composites were matched to one of the targets; and (iii) identification using a typical line-up procedure. It was found that naming rate was very low for Evo-fit (10% for the three hour delay and 3% for the two-day delay) and generally very low for all methods overall (2.8% for the two-day delay). Sketch artists produced the best naming score with 8% naming rate at the two-day delay. Sorting resulted in a higher accuracy rate after the two-day delay with Evo-fit scoring 39%, however, the best accuracy rate was again found for sketches produced by artists (54%). E-fit faired best in the identification task with a 60% accuracy rate at two days compared to 46% for sketches and 31% for Evo-fit.

Overall it was concluded that 'facial composite quality was very poor in general; those produced from PRO-fit and E-fit (the two leading UK computerized systems), were correctly named only twice out of 300 attempts' (Frowd et al, 2005b, 74–75). Problems with even this type of facial composite system is that they rely on a witness' ability to assess likeness from memory, and research (eg Kovera, Penrod, Pappas and Thill, 1997) has shown that this ability is far from perfect. It seems from all the research reviewed so far that a 'skilled police artist can still outperform all current systems that have been evaluated so far' (Davies and Valentine, 2007, 77).

In conclusion, the body of literature examining the efficacy of facial composites, whether they be drawn, mechanically constructed, computer-generated, or evolved from computer programming, has demonstrated serious limitations in all of these systems in terms of their ability to produce accurate facial likenesses when constructed from a witness' memory, and this is especially the case for memory for unfamiliar faces. Unfortunately, this situation reflects the forensic context, where a witness views a crime committed by an unknown person. It is believed that the underlying problem is that all of these systems rely on the ability of a witness to recall from memory the facial features of a perpetrator and this is a problematic process, and one that is contrary to the human memory system for processing person information (ie featural versus holistic). It is possible that no system will be able to help a witness in such a difficult task. Learning a face takes time and repeated exposure (Bruce, Green and Georgeson, 2003) and after all our primary use of person information in everyday life is to recognize faces rather than describe them in a recall task. As a result stereotypes may help fill in the gaps when witnesses are asked to produce a facial composite from memory. For example, Shepherd, Ellis, McMurran and Davies (1978) found that witnesses created facial composites that were later judged to be more intelligent and handsome when they were told that the target was a lifeboat skipper compared to composites produced when witnesses thought the target to be a murderer.

It is worth noting that there is limited research examining how the facial composite construction process actually interferes with the memory of the perpetrator's face and in turn subsequent identification attempts. Topp, McQuiston and Malpass (2003) found that when witnesses made a facial composite and then repeatedly viewed this, this process interfered with a subsequent identification task. More research is required on this important topic. This chapter will now turn to new technologies used to deliver identification parades: computer-based identification systems.

COMPUTER-BASED IDENTIFICATION SYSTEMS

As facial composite systems have developed over time with technological advancements, so have identification procedures. In the UK gone are the days where live foils line-up for the witness to examine. Instead, identification parades are constructed of images (including the suspect) randomly generated by a computer for the witness to view. In the UK two different systems exist: (i) VIPER (Video Identification Procedure Electronic Recording) and (ii) PROMAT (Profile Matching) both of which produce simulated video line-up formats, but each with its own database of images (Valentine, Darling and Memon, 2007). The line-up constitutes 15-second clips of each person shown one at a time (ie sequentially). The sequence begins with a head and shoulders shot of a person looking directly at the camera, who then slowly pivots their head to give a full right profile followed by a full left profile, the person then returns to the full-face pose (Valentine et al, 2007).

There are many obvious practical benefits to such a system. The old traditional 'live' line-ups often took a long while to arrange (approximately one to three months on average). This not only delayed the investigation but also, as memory for faces depreciates over time, this could have hindered the potential ability of the witness to select the correct person or reject the line-up if the perpetrator was not present. Furthermore, the longer the process takes the greater the room for contamination of memory (eg if the case is high profile with TV footage of witness composites etc). Computer-based identification systems on the other hand can usually produce a video line-up within two hours alleviating all the aforementioned problems (Valentine et al, 2007). It has been noted that 50% of live line-ups in the UK were cancelled (eg due to failure of someone to attend—bailed suspect, witness, lack of volunteers, lack of appropriate foils etc). Such cancellations contribute to further delay. Since the introduction of video-generated identification systems such cancellations have reduced to 5% (Valentine et al, 2007). The computer systems also have large databases of images at hand from which to select similar looking foils in order that the line-up is fairer to the suspect. Furthermore, having a large database of foils is likely to prevent delays from occurring if a suspect has an unusual appearance. It used to be very difficult for the police to find similar looking foils to match such suspects which again led to delays in the process. The new computer-generated system is also more victim/witness focused as the laptop which holds the parade can be taken anywhere, even to the witness/victim themselves (eg in hospital). This could potentially stop the witness/victim feeling threatened by the thought of the suspect being in the same location.

In conclusion, computer-generated video parades are a real practical improvement over the old traditional 'live' line-up method. However, the fact that a witness can only see the individual from the shoulders up should be investigated bearing in mind that gait could be important for identification purposes (Burton, Wilson, Cowan and Bruce, 1999; see Chapter 5 for a discussion of identification by gait).

CCTV-GENERATED IMAGES

In the UK (and elsewhere in the world) there are an increasing number of CCTV cameras watching our every move. Primarily CCTV has been implemented nationwide as a crime prevention method. Nevertheless, CCTV footage could also help in the actual investigation process. For example, CCTV footage could help with regard to outlining what happened in an incident and provide an investigator with basic information concerning the individuals involved (eg number etc). The key question with regard to CCTV images, however, is do images of perpetrators caught on camera help in the identification of these perpetrators? Unfortunately the research examining this very issue is not very promising.

Henderson, Bruce and Burton (2001) filmed, on poor-quality CCTV cameras (typical of those used in high street banks), a mock bank raid where two robbers were involved. The best still image of each robber was edited from the footage and 100 participants were shown these colour images in conjunction with two TP photo arrays (one per robber) of eight similar looking people and then asked to identify each of the two target robbers. The task was done poorly with a very low hit rate and there were many false positives (ie selection of the wrong individuals). With better-quality equipment the mock event was filmed again, but this time one robber wore a hat to conceal their external facial features (eg hairstyle), while the second did not. This time in a similar research paradigm participants were also either presented with a TP or TA line-up. It was found that for the robber without the hat correct identification performance across both line-up types (target present and absent) resulted in a 64% accuracy rate, however this dropped considerably when the target wore a hat. Indeed, even memory for unfamiliar faces that have certain dominant attributes (eg a hairstyle that stands out) are readily confused. Learning a face takes time and repeated exposure under different viewing conditions (Bruce et al, 2003). Thus, research shows that for individuals unknown to a witness/victim, recognition accuracy from poorly generated images is very low, and of not much use to an investigation. However, CCTV images may help in the prompting of memory for known faces (ie images on *Crimewatch*—a BBC programme—prompting memory of someone who knows them). Burton et al (1999) found that participants were able to match or reject with 92% accuracy for 'familiar' targets, but this reduced to 70% for unfamiliar targets even when the 'witness' was an experienced police officer, and when the participants had the photograph with them throughout the task (eg Bruce, Henderson, Newman and Burton, 2001).

In conclusion the most appropriate and beneficial use of CCTV images is therefore as a trigger to recognize a familiar face. Indeed, ACPO (2003) warn investigators that 'practitioners should be aware of the significance of probability factors, likelihood or repetition and likely range of variation in CCTV images, thus demonstrating awareness and an ability to analyse the effects of distortion caused by perspective, camera angle, motion blur, lighting and translation of data formats' (2003, 8) This demonstrates the awareness of the problem with this type of image and recognition potential, by the UK police service.

CONCLUSION

This chapter unfortunately has not brought with it good news. The whole task of answering the key investigative question 'Whodunnit?' is beset with difficulty. Innovative tools designed to help the witness do not seem to help and even when the offender is caught on camera, this still does not mean that they will be easily identified. All researchers and practitioners can do is attempt to create new systems in order to try to improve the difficult process of person description and identification.

FURTHER READING

DAVIES, G. and VALENTINE, T. (2007). Facial composites: Forensic utility and psychological research. In R. LINDSAY, D. ROSS, D. READ and M. TOGLIA (eds) *Handbook of Eyewitness Psychology Volume II*. NJ: Lawrence Erlbaum Associates, 59–83.

HANCOCK, P. (2005). Contemporary composite techniques: the impact of a forensically-relevant target delay. *Legal and Criminological Psychology, 10*, 63–81.

MCQUISTON-SURRETT, D., TOPP, L. and MALPASS, R. (2006). Use of facial composite systems in US law enforcement agencies. *Psychology, Crime and Law, 12*, 505–512.

TANAKA, J. and FARAH, M. (2003). The holistic representation of faces. In M.A. PETERSON and G. RHODES (eds) *Perception of Faces, Objects, and Scenes*. Oxford: Oxford University Press, 53–74.

REFERENCES

ACPO (2003). *National Working Practices in Facial Imaging Guidance*. Cambridge: National Improvement Agency.

ACPOS (2005). *Facial Imaging Guidance*. Scotland: TulleyAllen.

AMBLER, C. and MILNE, R. (2006). *Call handling centres—an evidential opportunity or threat?* Paper presented at the Second International Investigative Interviewing Conference, Portsmouth, July.

ASK, K. and GRANHAG, P.A. (2005). Motivational sources of confirmation bias in criminal investigations: the need for cognitive closure. *Journal of Investigative Psychology and Offender Profiling, 2*, 43–63.

BENNETT, P. (1986). Face recall: A police perspective. *Human Learning, 5*, 197–202.

BOYLAN, J. (2000). *Portraits of Guilt: The Woman Who Profiles the Faces of America's Deadliest Criminals*. New York: Pocket Book.

BRUCE, V., GREEN, P. and GEORGESON, M. (2003). *Visual Perception: Physiology, Psychology and Ecology*. Hove: Psychology Press.

——, HANNA, E., DENCH, N., HEALEY, P. and BURTON, M. (1992). The importance of 'mass' in the line drawings of faces. *Applied Cognitive Psychology, 6*, 619–628.

——, NESS, H., HANCOCK, P.J.B., NEWMAN, C. and RARITY, J. (2002). Four heads are better than one: Combining face composites yields improvements in face likeness. *Journal of Applied Psychology, 87*, 894–902.

—— and YOUNG, A. (1998). *In The Eye of the Beholder: The Science of Face Perception*. Oxford: Oxford University Press.

BURTON, A., WILSON, S., COWAN, M. and BRUCE, V. (1999). Face recognition in poor quality video evidence from security surveillance. *Psychological Science, 10*, 243–248.

CHRISTIE, D., DAVIES, G., SHEPHERD, J. and ELLIS, H. (1981). Evaluating a new computer-based system for face recall. *Law and Human Behaviour, 5*, 209–218.

—— and ELLIS, H. (1981). Photofit constructions versus verbal descriptions of faces. *Journal of Applied Psychology, 66*, 358–363.

CLARK. C. (2002). Facing up to changes. *Police Review, January*, 18–19.

CLIFFORD, B. and DAVIES, G. (1989). Procedures for obtaining identification evidence. In D. Raskin (ed.) *Psychological Methods in Investigation and Evidence* . New York: Springer-Verlag, 47–96.

—— and GWYER, P. (1999). The effects of the cognitive interview and other methods of context reinstatement on identification. *Psychology, Crime and Law, 5*, 61–80.

CUTLER, B.L., STOCKLEIN, C.J. and PENROD, S.D. (1988). Empirical examination of a computerized facial composite production system. *Forensic Reports, 1*, 207–218.

DAVIES, G. (1981). Face recall systems. In G. Davies, H. Ellis and J. Shepherd (eds) *Perceiving and Remembering Faces*. London: Academic Press, 227–250.

—— (1986). Capturing likeness in eyewitness composites: The police artist and his rivals. *Medicine, Science and the Law, 26*, 283–290.

—— and LITTLE, M. (1990). Drawing on memory: Exploring the expertise of the police artist. *Medicine, Science and the Law, 30*, 345–353.

——, MILNE, A. and SHEPHERD, J. (1983). Searching for operator skills in face composite reproduction. *Journal of Police Science and Administration, 11*, 405–409.

—— and OLDMAN, H. (1999). The impact of character attribution on composite production: A real world effect? *Current Psychology, 18*, 128–139.

—— and PATEL, D. (2005). The influence of car and driver stereotypes on attributions of vehicle speed, position on the road and culpability in a road accident scenario. *Legal and Criminological Psychology, 10*, 45–62.

—— and VALENTINE, T. (2007). Facial composites: Forensic utility and psychological research. In R. Lindsay, D. Ross, D. Read and M. Toglia (eds) *Handbook of Eyewitness Psychology Volume II*. NJ: Lawrence Erlbaum Associates, 59–83.

——, VAN DER WILLIK, P. and MORRISON, L.J. (2000). Facial composite production: A comparison of mechanical and computer-driven systems. *Journal of Applied Psychology, 85*, 119–124.

DOMINGO, F. (1984, June). Composite art: The need for standardisation. *Identification News*, 7–15.

ELLIS, H. (1986). Face recall: A psychological perspective. *Human Learning, 5*, 189–196.

——, DAVIES, G.M. and SHEPHERD, J.W. (1978). A critical examination of the PhotoFIT system for recalling faces. *Ergonomics, 21*, 297–307.

FISHER, R.P. and GEISELMAN, R.E. (1992). *Memory-enhancing Techniques for Investigative Interviewing: The Cognitive Interview*. Springfield, IL: Charles Thomas.

FROWD, C., CARSON, D., NESS, H., McQUISTON-SURRETT, D., RICHARDSON, J., BALDWIN, H. and HANCOCK, P. (2005a). Contemporary composite techniques: the impact of a forensically-relevant target delay. *Legal and Criminological Psychology, 10,* 63–81.

——, ——, ——, RICHARDSON, J., MORRISON, L., McLANAGHAN, S. and HANCOCK, P. (2005b). A forensically valid comparison of facial composite systems. *Psychology, Crime, and Law, 11,* 33–52.

——, HANCOCK, P. and CARSON, D. (2004). EvoFIT: A holistic evolutionary facial imaging technique for creating composites. *Association for Computing Machinery Transactions on Applied Psychology, 1,* 1–21.

GIBLING, F. and BENNETT, P. (1994). Artistic enhancement in the production of Photofit likenesses: An examination of its effectiveness in leading to suspect identification. *Psychology, Crime, and the Law, 1,* 93–100.

GIBSON, S., PALLARES BEJARANO, A. and SOLOMON, C. (2003). Synthesis of photographic quality facial composites using evolutionary algorithms. In R. Harvey and J. Bangham (eds) *Proceedings of the British Machine Vision Conference 2003.* London; British Machine Vision Association, 221–230.

GILLENSON, M. and CHANDRASEKAREN, B. (1975). A heuristic strategy for developing facial images on a CRT. *Pattern recognition, 7,* 187–196.

GREEN, D. and GEISELMAN, R.E. (1989). Building composite facial images: Effect of feature saliency and delay of construction. *Journal of Applied Psychology, 74,* 714–721.

GWYER, P. and CLIFFORD, B. R. (1997). The effects of the cognitive interview on recall, identification and the confidence/accuracy relationship. *Applied Cognitive Psychology, 11,* 121–145.

HASEL, L. and WELLS, G. (2007). Catching the bad guy: Morphing composite faces helps. *Law and Human Behavior, 31,* 193–207.

HENDERSON, Z., BRUCE, V. and BURTON, A. (2001). Matching the faces of robbers captured on camera. *Applied Cognitive Psychology, 15,* 445–464.

HENSS, R. (1991). Perceiving age and attractiveness in facial photographs. *Journal of Applied Psychology, 21,* 933–946.

JACKSON, R. (1967). *Occupied with Crime.* London: Harrap.

KITSON, A., DARNBROUGH, M. and SHIELDS, E. (1978). Let's face it. *Police Research Bulletin, 30,* 7–13.

KOEHN, C.E. and FISHER, R.P. (1997). Constructing facial composites with the Mac-A-Mug Pro system. *Psychology, Crime and Law, 3,* 209–218.

KŠHNKEN, G., MILNE, R., MEMON, A. and BULL, R. (1999). The cognitive interview: A meta-analysis. *Psychology, Crime and Law, 5,* 3–28.

KOVERA, M.B., PENROD, S.D., PAPPAS, C. and THILL, D.L. (1997). Identification of computer-generated facial composites. *Journal of Applied Psychology, 82,* 235–246.

LAUGHERY, K. and FOWLER, R. (1980). Sketch artist and identi-kit procedures for recalling faces. *Journal of Applied Psychology, 65,* 307–316.

McLEAN, M. (1995). Quality investigation? Police interviewing of witnesses. *Medicine, Science and the Law, 35,* 116–122

McLEOD, M.D. and SHEPHERD, J.W. (1986). Sex differences in eyewitness reports of criminal assaults. *Medicine, Science and the Law, 26,* 311–318.

McQUISTON-SURRETT, D., TOPP, L. and MALPASS, R. (2006). Use of facial composite systems in US law enforcement agencies. *Psychology, Crime and Law, 12,* 505–512.

MILNE, R. and BULL, R. (1999). *Investigative Interviewing: Psychology and Practice.* Chichester: Wiley.

—— and —— (2006). Interviewing victims of crime, including children and people with intellectual difficulties. In M.R. Kebbell and G.M. Davies (eds) *Practical Psychology For Forensic Investigations.* Chichester: Wiley.

MILNE, R. and SHAW, G. (1999). Obtaining witness statements: Best practice and proposals for innovation. *Medicine, Science and the Law, 39,* 127–138.

MILNE, R., SHAW, G. and BULL, R. (2007). Investigative interviewing: The role of research. In D. Carson, R. Milne, F. Pakes, K. Shalev and A. Shawyer (eds) *Applying psychology to criminal justice.* Chichester; Wiley, 65–80.

OSWALD, K. and COLEMAN, M. (2007). Memory demands on facial composite identification. *Applied Cognitive Psychology, 21,* 345–360.

PENRY, J. (1971). *Looking at Faces and Remembering Them; A Guide to Facial Identification.* London: Elek Books.

POWELL, M.B., FISHER, R.P. and WRIGHT, R. (2005). Investigative interviewing. In N. Brewer and K. Williams (eds) *Psychology and Law: An Empirical Perspective.* New York: Guildford, 11–42.

—— and SNOW, P.C. (2007). A guide to questioning children during the free-narrative phase of an interview about abuse. *Australian Psychologist, 42,* 57–65.

SCHECK, B., NEUFELD, P. and DWYER, J. (2001). *Actual Innocence: Five Days to Execution and Other Dispatches From The Wrongly Convicted.* New York: Doubleday.

SHAHERAZAM. (1986). *The Mac-a-Mug Pro Manual.* Milwaukee, WI: Shaherazam.

SHEPHERD, E. and MILNE, R. (1999). Full and faithful: Ensuring quality practice and integrity of outcome in witness interviews. In A. Heaton-Armstrong, D. Wolchover and E. Shepherd (eds) *Analysing Witness Testimony.* Blackstone Press.

—— and —— (2006). Have you told management about this?: Bringing witness interviewing into the twenty-first century. In A. Heaton-Armstrong, E. Shepherd, G. Gudjonsson and D. Wolchover (eds), *Witness Testimony: Psychological, Investigative and Evidential Perspectives.* Oxford: Oxford University Press.

SHEPHERD, J., ELLIS, H. and DAVIES, G. (1982). *Identification Evidence: A Psychological Examination.* Aberdeen: Aberdeen University Press.

——, ——, McMURRAN, M. and DAVIES, G. (1978). Effect of character attribution on Photofit construction of a face. *European Journal of Social Psychology, 8,* 263–268.

TANAKA, J. and FARAH, M. (2003). The holistic representation of faces. In M.A. Peterson and G. Rhodes (eds) *Perception of Faces, Objects, and Scenes.* Oxford: Oxford University Press, 53–74.

TAYLOR, K.T. (2001). *Forensic Art and Illustration.* Boca Raton, FL: CRC Press.

TOPP, L., McQUISTON, D. and MALPASS, R. (2003). *Exploring composite production and its subsequent effects on eyewitness memory.* Paper presented at the European Psychology and Law and American Psychology and Law conference, Edinburgh.

VALENTINE, T. (2001). Face-space models of face recognition. In M. Wenger and J. Townsend (eds) *Computational, Geometric, and Process Perspectives on Facial Cognition; Contexts and Challenges.* Mahwah: LEA, 83–113.

——, DARLING, S. and MEMON, A. (2007). Do strict rules and moving images increase the reliability of sequential identification procedures? *Applied Cognitive Psychology, 21,* 933–949.

WELLS, G., CHARMAN, S.D. and OLSON, E.A. (2005). Building face composites can harm lineup identification performance. *Journal of Experimental Psychology: Applied, 11,* 147–156.

—— and HRYCIW, B. (1984). Memory for faces: Encoding and retrieval operations. *Memory and Cognition, 12,* 338–344.

WOGALTER, M.S. and MARWITZ, D.B. (1991). Face composite construction: In-view and from-memory quality and improvement with practice. *Ergonomics, 34,* 459–468.

WRIGHT, A. and ALISON, L. (2004). Questioning sequences in Canadian police interviews: Constructing and confirming the course of events. *Psychology, Crime and Law, 10,* 137–154.

10

WHERE WE ARE NOW AND THE FUTURE

WHERE WE ARE NOW

The starting point for the present book was to give an up-to-date review of the literature on psychological aspects of identification and to discuss research that is relevant to current legislation and guidelines concerned with eliciting accurate identification evidence. In order to do this we have outlined what psychologists know about constructing and delivering identification procedures from the point of view of the witness, victim, and suspect. Whilst much progress has been made, there is still further research needed and this chapter, in addition to summarizing the present situation will aim to highlight possible future directions.

We know that identification evidence is a highly persuasive form of evidence (Cutler, Penrod and Stuve, 1988). However, we also know that although witnesses can be highly confident that they have correctly identified the perpetrator, Chapter 1 presented evidence that demonstrates that witnesses can make mistakes. These mistakes can lead to grave consequences as evidenced by the DNA exoneration cases, 77% of which involved faulty identification evidence. Over the years, as a result of a number of cases involving mistaken identification, in some countries legislation has been developed to improve the fairness of identification procedures. The 1976 Devlin Report innovatively highlighted the contribution that could be made by psychologists to increasing the understanding of the complex nature of identification evidence. Chapters 1 and 2 therefore outlined how psychological research applies to identification evidence. We saw that our ability to successfully remember a crime event and identify the crime perpetrator relies on our perception and encoding of the crime, storage of information, and then retrieval of that information. We know that many factors can affect any or all of these three stages and the subsequent performance of a witness. These factors can be internal, for example, attitudes and experiences, or they can be external, for example, the length of time between viewing the crime and reporting it, learning new information related to the crime, or the manner in which information about the crime is elicited by an interviewer. Thus, memory for a complex event, such as a crime, is likely to contain details not only of what was actually witnessed, but also new information related to the crime, and the witnesses' own inferences and understanding of what occurred. The resulting memory is therefore likely to contain accurate and inaccurate details.

Chapter 3 examined the accuracy of witnesses' descriptions of the perpetrator and the relationship between person descriptions and identification performance. Generally, there is little relationship between the quality of the initial description given by a witness and their subsequent identification performance (Meissner, Sporer and Susa, 2008). In terms of the nature of the descriptions themselves, research evidence is discussed that typically shows them to be very vague (Meissner, Sporer and Schooler, 2007) and only normally containing between seven and nine pieces of information (Lindsay, Martin and Weber, 1994) which tend to be more general characteristics such as gender and age. In light of this, it is important to consider if there is anything that can be done to improve the quantity and quality of person descriptions given and the cognitive interview was discussed as a possible method by which to elicit greater detailed person information. However, even if the cognitive interview is used, due to the cognitive demands of conducting an interview, the interviewer may have problems remembering accurately all of the information reported by the witness. Furthermore, the interviewer may have their own beliefs and expectations about who committed the crime (especially if they have a suspect in custody) and this may taint their account of the interview. In light of this it was recommended that all interviews with witnesses/victims be electronically recorded so valuable information relating to the crime, including person information is not lost or biased.

There are many other factors that are likely to affect both the accuracy of person descriptions and the accuracy of identification evidence. For example, in Chapter 3 the effect of violence of the event, and age of the witness on person descriptions was outlined. In relation to identification evidence these factors are referred to as estimator variables (Wells, 1978) and in Chapter 4 the effect of these on identification evidence was discussed. Such estimator variables can be further categorized into: (i) event factors, for example, crime duration; (ii) witness factors, for example, confidence of the witness; and (iii) perpetrator factors, for example, disguise. Throughout the chapter consideration was given to the likely effect of each individual factor on identification performance. Some factors, such as age of witness, are likely to have a robust effect on performance, whereas other factors, such as personality of the witness, are likely to have a negligible effect. Of course, in the real world it is important for the police to realize that any number of these variables will be operating in any one crime. Thus it may be more difficult to precisely estimate their likely effect on identification performance. However, research presented in Chapter 4 does provide the reader with useful information about such estimator variables.

Some of the same factors outlined in Chapter 4 were also referred to in Chapter 5 but with reference to voice identification rather than face identification. Research concerning earwitness ability on voice identification parades is fairly limited (compared with research on face identification parades) but generally the consensus is that identification of unfamiliar voices is likely to be considerably error prone. In light of the difficulties discussed in Chapter 5 in conducting voice identification parades (eg how many voices, duration of voices, what the voices should say) the government in England and Wales published guidance for conducting voice identification parades in 2003 which is a significant step forward to help ensure that better-quality voice identification evidence is gained. These guidelines also illustrate the growing cooperation between police and psychologists, and their willingness to work together in order to improve the reliability of witness evidence. Research into other methods of identification such as by walk/gait is at a very early stage and thus further research is required in order to understand the psychological processes that underlie how witnesses match their memory of the perpetrator's gait with that of members of a gait line-up. At the end of Chapter 5 the possibility of using multiple line-ups was discussed. Limited research has so far investigated identification by face-plus-voice and it would be premature to draw conclusions about the utility of multiple line-ups both in terms of their effectiveness and the practicality for use within the criminal justice system.

In Chapter 6 there was discussion of research that shows that human perception and memory are influenced by expectations and stereotypes and that these have an effect not only on witnesses but also on relevant professionals within the criminal justice system. We know from psychological research that witnesses' memory of a crime is subject to their own expectations and stereotypes. However, research has shown that 'black' faces rated as high in stereotypicality were more frequently labelled as criminal than 'black' faces rated low in stereotypicality by white American police officers (Eberhardt, Goff, Purdie and Davies, 2004). Also surprising are findings presented in Chapter 6 which highlight that expectations and stereotypes held by senior professionals working within the Criminal Justice System (fingerprint experts) can lead them to make biased decisions that could potentially affect the outcome of investigations. This research serves as a powerful reminder that we must be aware that we all have expectancies and stereotypes which may well influence the outcome of a criminal investigation regardless of whether we are a witness, a police officer, or a lawyer.

Throughout the book many factors relating to accuracy of identification evidence have been noted, but in Chapter 7, factors relating to how identification parades are constructed, presented, and delivered were discussed. This area of research has received a lot of attention because the manner in which a witness views a line-up is under the control of the police and the Criminal Justice System, thus if research demonstrates the utility of one procedure over another procedure then potentially changes can be made to legislation and new improved methods can be brought in. In Chapter 7 current guidelines for identification parades (in England and Wales—PACE Code D and in the US—*Eyewitness Evidence: a Guide for Law Enforcement*) and the psychological research which relates to or underlies those guidelines was discussed. In some cases the research findings are clear and recommendations are included in such guidelines. For example, that non-biased line-up instructions given to witnesses prior to a parade/line-up, informing them that the perpetrator may or may not be present, significantly reduces the rate of false identifications (Malpass and Devine, 1981). In other cases research findings are more ambiguous, for example, sequential line-up presentation versus simultaneous line-up presentation. Some research suggests that sequential line-up presentation reduces the rate of false identifications whilst having no detrimental effect on correct identifications of the perpetrator (Lindsay and Wells, 1985). Conversely, other research suggests that sequential presentation reduces the rate of correct identifications compared to simultaneous line-ups (Wilcock, Bull and Vrij, 2005). In terms of current recommendations *Eyewitness Evidence: A Guide for Law*

Enforcement gives instructions for both simultaneous and sequential line-ups which may be a little premature. There is yet other research where robust effects have been found but relevant recommendations have not been included in PACE Code D, for example, research shows that line-up administrators should be blind to the position of the suspect in the line-up because they may inadvertently give off cues to the witness as to the suspect's position (Phillips, McAuliff, Kovera and Cutler, 1999). Discussions in this chapter again highlight the cooperation between police and psychologists and their shared goal of ensuring the accuracy of identification evidence. However, psychologists must be careful to develop a thorough theoretical understanding of the impact of various procedures before they make recommendations.

One topic on which there is a growing body of research but nevertheless a need for further research before we can make any firm recommendations is the important topic of vulnerable witnesses. In Chapter 8, research conducted with children, older adults, and people with a learning disability was discussed. The research presented suggests that vulnerable witnesses may be particularly prone to making false identifications from line-ups in which the suspect is innocent. Knowing that vulnerable witnesses may be less accurate than ordinary witnesses has led researchers to (i) try to understand why this group of witnesses make mistakes and (ii) investigate methods of aiding their performance. These have included practice line-ups, different sorts of line-up instructions, and different line-up presentation methods. Thus far the outcomes of this research have largely been negative/unsuccessful but are likely to lead to new directions in future research.

Other methods of aiding witnesses with the very difficult task of remembering 'whodunnit' are outlined in Chapter 9. Methods for constructing facial composites have developed over the years in line with technological advances and include sketch artists' impressions and different types of computer-generated composite systems. Despite advances in technology, it appears that the most recent methods such as PRO-fit and E-fit still have a way to go until they should be fully utilized in the real world. However, the speed with which technology advances and our growing knowledge of how people process faces suggests that the quality of composites is likely to improve and with that their effectiveness in investigations should also improve.

THE FUTURE

It is clear from the preceding chapters that psychologists have had and will continue to have an important role to play in understanding the complexities of witness identification evidence both in terms of witnesses' memorial ability but also in terms of how parades are constructed and delivered. However, it is vital that psychologists critically examine the nature of the research they conduct. Much of the research discussed in this book has been conducted using a mock witness paradigm where participants (typically psychology undergraduate students) view a simulated crime event and then after a delay view a line-up normally presented photographically. Whilst this method has the advantage of experimenters being able to isolate a certain factor to investigate its impact on identification accuracy, it does not equate to the real-life circumstances in which a crime typically occurs. For example, in a laboratory situation a mock witnesses' attention is artificially drawn to the mock crime event, which may well not always happen in real life. Furthermore, in a laboratory situation we cannot replicate the stress that is likely to be associated with witnessing some real crimes. Similarly, the consequences of witnesses' performance on a photographic line-up presented in a laboratory situation do not equate to those present when witnesses and victims of actual crime view a police identification parade.

Some researchers have attempted to address the problems of research conducted in a laboratory setting by using archival studies, sometimes referred to as field studies. Such research is highly ecologically valid but also has a number of problems associated with it. For example, it is difficult to establish the ground truth of what really happened. There may also be a number of factors operating at any one time so it is difficult to establish the effect of a particular factor on witness accuracy. Recently published research discusses the Illinois Pilot Project where field data was collected for a year by the police to investigate the effect of a double blind sequential procedure and simultaneous (non double blind) procedure on line-up performance (Mecklenburg, Bailey and Larson, 2008). Because all simultaneous line-ups were not double blind and all sequential line-ups were double blind, one of the problems with this data is that we do not know whether the findings are due to line-up presentation (simultaneous/sequential) or line-up administrator (blind or not blind) (Schacter et al, 2008). A further problem with field research stems from the practicalities of obtaining data from real witnesses. It relies on cooperation between researchers and police and normally takes a much greater length of time to collect data.

If one compares the results of archival studies with those of laboratory studies we are sometimes led to drawing different conclusions. For example, if we examine the effect of delay on identification performance field studies show that the rate of correct identifications falls after one week (Behrman and Davey, 2001; Valentine, Pickering and Darling, 2003), however, results from a laboratory study demonstrate that there was no significant difference in the rate of correct identifications between the one week, one month, and three month delay conditions (Shepherd, 1983). In fact the rate of correct identifications only declined after a delay of 11 months. This highlights the importance of researchers not relying solely on one method of research. Instead, we should conduct research using a variety of methods to allow us to build up as accurate and complete a picture as possible.

A further problem with laboratory research is that some researchers are not that aware of the issues that arise for police officers conducting identification parades. For example, it was only after discussions between the first author and the police that it transpired briefings given to witnesses prior to a parade to tell them what the procedure involves, could be improved. Furthermore, the briefing ideally should be given at an earlier point in time to encourage and support witnesses to go through with the viewing. As a result, a new more accessible witness briefing is now being developed which will hopefully go some way to address these problems. Such cooperation between academics and the police is important to ensure that fruitful research is conducted which addresses the problems that occur in the real world.

There is a need to increase the amount of research that involves careful consideration of real-world problems while maintaining high methodological rigour. For example, Valentine, Darling and Memon (2007) used a live surprise (simulated) theft and VIPER line-up parades to investigate the effect of the way in which video parades are currently shown in England and Wales, compared to a sequential line-up presentation as has been suggested by researchers, on witness performance. This piece of research therefore addressed a current applied question using a well controlled but ecologically valid piece of research. As mentioned in Chapter 9, in the UK and in many other countries there are increasing numbers of CCTV cameras watching us and being used as a possible crime prevention method. With advances in technology the picture quality of CCTV is likely to improve. It may therefore be possible for psychologists and the police to work together to produce large-scale studies examining CCTV footage of crimes that have occurred and follow the investigations through the criminal justice system to build up a picture of factors likely to affect the chances of the perpetrator being correctly identified from a line-up. By using such CCTV footage one would overcome the problem with many field studies of establishing ground truth.

Few people would now argue that psychology cannot make any contribution to the Criminal Justice System. Indeed, there has been a wealth of psychological research concerned with witness identification conducted in the past few decades and, as has been discussed though out this book, findings from some of it have been adopted within the relevant official guidance. However, at present there is no single comprehensive document available to investigators which contains guidance encompassing all procedures necessary for and related to eliciting accurate identification evidence from the time that a witness reports a crime to the police and a person description being sought, through to a witness leaving the police after having viewed an identification procedure. Such a document would be immensely valuable and it would ensure that all areas related to identification are given due consideration.

Although psychologists may well contribute to such a document, there are still many unresolved theoretical and applied questions regarding psychological aspects of identification evidence which remain. In order to answer these questions and help ensure that witness identification evidence is as accurate as possible, the levels of trust and cooperation between members of the Criminal Justice System and researchers needs to increase. We have already referred many times to the importance of the relationship between the police and psychologists, and in the UK and US it is developing well but in some other countries it is more faltering, or in fact non-existent. This situation must be remedied if future research is to be of maximum value. Future research needs to: (i) address existing everyday problems or questions the police have by drawing on well-researched psychological theories or models; (ii) be as ecologically valid as possible; and (iii) investigate possible innovative methods which could realistically be used in the future by the police to improve the performance of witnesses, especially vulnerable witnesses.

CONCLUSION

To conclude, it is clear that psychology has made a significant contribution to our understanding of identification evidence. The current book has presented an up-to-date review of psychological research and this can be used to inform those who conduct identification procedures or those with an interest in witness identification. There is still much more research that needs to be conducted and we must consider carefully how we do that research to ensure that the results are applicable in the real world and that identification evidence is as reliable as possible.

REFERENCES

BEHRMAN, B.W. and DAVEY, S.L. (2001). Eyewitness identification in actual criminal cases: An archival analysis. *Law and Human Behavior, 25,* 475–491.

CUTLER, B.L., PENROD, S.D. and STUVE, T.E. (1988). Juror decision making in eyewitness identification cases. *Law and Human Behavior, 12,* 41–55.

EBERHARDT, J., GOFF, P., PURDIE, V. and DAVIES, P. (2004). Seeing Black: Race, crime and visual processing. *Journal of Personality and Social Psychology, 87,* 876–893.

LINDSAY, R.C.L., MARTIN, R. and WEBBER, L. (1994). Default values in eyewitness descriptions. A problem for the match to description lineup foil selection strategy. *Law and Human Behavior, 18,* 527–542.

—— and WELLS, G.L. (1985). Improving eyewitness identifications from lineups: Simultaneous versus sequential lineup presentation. *Journal of Applied Psychology, 70,* 556–564.

MALPASS, R.S. and DEVINE, P.G. (1981). Eyewitness identification: Lineup instructions and the absence of the offender. *Journal of Applied Psychology, 66,* 482–489.

MECKLENBURG, S.H., BAILEY, P.J. and LARSON, M.R. (2008). The Illinois field study: A significant contribution to understanding real world eyewitness identification issues. *Law and Human Behavior, 32,* 22–27.

MEISSNER, C., SPORER, S. and SCHOOLER, J. (2007). Person descriptions as eyewitness evidence. In R.C.L. Lindsay, D.F. Ross, J.D. Read and M.P. Toglia (eds) *Handbook of Eyewitness Psychology Handbook Volume 11.* Mahwah, NJ: Lawrence Erlbaum Associates, 1–34.

——, —— and SUSA, K. (2008). A theoretical review and meta-analysis of the description-identification relationship in memory for faces. *European Journal of Cognitive Psychology, 42,* 57–65.

PHILLIPS, M.R., MCAULIFF, B.D., BULL KOVERA, M. and CUTLER, B.L. (1999). Double-blind photoarray administration as a safeguard against investigator bias. *Journal of Applied Psychology, 6,* 940–951.

SCHACTER, D.L., DAWES, R., JACIBY, L.L., KAHNEMAN, D., LEMPERT, R., ROEDIGER, H.L. and ROSENTHAL, R.(2008). Policy forum: Studying eyewitness investigations in the field. *Law and Human Behavior, 32,* 3–5.

SHEPHERD, J.W. (1983). Identification after long delays. In S.M.A. Lloyd-Bostock and B.R. Clifford (eds) *Evaluating Witness Evidence.* John Wiley and Sons.

VALENTINE, T., DARLING, S. and MEMON, A. (2007). Do strict rules and moving images increase the reliability of sequential identification procedures? *Applied Cognitive Psychology, 21*, 933–949.

——, PICKERING, A. and DARLING, S. (2003). Characteristics of eyewitness identifications that predict the outcome of real lineups. *Applied Cognitive Psychology, 17,* 969–993.

WELLS, G.L. (1978). Applied eyewitness testimony research: System variables and estimator variables. *Journal of Personality and Social Psychology, 36,* 1546–1557.

WILCOCK, R.A., BULL, R. and VRIJ, A (2005). Aiding the performance of older eyewitnesses: Enhanced non-biased lineup instructions and lineup presentation. *Psychiatry, Psychology and Law, 12,* 129–140.

INDEX